The Judge
and the
President

Stealing the 2020 Election

David H. Moskowitz

www.thecreativepositivist.com

First published by Huge Jam,
Gravenhurst, England, 2023

www.hugejam.com

ISBN: 978-1-916604-11-7

Dedicated to
the brave women and men
who saved our Capitol
on January 6, 2021.

The Judge and the Creative Positivist
David H. Moskowitz

Other books in this series:

Volume One: The Judge and the Umpire: Evaluating Judicial Decisions
Huge Jam, 2022 ISBN: 978-1739182915
Volume Two: The Judge and the Philosopher: Determining What Is the Law
Huge Jam, 2023 ISBN: 978-1739182922
Volume Four: The Judge and the Incorrect Decision: Roe v. Wade (2024)

ACKNOWLEDGMENTS

Writing books is a lonely, solitary experience especially when you are not in an academic setting. Consequently, I have found it very important to engage jurisprudential scholars and friends interested in legal philosophy in discussions about my ideas in order to get feedback. Among those to whom I want to acknowledge their assistance, I would include Mark Freed (who was an enormous help regarding pipeline research), Jim McErlane (who was a 2016 member of the Electoral College); Michelle Dempsey, Mitchell Berman, Lou Kupperman, Bob Martin, Dan Williams, Leo Zamparelli, Ken Mumma, Eli Silberman, Manny DeMutis, and the additional folks named in the acknowledgements sections in volumes 1 and 2 who also read the draft of volume 3. Mary Lawrence read this book and offered an analysis of it. Mindy Brook read several versions of this book and functioned as an editor. Jacqueline Tobin edited two versions of the book. And my wife Marian graciously discussed various issues every night at the dinner table and read the manuscript and contributed her ideas. This book would not have happened without this help, and I want to thank each of you.

D.H.M., September 2023

Contents

Introduction

This book is the third book in a series of four which I call *The Judge and the Creative Positivist*. Creative positivism is the legal philosophy that is presented in the four books. The fundamental issue in legal philosophy is to describe what is the law and how we find it.

The leading legal philosopher in the 20th century was H.L.A. Hart. In his classic book, *The Concept of Law*, he presents his view of the law and describes the rule of recognition. This rule can be defined as a social fact in every legal system. In every legal system, there is a consensus among legal officials about what is the law and how it may be ascertained and applied. When we are considering what is the law according to the rule of recognition, then we have to specify the legal system we are discussing. There are multiple overlapping legal systems in some areas of the law.

I review in this book the subject of the election of the U.S. president. This area of the law is complicated. It is approximately one-third each of federal law, state law and local law. These legal systems consist of constitutional norms, statutes, precedents, and customary rules. I refer to "rules", "norms", and "laws" interchangeably, all meaning the same thing. These three legal systems are interrelated, cross-pollinating, and, in combination, provide the legal structure for the presidential electoral process.

Much of the law related to the election of the president is based upon customary rules. Some of these customary rules are part of the written and unwritten Constitution.[1] Others are non-constitutional customary rules with the force of law, and some are customary rules that lack the force of law. It is the distinction between these types of customary rules that lies at the heart of the peaceful transfer of power after the national presidential election popular vote.

In chapters 1-3, I describe the system in the United States for election of the president, and the 2020 presidential election specifically, to illustrate how this confusing network of legal rules operates. When we vote for the president in the U.S., we do not vote for the actual candidates.

When the Founding Fathers, the authors of the Constitution, met in the constitutional convention, they were faced with the question of whether their country would be ruled by a monarchy or by an elected official whom they would call "the president". At that time, there was no nation in the world that directly and consistently elected its rulers. They decided that the president should be elected by the citizens of this country that they were forming.

The representatives in the constitutional convention were the leading citizens of this new country. They were all white men who were well-educated and the owners of property. They were the elite, the aristocrats. But they did not want this new country to be controlled by the aristocracy. They wanted all the white males who were over 21 years of age to be able to vote for the president.

There was a problem with this idea. Many of the citizens were illiterate. Most were not well-educated. Most of the country was rural. The people in one colony did not know the leading figures in the other colonies. There were no national newspapers. How could these citizens be trusted to make a wise choice?

The gentlemen in the constitutional convention decided upon a compromise. The voters would not vote directly for the president. They would vote, instead, for the leading local citizens who would become the Electoral College every four years. So, even today, when you voted in 2020 for the president, you did not vote for either Joe Biden or Donald Trump. You, instead, voted for people whose names you did not know who would actually vote for the president and the vice president. This is the system that I describe in this book.

Ultimately, we will arrive at the crucial question about our governmental system, the predominant question of the U.S. democracy. This inquiry concerns whether the presidential electors in the Electoral College are legally required to vote for the candidate who won the popular vote in the state that has selected them to be an elector.

The U.S. democracy will survive only if there is a peaceful transfer of power after the members of the Electoral College meet and cast their votes for the winner of the election. The election is a contest. Like all contests, it must result in a winner (unless there is a tie). If the winner of the election does not become the president, there will be no democracy and the election will become irrelevant.

We will look at the aftermath of the 2020 election and the indictment of former President Donald Trump for four criminal offenses after he attempted to prevent the peaceful transfer of power on losing the election, including (in 3.12) the Georgia indictment of August 2023. Were this effort to have been successful, Joe Biden would not have become the President and Donald Trump would have remained in office. Fortunately, Trump failed to overturn the results of the 2020 election.

It is customary norms that establish which rules are legal rules and which rules are not. In short, customary norms identify what the law is. My description of this electoral process requires a further understanding of customary rules and their place in the legal system which is the topic that I discuss in chapter 4 after the description of the electoral process.

As part of the examination of customary legal norms, we look at various situations in which customary norms distinguish what is law from what is not law. There is no clear dividing line between law and non-law. What is law one day may become non-law the next day. This will occur when a statute is repealed, or a precedent is overruled. Non-law may become law the next day, such as when a statute is adopted, or a precedent is decided. Just as every judicial decision is either correct or incorrect, every potential act is either prohibited or not prohibited.

Moreover, there is no universal agreement on how the word "law" is used. We say to our children that the law in this house is that smoking is prohibited. Determining what is the law is also confusing when we consider laws that have no penalty. Has a law been established when the health officials decide that wearing masks because of COVID-19 is required, even though the violation of the clear mandate that you wear a mask does not include any penalty for not wearing a mask?

While I am not attempting to provide a definition for what is law, Hart's version of the rule of recognition has to be stretched or expanded to incorporate within the rule of recognition various factual situations and social practices in a modern mature society. Hart's rule of recognition provides the framework for identifying what is law, but it does not encompass all the facets of the legal system. In chapter 5, I point out that there are laws which by their terms are non-reviewable. In addition, some acts are non-reviewable because of lack of standing to challenge them. There are also acts that are enforced by legal officials, even though the acts themselves are not the subject of legal enactment. There are many legal acts, including some judicial decisions, that are not precedents.

In chapter 6, I discuss non-justiciability. I also describe laws that provide for regulatory authority, but where no regulations have been adopted. In addition, there may be violations of the law with no potential recourse for the violation. An example of this is in chapter 7 where I consider litigation involving racial discrimination. Many of the situations described in the previous chapters are illustrative of how the law works or fails to work regarding various racially discriminatory practices.

We look in chapter 8 at how the law functions when we consider the real rules and compare them to the paper rules. The real rules are not part of the law, but they are descriptive of how the legal system operates. When a real rule is applied in a judicial decision, the real rule will also become an enacted law (a paper rule). These practices that are represented in the real rules may not be part of the law even though they are features of the legal system in a specific society.

When the judge creates a new legal rule, the judge must have considered an alternate source for creating the new legal rule. Justice and wisdom are two alternate sources, and these sources were introduced in *The Judge and the Umpire*. In chapter 9 of this book, volume 3, I consider other alternate sources that may be cited in judicial decisions, though they may not result in a correct decision.

In chapter 10, I review the obligation to make the correct decision and the evaluation of the judicial decision. Appendix A contains a summary of the issues discussed in volumes 1 and 2 and a preview of volume 4. Appendix B lists the references relating to the indictment of Trump for attempting to overturn the results of the 2020 election.

I.
Electing the US President

When the Founding Fathers were meeting in Philadelphia to write the Constitution about 250 years ago, one of the most difficult subjects they discussed was the method to be used to elect the President of the United States (POTUS). The ultimate decision reflected a compromise. In addition, the procedure for electing POTUS has evolved over the years. The election in 2020 for POTUS provides a vivid example of how the American legal system for the election of POTUS works.

The goal of this chapter and the next two chapters is to demonstrate how constitutional norms, legislative norms, norms derived from precedents, and customary norms with the force of law create a body of legal norms that control the procedure for the election of POTUS. In addition, there are a multitude of legal systems at the national, state, and local level that have a role to play. These norms that constitute the law governing the election of POTUS are supplemented by customary norms without the force of law. This legal/political structure with its various types of norms in its multiplicity of legal systems, acting in combination and coordination, prevented a coup d'état on January 6, 2021.

In the election of POTUS, you might expect that the candidate who wins the national popular vote will win the election. That is not even a customary rule because several presidential candidates failed to win the popular vote but still became the president. The 2000 election is an example where George W. Bush won the election and Albert Gore lost, though it was Gore who won the popular vote. This 2000 election resulted in a lawsuit that is considered below.

If you contend that the candidate who wins the election in the most states will be the winning candidate, that is also not necessarily true. To win the election, the candidate must win a majority of the electoral college votes. The candidate needs at least 270 electoral college votes to become the president.

To win the 270 electoral college votes, the candidate must win the popular vote in enough states computed by adding each state's number of electoral college votes for the particular candidate. The number of electoral college votes in a state is based upon the census every ten years and is the combination of the two senatorial seats and the number of members of the House of Representatives in a particular state.

Most of the states are winner-take-all states in which all the members of the Electoral College in a particular state are supposed to vote in accordance with the popular vote in that state. This winner-take-all system is based upon a legal rule in some states (by statute) and a customary rule in other states.

In some states, the requirement that the members of the Electoral College vote in accordance with the popular vote in the state is the subject of a statute with a sanction (for example, a fine of $1,000). In other states, there may be a disqualification of the faithless elector (this term refers to an elector who does not vote for the winner of the popular vote in the state) and a substitute elector is appointed. In some states, the electors sign a pledge regarding how they will vote. We will return to these issues below. Let's start with the constitutional norms.

1.1 Constitutional norms

The United States has a written Constitution supplemented by an unwritten Constitution, the latter consisting of customary norms, legal/political concepts (for example, the peaceful transfer of power after the presidential election), and interpretation of the constitutional norms. Article II, Section 1 of the Constitution describes how the president and vice president shall be elected, as follows:

> Each state shall appoint, in such manner as the Legislature thereof shall direct, a Number of Electors, equal to the whole number of Senators and Representatives to which the state may be entitled in the Congress, but no Senator or Representative, or person holding an office of trust or profit under the United States, shall be appointed an elector.
>
> The Electors shall meet in their respective states, and vote by ballot for two persons, … And they shall make a list of all the persons they voted for, and of the number of votes for each, which list they shall sign and certify, and transmit sealed to the seat of the government of the United States, directed to the President of the Senate. The President of the Senate shall, in the presence of the Senate and the House of Representatives, open all the certificates, and the votes shall then be counted… [2]

The reference to the "President of the Senate" really applies to the sitting vice president because the Constitution makes the vice president the president of the senate.[3] This provision has some interesting situations when the vice president is a candidate himself for either the presidency or the vice presidency. This role of the vice president became an issue of enormous importance in the 2020 election, and we will consider below what happened in that election.

The Founding Fathers intended that the votes of the citizens (not all the citizens but the adult males who own property) would not be binding on the wise men elected to be members of the Electoral College. The electoral college system is the result of the Founders wanting a federal republican form of government. Electors were supposed to be free agents. The electors were able to select whomever they wanted to be president and vice president.

These electors were supposed to be selected in each election to serve for only that election. Membership was not fixed beforehand. The persons to be selected could not be federal office holders. They were expected to be the prominent citizens of the state. The citizens of the individual states were not given the right to vote directly for POTUS.

The system that was designed by the Founders is not what we would today regard as democratic. Voting was very restricted. The number of electoral college votes in the individual states was not of equal weight for at least two reasons. First, each state, large or small, would have two senators, which means they would have at least two electoral college votes, regardless of the number of citizens in that state (actually, at least three votes, because every state would have at least one member of the House of Representatives). Second, slaves were counted on a 3/5ths formula, even though they could not vote. This gave an advantage to slave-owning states when compared to states that prohibited slavery.

To be elected, the president must receive a majority of the total number of the votes of the members of the Electoral College whose votes are counted. If there are an equal number of votes for two candidates so that neither has achieved a majority, the House of Representatives elects the president. In choosing the president, the votes in the House are counted with each state having one vote. There must be a majority of the votes of the states to make the choice.

The Constitution also provides that the Congress will act regarding the timing of the activities related to the election: "The Congress may determine the Time of choosing the Electors, and the Day on which they shall give their Votes, which Day shall be the same throughout the United States."[4]

Therefore, the Constitution establishes the number of electors per state. There is nothing in the Constitution dictating how the electors are chosen, except that how the electors shall be selected is left to each state legislature. As I mentioned above, there is no uniformity among the states regarding how the electors must proceed, though they all meet on the same day in their respective state capitols and vote as separate groups.

Each state controls its own popular voting system for president and vice president. The Constitution does not describe who or what is on the ballots. In theory, the votes in each state are cast for a slate of electors in each state (who are not named on the ballots). In summary, each state legislature decides how electors are chosen in their state (this is called "the elections clause"). In the early elections in the U.S., the state legislatures selected the slates of electors in their individual states.[5]

The states do not select the electors in a uniform manner. In many states, the electors are selected by the political parties, either in state party conventions or by state party committees. There is no federal law governing how electors are selected or how winning the popular vote relates to how electors vote when the Electoral College meets. This part of the electoral process is subject primarily to customary rules, which is why I started this section by stating that there is an unwritten Constitution in addition to the written Constitution. Some of these customary rules have been incorporated into statutes.

I mention above that most of the states, but not all, have a system in which the winning candidate receives all the votes of the state, and these states are known as winner-take-all states. In other words, for the winner-take-all states, the winner of the popular vote in the state will receive all the electoral college votes in that state. It makes no difference how close the election is in the state.

Maine and Nebraska are not winner-take-all states. In these two states, the votes are awarded on a district-by-district basis. The districts are those that are established for the House seats. There is one electoral college vote for each congressional district. The winner of the statewide vote receives the two electoral college votes for the two senators in the state. In the 2020 election, Biden received three votes in Maine and Trump received one. In Nebraska, Trump got four votes and Biden got one.

This method for selecting the president was a great advance in the creation of a democratic system, but, as I mentioned, it did not establish a democracy. The original system limited the right to vote to white males who own property. The voting rights were left to the individual states to determine. This system was a compromise that may have been necessary to achieve ratification of the Constitution.

1.2 Controversy in the presidential elections

It did not take long for the system created by the Founding Fathers to be enveloped in controversy. While our focus is on the 2020 election, and the unprecedented political crisis that followed this election, this is not the first crisis in a presidential election. From the beginning, there have been problems because of the vague language in the Constitution and the system that has developed over the centuries since the Constitution was written.

Two elections before 2020 expose the complexity of the electoral process for electing POTUS. The first was in 1800. Pursuant to the original system of the Founding Fathers, the first-place finisher in the electoral college system became the president and the runner-up became the vice president. The Constitution did not anticipate the development of political parties and that the presidential and vice-presidential candidates would run as a slate of candidates. In the 1800 election, there was a tie in the votes for Thomas Jefferson and Aaron Burr. This led to the House of Representatives selecting the president. After 36 ballots, the House selected Jefferson.

Several amendments to the Constitution have been adopted. The 1800 election led to the Twelfth Amendment which adopted before the next presidential election in 1804. The Twelfth Amendment called for separate elections for the president and the vice president.[6]

The Fifteenth Amendment does not allow denial to vote to be based on race, color, or previous servitude.[7] Women acquired the right to vote in the Nineteenth Amendment.[8] Poll taxes were prohibited in the Twenty-Fourth Amendment.[9] The age to vote became 18 or older in the Twenty-Sixth Amendment.[10]

In summary, in accordance with the Constitution, when the citizens of a state cast their votes in the presidential election, they are in theory selecting a group of electors who will act for the specific state that elected them. Political parties, like present-day political parties, did not exist when the Constitution was drafted. When political parties were formed, like those we currently have, the selected electors were expected to vote for the candidates of their respective political party.

In order to avoid the formation of a national clique that would support a particular candidate, the electors must meet in their respective state capitols (not all electors in the entire country in one location) and they cast one ballot for the president and one for the vice president. There are 538 electors, which number is based upon there being 435 members of the House, 100 members of the Senate, and three electors for the District of Columbia. To be elected, a candidate needs to receive a majority of the 538 votes, or 270 votes.

The Founding Fathers expected the electors to act as free agents who would exercise their own discretion in selecting the best persons to be the president and vice president. This system has evolved into a general popular election of electors who do not, in general with some exceptions, exercise discretion. The customary norms have developed into 50 different state voting systems. In approximately 33 states and in the District of Columbia, there are statutes that require pledges from the electors selected by the political parties that they will vote in accordance with the popular vote in their state. These pledges may or may not be legally enforceable. In approximately 14 states, the state statute permits replacement of an elector who refuses to vote in accordance with the popular vote.

1.3 The Electoral Count Act

The most important of the statutes adopted by Congress relating to the election of POTUS is the Electoral Count Act.[11] This is the federal statute adopted in 1877 to provide for the voting procedures that the Constitution called for the Congress to adopt. The Act was in direct response to the second contested presidential election in 1876 when a divided Congress spent several weeks trying to determine the winner of the election. As happened again in 2020, which we consider below, several states sent certificates of alternate groups of electors to the Congress to be counted.

In the 1876 presidential election, both the Democratic candidate Samuel Tilden and the Republican candidate Rutherford B. Hayes claimed that they had won the election. There were three contested states: Florida, Louisiana and South Carolina. Without counting the electoral college votes in these three states, Tilden had 184 votes and Hayes had 165 votes. If Hayes won all 20 votes in these states, he would win. If Tilden won one of the votes in these states, he would win.

The Democrats controlled the House, and the Republicans controlled the Senate. An Electoral Commission was appointed to decide who won each state. Supreme Court Justice David Davis was appointed to the Electoral Commission as the deciding vote, the other members being equally divided between the Republicans and the Democrats. The Illinois state legislature controlled by the Democrats elected Davis to the Senate and he resigned from the Electoral Commission. His replacement was Supreme Court Justice Joseph Bradley.

The eventual resolution of the dispute was that Hayes became the president based upon an agreement between the parties. The Southern Democrats agreed because they received the commitment from the Republicans that all federal troops would be withdrawn from the South. This ended the reconstruction process. In addition, in 1877, the Electoral Count Act was adopted to provide a framework for how future disputes would be handled. This format was challenged by the riot at the Capitol after the 2020 election.

The Constitution left the actual rules of the voting process to the states to resolve, and the Electoral Count Act is consistent with that methodology. The intent of the Act is to make the procedures more uniform and to provide a road map for what the states should do. The certification of the votes of the Electoral College is left to the governors of the states. The Act also includes a provision for a criminal offense related to "any false writing or document" submitted in the election process, and this became an issue after the 2020 election.

The Act includes the procedure for resolving the situation of alternative slates of electors. The Act clarifies what the respective roles of the Congress and the state legislatures are regarding alternate electors. While the procedure set forth in the Act has not been an issue of dispute itself, the validity of the Act has been challenged, and this is also a central theme in the 2020 election dispute.

Election Day is on the Tuesday after the first Monday in November. Each state has the initial responsibility of determining who the electors are in that state. This initial determination is made six days before the date fixed for the meeting of the electors. The electors in each state meet and vote on the first Monday after the second Wednesday in December. This does not mean the state must make its final determination of electors by the sixth day before the electors meet. The Act has been interpreted as having established a "safe harbor" regarding the state action in selecting the electors.[12] For the determination by the state to be conclusive, it must be made during the safe harbor timeframe. Deciding within the safe harbor makes the decision binding upon the Congress.

When the electors meet on the first Monday after the second Wednesday in December (December 14, 2020, for the 2020 election), either the governor or the secretary of state is the presiding official. To resolve the issue of alternate electors at the congressional level, the Act provides for a "certificate of ascertainment" to be prepared by the governor in each state (seven copies is stipulated, though some states provide as many as nine copies). The certificate should include the seal of the state. It identifies the electors appointed by the state and certifies that they were appointed pursuant to the laws of the state. The certificate is signed by each of the electors and the presiding officials. The certificates of ascertainment are sent to various officials including the National Archivist of the United States.

The votes that are cast by the electors are set forth on a "certificate of vote".[13] When the electors meet on the first Monday after the second Wednesday in December, they sign, seal, certify and transmit their votes to the president of the Senate. The certificate of vote is sent with the certificate of ascertainment to the Senate, the National Archivist at the Library of Congress, the state's secretary of state, and the chief judge of the U.S. District Court closest to where the state capitol is located. The electors also sign and send at least four ballots. These documents must be received by December 23. As I discuss in section 2.3, in the 2020 election, this procedure was followed by both the duly appointed electors and by the alternate electors in the seven battleground states.

The Act sets forth the procedure for the counting of the votes which is the paramount purpose for adopting the Act and its most important feature. The Twelfth Amendment states only that: "The President of the Senate shall, in the presence of the Senate and House of Representatives, open all of the certificates and the votes shall be counted." The specific details of the Act go far beyond this short sentence of the Twelfth Amendment. This disparity between the constitutional amendment and the Act forms the legal basis for the memoranda concerning the 2020 election that gave rise to the insurrection on January 6, 2021. We consider these memoranda below.

Under Section 4 of the Act, Congress must meet in a joint session on January 6 following the presidential election. The Senate and the

House both meet in the House Chamber at 1:00 p.m. The sitting vice president, acting as the president of the Senate, presides at the meeting. He opens all the certificates with the electoral college votes. The four tellers make a list of the votes from the states as they are examined in alphabetical order.

For an objection to the votes in a state, at least one representative and one senator must challenge the votes of a particular state (in writing signed by both legislators). That issue, that challenge to the votes of a state, must be resolved before the votes of the next state are considered. For a certificate to be rejected, both chambers must agree that it should be. In the 2020 election, on January 6, 2021, there were objections to the votes of Arizona and Pennsylvania.

Section 5 of the Act calls for the two chambers to decide upon objections in separate meetings. There are two hours of debate. They each vote. The acceptable reasons for rejecting a certificate are subject to customary rules as to which reasons are acceptable.[14]

An objection to the vote of a faithless elector occurred in 1968 when an elector from North Carolina voted for George Wallace instead of Richard Nixon. The vote of this faithless elector was rejected by both Houses of Congress. This then raises the question of whether the customary rule concerning the invalidity of the vote of the faithless elector has the force of law or whether it is just an acceptable reason for rejecting a vote. If it is the latter, it would appear to be a customary rule without the force of law because the votes of faithless electors are generally counted for the candidate for whom they voted.

After resolving the objection, the two Chambers then reassemble in their joint meeting and the results are announced. The votes from the various states continue to be counted until the votes in all the states have been tabulated.

The discussion so far has not considered in detail the possibility of multiple returns from a single state, such as when there are alternate electors and two competing certificates have been filed. The standard is whether one of the certificates qualifies as "regularly given". The ultimate test will be whether the certificate has been submitted in accordance with state law. If the two Chambers agree, the matter is resolved. If the two Chambers do not agree, then the votes of the electors who have been certified by the governor of the state shall be the votes that are counted. If one certificate is submitted within the safe harbor guideline and the other is not, that may be a factor in making the decision.

This still leaves open the question of whether state law is determinate on the issue of which votes should be counted. Suppose that there is a conflict between the state legislature and the governor about what the state law is. Or, what happens if there is a conflict between the governor and the highest court in the state? Or a conflict between the highest court in the state and the state legislature? Once again, the 2000 and the 2020 elections will give us some insight into how these issues are resolved.

After the votes are counted by the four tellers, the results are given to the president of the Senate, and he announces the tally of the vote. Since he is also the vice president, and often may be a candidate himself, the intent of the Electoral Count Act is to minimize the role of the president of the Senate. This reading of the Act became crucial in the 2020 election.

The Act leaves many open issues. For example, if the vote of a state is rejected, does that affect whether a candidate has received a majority of the votes, or is the majority based upon the total possible vote, to wit, 538 votes? The answer to this question is also one of the 2020 election controversies. Since the answer to this question is uncertain, is this question then subject to determination by a joint session of the Congress? After all, it is the Congress that decided not to count the votes of a state or states.

If, instead, the Chambers meet separately in deciding whether the votes of a state should be counted, do they also decide separately on what a majority of the electors will be when the number of votes counted is less than 538? The Act does not disclose whether that is the appropriate procedure to resolve the issue. And the two Chambers may disagree in answering the question of what constitutes a majority.

There is a default procedure in the Twelfth Amendment for what happens if no candidate receives a majority. The House, voting state by state, elects the president and the Senate elects the vice president. This creates the possibility that the House, in its desire to elect the president, is uncooperative with the Senate in resolving the issue of what a majority vote will be. In deciding the 2020 election, the House was controlled by the Democrats and the Senate by the Republicans, so the House would have an incentive to declare a deadlock.

Since the vote in the House, however, is by states, the party with a majority of members in the House might not be the party which will receive a majority of the states voting for its candidate. Moreover, the country could have a president with a vice president from the opposing political party if the Twelfth Amendment deadlock procedure is utilized.

The various open issues and ambiguities within the Electoral Count Act create a political minefield of potential conflict in determining the outcome of a presidential election. Examples of this confusion were a factor in the 2020 election. Before considering that election, let's take a detour and consider the contest in 2000.

1.4 The 2000 election and *Bush v. Gore*

In addition to constitutional norms and statutory norms, the election of POTUS is also affected by judicially created norms. A good example of how this occurs is in the *Bush v. Gore* case that resolved the issue of which candidate won the 2000 election. This was a close election. The Florida Division of Elections announced that Bush won by 1,784 votes. When the machine recount was finished in all but one county, Bush had won by the margin of just 327 votes.[15]

The Florida Supreme Court decided that there should be a selective manual recount of Florida's presidential election ballots. This would be a statewide recount of over 61,000 ballots of undervotes (ballots that are incomplete) that the state vote election tabulation machines had not counted. This decision was then appealed to the U.S. Supreme Court.

The U.S. Supreme Court, in a 7-2 per curiam decision, based upon the equal protection clause, stops the recount.[16] The reasoning of the Court is that the use of different standards within the Florida counties violates the equal protection clause. The Court votes 5-4 against remanding the case to Florida to complete the recount. The majority maintains that the discretionary December 12 "safe harbor" deadline established by Section 5 of the Electoral Count Act is legally significant. The contention is that missing the deadline would violate the Florida Election Code.

The effect of the U.S. Supreme Court's decision is to reverse the Florida Supreme Court decision. The result gives the 25 electoral college votes to George W. Bush, the Republican candidate. This gives him the victory. Bush receives 271 electoral college votes once you add in Florida's votes, which is one more than the 270 votes necessary to win. Albert Gore, the Democratic nominee, would lose the election as a result of this decision.

As I mentioned earlier, there was only a 1,784-vote difference between the two candidates in Florida's original count. After the machine recount, Bush was winning by 327 votes out of six million votes. The decision gives Bush the victory, even though it could be argued that the Florida Supreme Court is supposed to be the final voice in resolving the matter. The Constitution, and the Electoral Count Act, establish that the conducting of the presidential election is a matter of state law, subject to state control. The Florida Supreme Court decided that there should be a selective manual recount of Florida's presidential election ballots. The recount was supposed to be a statewide recount of over 61,000 ballots of undervotes that were incomplete that the state vote election tabulation machines had not counted.

There is a well-reasoned dissenting opinion by Justice John Paul Stevens in *Bush v. Gore*. He reviews the constitutional framework, the principles of federalism and the customary rule of deference to state courts when the state court interprets its state statutes. This is a customary rule without the force of law (perhaps it is a principle). Justice Stevens goes further and gives the rules of judicial restraint (this could also be a competing principle) the status of customary rules with the force of law: "On questions of state law, we have consistently respected the opinions of the highest courts of the States."[17] Since this is a dissenting opinion, it does not create a legal rule, so it is not clear if the customary rule that Justice Stevens recites has the force of law or only sometimes has the force of law.

The other issue that Justice Stevens stresses is non-justiciability.[18] The U.S. Supreme Court usually refuses to interfere with other branches of the federal or state government when these governmental agencies are staying in their own lanes, making decisions within their areas of expertise. This is especially true of federal constitutional questions that have not been thoroughly reviewed at lower levels of the federal judicial system. Justice Stevens concludes that the result of the majority opinion "is acting unwisely". In other words, this is not a wise decision that the Supreme Court is making.[19]

Justice Ruth Bader Ginsburg also dissented. Her contention is that, notwithstanding the dates in the Electoral Count Act, Congress would still have to count Florida's votes even if the certification is not within the safe harbor provision and is, therefore, late. The safe harbor deadline insulates results from being disputed. Certifications from states after the safe harbor are still counted, though they may be disputed. Therefore, Florida could have proceeded in accordance with the decision of its Supreme Court and filed its certification after the safe harbor deadline. The basis for the majority opinion is that, if the case is remanded to Florida, the certification would not be within the safe harbor deadline. As Justice Ginsburg points out, that would not be fatal and the votes that are certified could still be counted.

One oddity of the *Bush v. Gore* case is that it is decided by a per curiam opinion. It is a customary rule, apparently without the force of law, that per curiam opinions are usually issued only if the decision is unanimous. Since Justices Stevens and Ginsburg dissented, this decision was not unanimous. The decision in *Bush v. Gore* does not resolve the question of whether the Constitution gives the power to make the selection of the winning candidate to the state legislature and not to the judicial branch in the state or the state official who certifies the election. This, like many other issues of the presidential election process, remains unclear and subject to customary rules that lack the force of law.

The concurring opinion in *Bush v. Gore* (Chief Justice Rehnquist, and Justices Scalia and Thomas joined him) adopted the theory that Article II, Section 1 of the Constitution established state legislative ultimate authority over the election process. This theory is called the "independent state legislative" theory. If this theory is adopted by the conservative majority of the 2023 Supreme Court Justices, the state supreme court (such as the Florida Supreme Court in the *Bush* case) would lack the authority to overturn a state legislative pronouncement that specific electoral regulations violated the state constitution. This could be in the form of a state statute that would thereby achieve immunity from a judicial determination of its invalidity.

If the independent state legislative theory became law, the legislature could potentially reverse the popular election results, which is what former President Trump attempted to achieve after the 2020 election. Under this theory, state and federal courts would have to defer to state legislative statutes or certifications of electoral results. If Justices O'Conner and Kennedy had joined in Chief Justice Rehnquist's concurring opinion, there would have been five votes for adoption of the independent state legislative theory. There may be five votes for this theory with the conservative majority in the Supreme Court that would rule upon an electoral dispute in the 2024 presidential election. We will return to this issue when we discuss "gerrymandering" in section 6.3.

One final point, which we revisit further on, Al Gore received 266 votes, not the 267 votes that he should have received. One faithless elector from the District of Columbia failed to cast the vote for him and abstained instead. I discuss the faithless elector issue in section 3.4.

2.
The 2020 Presidential Election

2.1 The legal systems and the 2020 presidential election

Let's consider the 2020 presidential election to illustrate how the legal systems (federal, state, and local) work. Vice President Mike Pence is one of the unlikely heroes of the thwarting of the effort to overturn the results of the 2020 election (unlikely because of his four-year record of lock-step loyalty to President Trump). A second hero would be General Mark A. Milley, the Chairman of the Joint Chiefs of Staff, and the members of the U.S. military forces. A third would be most of the members of the U.S. Congress. They not only finished the electoral process on January 6 and January 7, but the House formed the January 6 Committee to add to our understanding of the insurrection that occurred on January 6.

The courts – the approximately 90 judges who heard the 62 election fraud cases – are also entitled to praise for their law-ascertainment and law-application of the web of norms in the election process. Some of the judges were appointed by President Trump. The cases were filed by Trump supporters citing fictitious fraudulent efforts by voters and election officials.

The judicial system continued its work by supporting the subpoenas issued by the January 6 committee. Ultimately, we are left with the thin and tattered threads of the legal systems that were stretched but did not break.

It is important to note that the legal systems withstood this onslaught by mobilizing not only the legal norms that make up the law, but also leaning on the customary rules that lack the force of law.[20] Customary norms without the force of law can serve an important role in creating guideposts within the legal system, even though they are not law.

An intriguing example of a customary rule without the force of law is the conversation that occurred two days after Joseph Biden had obviously won the election. The telephone conversation was between General Mark A. Milley, the Chairman of the Joint Chiefs of Staff and the Speaker of the House, Nancy Pelosi. Bear in mind that the sitting president is the commander-in-chief of the armed forces. The military was subject to the control of President Donald Trump. Notwithstanding this clear chain of authority, General Milley assured Speaker Pelosi that he would override the command to start a war or fire a nuclear missile if ordered to do so by the President.

Speaker Pelosi was concerned that President Trump might prevent the peaceful transfer of power after losing the election. He might take some military action, including even potentially involving the use of nuclear bombs, to extend his presidency. Chairman Milley wanted to assure her that this would not happen. He made the following statement:

> The one thing I can guarantee is that, as the chairman of the Joint Chiefs of Staff, I want you to know that — I want you to know this in your heart of hearts, I can guarantee you 110 percent that the military, use of military power, whether it's nuclear or a strike in a foreign country of any kind, we're not going to do anything illegal or crazy.[21]

What I find the most interesting aspect of this statement is that Milley would override the command of his superior officer not just because the act in question would be illegal but also because it might be crazy. There might be authority, though it would not necessarily count as law, for disobeying an illegal order. To disregard an order because it is thought to be crazy goes beyond that potential law and may not even rise to the status of a customary rule that lacks the force of law. The justification for such an act would ultimately be supported by reference to inherent values that give rise to implicit authority based upon something like a customary rule.

Even before the 2020 election, Trump claimed that, if he lost the election, it would be the result of fraud. He continued to make this claim after the election when Biden was granted the victory by the television pundits. A movement to overturn the election started soon after the result of the election was clear.

James R. Troupis, 15 days after the election, while working for the Trump campaign in Wisconsin, received a November 18 memo outlining the strategy for overturning the results of the 2020 presidential election.[22] The memo was from Kenneth Chesebro, another Trump supporter. This memo called out January 6 as a hard deadline for the outcome of the multiple lawsuits that the Trump team had filed. It suggested that alternate electors should meet in Madison, the state capitol of Wisconsin, on December 14 to vote in an alternate electoral college proceeding. I refer to Troupis and Chesebro again in section 3.5.

Another memorandum was distributed three weeks later, on December 8, and it gave more details on the plan. This memo called for alternate electors in six battleground states, one of which was Wisconsin. Even before the memos were written, Republican legislators in Wisconsin and Arizona had asked their lawyers to advise them on how to proceed with the appointment of electors.[23] They suggested that there should be a pressure campaign to get Vice President Mike Pence, acting as the presiding official in the Congress when the electoral college votes would be counted, to consider a challenge to the certificates of the duly-elected electors, approve the certificates of alternate electors, and, ultimately, stop Congress from accepting that Biden had won the election.

These two memos preceded the efforts by Rudolph W. Giuliani and John Eastman to develop the strategy to take advantage of ambiguities in the Electoral Count Act. The original memo was related to challenging the vote in Wisconsin. The second memo extended the concept to six battleground states. Eastman and Giuliani expanded this project to a seven-state effort, which included challenges to the elections in Wisconsin, Arizona, Michigan, Georgia, Nevada, New Mexico, and Pennsylvania.

2.2 The Eastman memos

Before the election, President Donald Trump saw John Eastman interviewed on a *Fox News* talk show. Eastman was a constitutional law professor and dean of Chapman Law School. Eastman clerked for Supreme Court Justice Clarence Thomas and Court of Appeals Judge J. Michael Luttig. Two months after the television appearance, Eastman met with President Trump at the Oval Office in the White House for an hour-long meeting. Eastman became a member of Trump's Election Integrity Working Group. After the election, he wrote two influential memoranda. These memos outline the procedure by which Vice President Pence could act to keep Trump in office.[24]

The two memos were written by John Eastman in late December 2020 and early January 2021. The memos were undated. They were delivered to the Trump campaign on December 22, 2020, and January 3, 2021. They were designated as "Privileged and Confidential." These memos had more detailed versions of the plan to thwart the ascendency of Joe Biden to the presidency than the memos previously discussed. The two Eastman memos were particularly influential:

John Eastman's path from little-known academic to one of the most influential voices in Donald J. Trump's ear in the final days of his presidency began in mid-2019 on Mr. Trump's favorite platform: television.[25]

The first memo was two pages and was prepared in late 2020. The second and longer memo (six pages) appears to have been prepared between the end of the year and January 3, 2021.[26] This first memo is based upon Eastman's interpretation of the Twelfth Amendment and the Electoral Count Act. It is entitled *January 6 Scenario*.

Eastman bases his strategy on the claim that the Electoral Count Act is unconstitutional. His theory is that Vice President Pence does the counting of the votes when acting as the president of the Senate. In such capacity, Pence, according to Eastman, has the authority to resolve disputed electoral college votes. Since he is responsible for the counting, resolving electoral disputes does not involve the members of the Senate doing anything. Eastman's historical basis for this claim is that in the 1796 and 1800 elections, John Adams and Thomas Jefferson, in the same role as Pence, did the counting. Both Adams and Jefferson, acting as vice president, were elected to be president.

The two-page memo had six steps to be taken in implementation of what came to be called "the Pence Card". Pence could open and count the ballots. When he came to count the Arizona votes, he could announce that he had received conflicting certificates from that state. He would put those aside and proceed with the other states. When he arrived at the end of the counting, there would be seven states which had not been counted because there were conflicting certificates in those states.

The Twelfth Amendment refers to the total number of "electors appointed" by the state legislators. Because the votes in seven states would not be included in the total count, the number of votes of the remaining 43 states would not be 538 but would be 454. The majority of electors who had been appointed would then be 228 rather than 270. Without counting the seven disputed states, Trump would have 232 votes and Biden would have 222 votes. Pence could then declare that Trump had won the election.

The Democrats might protest that 270 votes were still required. So, Eastman's alternate plan is that the House could then vote for the president. For this purpose, per the Twelfth Amendment, the votes shall be taken by states, with each state having one vote. Republicans controlled at that time 26 of the state delegations. They would vote for Trump and Trump would be declared the winner by the House vote.

The fifth step refers to another alternate possibility, with the Electoral Count Act process being employed. This step starts with the objection to the Arizona competing electoral certificates. When the Chambers split to consider the objection, the Republican members of the Senate could insist that the current Senate rules will prevail, and that they may filibuster the vote. The theory here is that the methodology of the Electoral Count Act with its two-hour limit for debate should not apply, since predecessor senates may not control the voting process of the currently acting Senate. Each Senate decides its own procedural rules. This dispute would create a barrier to the Senate voting and the decision-maker would, by default, be the state legislatures.

The final and sixth step is that Pence should act on his own volition without seeking advice from the Joint Session of Congress or from the Supreme Court. If the Democrats sought Supreme Court resolution, the argument before the Supreme Court should be that this would be a non-justiciable political question.[27] This would then default to Vice President Pence to resolve the issue.

As mentioned above, the six-page second memo is longer. It considers alternative possibilities. In six battleground states (leaving New Mexico out), there is the claim that fraud occurred. Once again, the Electoral Count Act is regarded as unconstitutional. Vice President

Pence has unilateral power to accept or reject votes. He follows the procedure outlined in the first memo (above).

An alternative possibility involves the seven battleground states. There are multiple courses to follow for Trump to be declared the winner. The Electoral Count Act is, according to the memo, unconstitutional, so Vice President Pence asserts that he has the authority to act on his own initiative in counting the votes.

One method he could follow is to accept the certificates of the alternate electors if the state legislatures have acted to declare that the official certificates are those that name Trump the winner. If the state legislatures have not certified the alternate electors as the legal electors, but the state legislatures challenge the action of the governors of the states to certify the Biden electors, Vice President Pence should acknowledge that fraud has occurred. He should not count the votes in the disputed states. Trump gets 232 votes and Pence could declare that he won the election.

Another alternative is that Pence acknowledges the competing certificates and declares that neither candidate received 270 votes and the state delegations in the House will have to decide the winner. Yet another possibility for Pence is to acknowledge the fraud and require the state legislatures to audit the votes in their states and report back.[28]

In addition to writing the two memos, Eastman acted as a member of the Trump legal team that met at the Willard Hotel to plan the post-election strategy. He also met with Pence and Pence's legal advisor in the Oval Office at the White House on January 4, 2021. He tried to convince Pence to act in accordance with the Pence Card strategy.

John Eastman is the mastermind behind the legal theory that Vice President Pence could use his authority as the presiding officer in the Senate to overturn the results of the 2020 election. The Pence Card is the theory that Pence as the Vice President acting as the leader of the Senate has unilateral authority to reject electoral votes in the states in which he concludes that the elections were fraudulent.

On January 6, 2021, when the Congress would meet to count the electoral college votes, Pence could disregard the votes of the legally appointed electors from the seven battleground states. These are the states in which alternate electors met and certified that they were voting for Trump and the certificates were submitted to the National Archives, the Senate and to the local federal District Court. The theory would then have Pence declare Trump the winner because Trump had 232 votes and he would need only 228 votes when the votes from the seven states were excluded from the count.

2.3 Vice President Pence's decision

Vice President Pence sought advice upon realizing that Trump was attempting to avoid the peaceful transfer of power after Biden had won the election. Pence conferred with several influential sources. Pence called Dan Quayle who had also served as vice-president. Quayle, like Pence, is from Indiana, and he is also a Republican.

The question was whether the vice president had the legal authority to make Trump the president on January 6 when the votes would be counted. Eastman had argued that the vice president could control the process of how Congress certified the final count because the vice president is the presiding officer when the Congress meets to perform this task. If the Congress could not decide the winner of the election, the next step was to present the issue to the House of Representatives.

The House of Representatives could meet and the Twelfth Amendment to the Constitution called for the voting to be counted with one vote for each state. The Twelfth Amendment declares:

> If no person have such majority … the House of Representatives shall choose immediately, by ballot, the President. But in choosing the President, the votes shall be taken by states, the representation from each state having one vote.

In other words, the outcome would not be decided by a majority vote of the members of the House. While the Democrats were a majority of the members of the House, the Republicans could deliver to Trump a majority of the state delegations.

Quayle advised Pence that Eastman's plan would not work. The vice president, even though he is president of the Senate, must certify the election results based on the voting of the members of the Electoral College. The vice president's role was just to count the votes. Lawmakers are the ones who object to the certifications, not the vice president. Quayle based his opinion on the Twelfth Amendment: "The President of the Senate shall, in the presence of the Senate and House of Representatives, open all the certificates and the votes shall then be counted." Quayle concluded that the vice president had no flexibility in performing this task. His clear advice to Pence was to disregard Trump's request.[29]

On the morning of January 6, 2021, Vice President Pence was meeting with two members of his staff, Marc Short and Greg Jacob, to finish a letter that he was writing to deliver to President Trump. Jacob called Richard Cullen, who was Pence's personal lawyer in 2017. Cullen called J. Michael Luttig, who had retired as a federal judge. Years earlier, Luttig had as his law clerk John Eastman. Luttig told Cullen: "You can tell the vice president that I believe he has to certify the electoral college vote today."[30] Luttig sent a statement to Cullen, who incorporated it into Pence's letter.

Pence released his short letter minutes before 1 p.m. on January 6:

As a student of history who loves the Constitution and reveres its Framers, I do not believe that the Founders of our country intended to invest the Vice President with unilateral authority to decide which electoral votes should be counted during the Joint Session of Congress, and no Vice President in American history has ever asserted such authority.

This leaves open the question of whether the limited authority of the vice president is based upon the enacted law or a customary rule, and, if it *is* a customary rule, is it a customary rule with or without the force of law? Ultimately, regardless of the answer to that question, Vice President Pence decided not to proceed in accordance with Eastman's plan. Hence, he should be credited with having saved American democracy and the peaceful transition of power after a presidential election.

In a pivotal case, *Gohmert v. Pence*, Pence's authority to control the outcome of the election was not the direct issue resolved in the case.[31] The issue that was resolved in this case was that Gohmert and the alternate electors who were the plaintiffs in the case did not have standing to challenge the validity of the electors certified by the Arizona Governor. The electors appointed by the Governor cast their votes for Biden who had won the popular election in Arizona. I will return to this case below.

2.4 The alternate electors

While it was not generally known at the time, when the duly appointed electors were meeting on December 14, 2020, the day of the Electoral College's official vote, other meetings were taking place. There was an organized effort to implement the strategy of the Eastman memos. Republicans in Wisconsin, Arizona, New Mexico, Nevada, Georgia, Michigan, and Pennsylvania were meeting in their respective state capitols as alternate electors. Trump had lost the popular vote in all seven battleground states. The strategy was to submit to Congress phony certificates declaring that the alternate electors were the true electors.

On December 14, 2020, Republican electors met in the state capitols in the seven states. They proclaimed that they were "duly elected and qualified" members of the Electoral College, and they sent signed certificates stating that Donald Trump had won the election in their respective states. All seven of these states were states in which Biden had won the popular vote. The officially approved Biden electors also met in the state capitols. They also sent signed certificates stating that the electoral college votes in their respective states were being cast for Biden.

The plan was to have alternative slates of electors. Both groups of electors, the legal electors, and the alternate electors, met on December 14 to cast their votes for president and vice president. The alternate electors in the seven battleground states also met in their state capitols and cast their votes for Trump even though Biden had won the popular vote in those states. Congress and/or Vice President Pence could consider these alternate slates of electors to be the legitimate electors in those states. This had happened before. In the 1960 election, Hawaii had two slates of electors. One had been supported by the Republican Governor and the other by the Democrats.

The Republicans claim that in 2020 they were doing the same thing that the Democrats did in the 1960 election. In 1960, Senator John Kennedy was running against Vice President Richard Nixon. It was a very close election in Hawaii and the difference was only 200 votes. Nixon was declared the winner, but, on a recount, it appeared that Kennedy had won the state. Meanwhile, there were two slates of electors appointed who both sent in certificates proclaiming their candidate as the winner.

On January 6, 2001, Richard Nixon, who was the Vice President and the presiding officer in the Senate for the counting of the votes, suggested that the Democratic electors' certificate should be counted. At the time, Nixon said he did so "without the intent of establishing a precedent". In other words, Nixon was acting in accordance with a customary rule without the force of law in accepting the certificate of the candidate who won the election in Hawaii. Kennedy did not need the three electoral college votes from Hawaii to be the winner in the national election.

In five of the seven battleground states in 2020, the alternate electors used the exact same language in the certificates that they all signed. In two of the seven states, New Mexico and Pennsylvania, the wording of the certificates was altered. In these two states, the alternate electors were submitting their certificates only if the lawsuits filed by the Trump supporters were successful in establishing that the election had been fraudulent.

In Michigan, Dana Nessel, the Attorney General of the State of Michigan, had been in the Senate Chamber in the state capitol when the electors met to cast their vote. She observed the process as an interested spectator. She did not know at that time that there was an alternate group of Republican electors also meeting in the state capitol, following the same procedure as the lawful electors. She referred the issue of the alternate electors to the Department of Justice as an illegal conspiracy to obstruct the peaceful transfer of power after the election. She maintains that Michigan law requires that the electors meet in the Senate Chamber, and she was there when the electors met. The alternate electors were not there. It is her contention that submitting the false certificates to historical archives and governmental officials constituted an "open-and-shut case of forgery of a public record," which is a criminal offense.[32]

These activities in the seven battleground states were part of a planned scheme to change the result of the election and keep Trump in office. The effort was organized by the Trump campaign workers and Trump's attorneys. There can be no doubt that this effort was organized and conducted to prevent the peaceful transfer of the power of the presidency.

The New Mexico Attorney General, Hector Balderas, said that he also had referred the matter to federal prosecutors. The Attorney General in Wisconsin, Josh Katal, also agreed that the sending of the false certificates was a criminal act.

As more information is becoming available, there can no longer be any doubt that the scheme of having alternate electors was an organized attempt to interfere with the peaceful transfer of power. It is also apparent that many of the participants in this conspiracy were aware that the purported legal basis for the proposed action was weak. In other words, the participants knew that what they were doing was illegal.[33]

The House of Representatives has appointed a Select Committee to investigate the events involving the counting of the votes on January 6, 2020, when a mob attempted to disrupt the proceedings. I will briefly discuss the activities of the Committee in relation to the Eastman memoranda in section 3.3. This Committee has subpoenaed several of the alternate electors to testify before the Committee. As of this writing, they did not testify.[34]

2.5 Arizona and *Gohmert v. Pence*

Gohmert v. Pence involves the events in the 2020 Arizona election. Former President Donald J. Trump did not prevail in Arizona. He lost by a little more than 10,000 votes. He had won the election in Arizona in 2016 by approximately the same margin. Both before the election in 2020 and after the election, he claimed that the voting in Arizona would be, and was, rigged and that he had won the 2020 election in Arizona by a wide margin.

After the election, Trump and his attorney Rudy Giuliani called Rusty Bowers, the Republican Speaker of the House of Representatives in Arizona. They asked him to reverse the election results because it was a fraudulent election. They asked him to reconvene the Arizona Legislature and to recall the Biden electors. He was skeptical about their claim and asked for evidence. This was followed by a meeting on December 1, 2020, in a conference room of the Arizona Senate. In attendance at this meeting were Giuliani and his associates, Speaker Bowers and Senate President Karen Fann, also a Republican. Bowers was still unconvinced, but Fann seemed more receptive to doing something in response to the claim of a fraudulent election.

During the next few weeks, there was an effort by the two Chambers in Arizona to agree upon a course of action. Both Chambers were controlled by the Republican Party. Their focus and that of Trump and his allies was on Maricopa County. Trump lost that county by 45,100 votes, though he had won it by a similar margin in 2016.

The three Republican Representatives in Congress from Arizona sent a letter to the Maricopa County Board of Supervisors before the election results were certified, asking them to audit the voting in that county. The Board, however, decided to certify the votes. The Republican Governor Doug Ducey and Democratic Secretary of State Katie Hobbs signed the official canvas confirming the Arizona election results for Biden. As Ducey was signing the certification, he received a phone call from the White House, which he silenced.

The Republicans in Arizona, even though their candidate had lost the election, selected an alternate group of electors. This was part of the Eastman plan to overturn the election results. The Congress received two certifications of the voting in Arizona, one from the official electors and one from the alternate electors.[35] One was legal, and one was not legal. This conclusion is based upon a mixture of constitutional law, federal law, state law and customary rules.

Trump and his allies filed eight lawsuits specifically challenging the Arizona election results, one of which is *Gohmert v. Pence*. The plaintiffs in the *Gohmert* case are Louis Gohmert, a member of the U.S. House of Representatives from Texas and the slate of Republican electors for the State of Arizona. They were not the official electors since Trump did not win Arizona.[36] Gohmert is a congressman, an attorney, and a former judge. Judge Jeremy Kernodle, who decided the case at the trial level, was appointed by Trump.

The defendant is Michael R. Pence, in his official capacity as the vice president of the U.S. The vice president of the U.S. is, as I have already mentioned, the presiding officer in the U.S. Senate with the ceremonial role in the election vote counting procedure. The case was filed in the United States District Court for the Eastern District of Texas, Tyler Division. The issue in the lawsuit is that "Vice President Mike Pence should ultimately decide which electoral college votes to count when Congress meets January 6 to accept the election results". The relief requested specifically seeks to require that Pence not accept the electoral college votes from five states (Arizona, Georgia, Pennsylvania, Wisconsin, and Michigan), which would be enough to overturn the results of the election.

The lawsuit claims:

> Under the Twelfth Amendment Defendant Pence has the exclusive authority and sole discretion to open and permit the counting of the electoral votes for a given state, and where there are competing slates of electors, or where there is objection to any single slate of electors, to determine which electoral votes, or whether none, shall be counted.

This legal theory is one of the alternatives mentioned in the Eastman memoranda.

The plaintiffs lost the case.[37] The procedure for selecting the electors is left to the state legislatures.[38] The Arizona legislative leaders did not accept the argument that they had the authority to overturn the results of the election. After the disputed presidential election in 1876, a dispute that was resolved peacefully, the Congress adopted the Electoral Count Act.[39] This Act makes the certifications of the respective states "conclusive" regarding the counting of the electoral college votes.

On December 14, 2020, the members of the Electoral College met in their respective states and cast their votes in accordance with the popular vote in their state.[40] Since the Democratic Party had won the popular vote in Arizona, the 11 electors selected by the Democrats voted for Biden and Harris. Their votes were then certified by

Governor Ducey and Secretary of State Hobbs and sent to the Congress.

The plaintiff Republican electors in the *Gohmert* case claim that they also met in Arizona on that date and cast their votes for Trump and Pence (the same Pence who would preside in the Senate). In total, 73 electoral college votes were challenged in the so-called "contested states" (in addition to Arizona, Georgia, Wisconsin, Michigan, Nevada, New Mexico and Pennsylvania). In the Gohmert lawsuit, the Vice President did not support the plaintiffs' motion for an injunction that would have prevented him from performing his duties under the Electoral Count Act.

The Court of Appeals did not reach the merits of the case and did not decide what the role of the vice president is in the electoral process.[41] The Court of Appeals made its decision with a per curiam opinion. The case was decided by a panel of three Circuit Judges, without naming an author of the opinion. This is not an uncommon practice.[42]

2.6 The Pennsylvania experience

The official Pennsylvania Delegates (the electors for the Electoral College) for the Democratic Party convened in Harrisburg, the state capitol, on December 14, 2020. Harrisburg is a small city (49,247 residents) that is in the middle of the state. It is 200 miles from Pittsburg, the largest city to the west (301,296 population) and 106 miles from Philadelphia, the largest city to the east (1,782,000 population).

For the purpose of transparency, I should mention at this point that my wife, Marian D. Moskowitz, was one of the 20 Pennsylvania electors. My wife was also the chairwoman of the Board of Elections in Chester County during the 2020 election. Much of the information in this section comes from discussions with her.[43]

This was not a typical meeting of the Pennsylvania Electoral College, the type that usually occurred every four years. There are two dramatic differences between the 2020 meeting and all the prior meetings. The first variant is that this meeting occurred during the height of the COVID-19 pandemic. This resulted in a few changes, such as the elimination of much of the traditional ceremony. The second dramatic difference is that this meeting occurred during then-President Donald J. Trump's attack on the electoral system itself.

The meeting opened with this declaration: "Today you will follow the tradition of the first Electoral College that convened in Pennsylvania 231 years ago and cast your votes based on the outcome of that election to carry out the will of the voters of the Commonwealth of Pennsylvania." The outcome of the election in Pennsylvania was not in doubt because Biden had received 80,000 more votes than Trump.

Given the stridency of the opposition to the traditional procedure for electing the president and the peaceful transfer of power, there was great concern about potential efforts to prevent this meeting in Harrisburg, Pennsylvania on December 14 from occurring. The delegates were not told where the meeting would be and only told where to park their cars, and not to disclose the location of the parking garage to anyone. The delegates did not know that, while they were meeting, there was another meeting of "delegates" also occurring in Harrisburg. This group of alternate electors was also meeting at an unannounced location.

My wife's meeting was on C-Span, so that I was able to watch the entire proceeding (I was not permitted to attend the meeting in person). This other meeting of the alternate delegates, occurring at the same time, had no press coverage. At this second meeting, 20 prominent Republicans met in an unknown location in an unpublicized meeting, with no announcement or disclosure that the meeting was occurring.[44]

Not all potential Trump electors were willing to cooperate in this effort. Bunny Welsh, a former sheriff in Chester County, Pennsylvania, and a fervent Trump supporter, was one of the members of the Trump slate of electors who refused to participate in the scheme. She, like the others who refused, was replaced with a compliant party supporter.[45]

The meeting of the alternate electors was "at the request of the Trump campaign". The alternate electors cast what they referred to as a procedural vote that claimed that Trump had won the election in Pennsylvania. The certificate they signed was in a format with much of the same language as that of the actual electors. It had this important difference—the ballots of the Pennsylvania alternate electors were cast based upon the supposition that there would be a trial or some other official proceeding that would overturn the results of the Pennsylvania election. It is more likely that it would be a judicial proceeding, though some Pennsylvania legislators were promoting legislative action.

As explained in section 2.4, this aspect of the certificate of the alternate electors in Pennsylvania is the same as the one signed by alternate electors in New Mexico but is different from the certificates signed by the alternate electors in five other battleground states: Wisconsin, Nevada, Arizona, Michigan, and Georgia. The certificates in those five states looked like the official certificates.

Before I describe the events leading up to and occurring at the Pennsylvania Electoral College meeting on December 14, 2020, I should provide some background information about how my wife Marian became a member of the 2020 Pennsylvania Electoral College. Marian is not a professional politician.

In 2013, Marian was approached by Democratic members of the House of Representatives and asked if she would be willing to run for Congress. At that time, she had never run for an elected office or had any governmental job, except for an internship in a municipal office in her teens. Her only involvement in politics had been working at the polling place on election day. She had been appointed to serve on the

Council of Trustees of West Chester University by several Governors, both Democratic and Republican, and she has been on that Board for over 12 years.

She decided not to run for Congress. She did agree to be a candidate for the Pennsylvania General Assembly. She did not win the general election in 2014. In 2018, she decided to be a candidate for Chester County Commissioner in the 2019 election. This time, she won in both the primary and the general elections. On January 6, 2020, she was sworn in as the Chairwoman of the Board of Commissioners of Chester County.

Marian did not apply for the role of elector in the 2020 primary election. She was approached by the Biden/Harris campaign committee and asked if she would agree to be a candidate for the Electoral College as a delegate for Biden and Harris. She agreed. And she was elected in the primary election. On August 20, 2020, Marian received the official notification from Kathy Boockvar, Secretary of the Commonwealth of Pennsylvania, that she had been elected on June 20, 2020, to be a Delegate to the Democratic National Convention for the Sixth Congressional District of Pennsylvania, "having received 69,589 votes in the primary election". She would serve as a member of the Pennsylvania Electoral College only if Biden/Harris won the November election in Pennsylvania, which would mean that she had been selected to be an elector.

The 2020 Democratic National Convention was a virtual convention because of the COVID-19 pandemic, so Marian did not attend the convention in person but did participate in the Zoom version. Biden and Harris were nominated at the convention to be the candidates in the general election in November 2020. Marian, who by then had been a member of the Democratic State Committee for several years, actively supported the Biden/Harris ticket.

In Pennsylvania, each presidential candidate picks their electors within 30 days of their party's national convention. Their names are submitted to the Secretary of the Commonwealth. Marian's name was on the list submitted to the Secretary. On election day, November 3, 2020, voters actually vote for the electors to represent their candidate of choice (in this instance, Biden, Trump or the Libertarian candidate). The voters select, in effect, the electors for a candidate. The electors are then appointed based on which candidate won the election. Since Biden/Harris won, Marian was going to be an elector.

If the election in Pennsylvania was fraudulent, the Pennsylvania legislature, which was controlled by the Republicans, could decide that the voters have "failed to make a choice". The legislature can then decide how the electors shall be appointed. One potential interpretation of the constitutional provisions is that state legislatures decide how electors are appointed. Therefore, theoretically speaking, the legislators could decide that the election was fraudulent, and that Trump was in fact elected on November 3, 2020. I will return to this issue in section 3.6.. As of November 13, 2020, one week after the election, Republicans had called for an investigation into Pennsylvania's election.[46] This was consistent with John Eastman's legal theories and he, in fact, specifically suggested to Pennsylvania legislators that they follow this strategy.

As I explain below, the suggested legislative action in the absence of there being proof of a fraudulent election would violate a customary norm with the force of law if the consequence of such action was to overturn the result of the election. In other words, there is no legislative authority to select alternate electors if the election is not fraudulent and if doing so would give the presidency to a candidate who did not win the election.

2.7 Pennsylvania election law

The law related to the members of the Electoral College is primarily state law. There is no federal statute that requires electors to vote either for the candidate who won the popular vote in their state or for the candidate for whom they pledged to vote. There are statutes in some states regarding this issue. Pennsylvania does have a statute, but it does not relate to how the electors must vote.[47] Pennsylvania does not require electors to pledge who they will vote for. In theory, a Pennsylvania elector has discretion to vote for whomever they select, and the vote will be counted.[48] For an individual Pennsylvania elector to be a faithless elector and to not vote for the candidate for whom they had been elected to be an elector would violate a customary norm. But this is a customary norm without the force of law if it does not affect the outcome of the national election.

In summary, in Pennsylvania, there is no constitutional provision, federal statute, or state statute that controls how an elector will vote. The electors who are chosen to vote do not sign a pledge as to how they will vote. There is no penalty for "faithless electors" in Pennsylvania.[49] Election law in Pennsylvania includes constitutional, federal, state and local norms. The overlapping legal systems demonstrate the complexity that Hart's rule of recognition does not accommodate. In short, the present state of election law does not ensure the peaceful transfer of power after a presidential election.

2.8 The Pennsylvania electoral college meeting

On November 24, 2020, a letter was sent to Marian and to the 19 other Pennsylvania Democratic electors that the Electoral College would meet on December 14. The letter did not state where they would meet. It instructed her where to park and stated that she would be taken to the still-undisclosed location where the meeting would occur. There would be a van in the aforementioned parking garage that would take the electors to the meeting. They would be issued a mask (in accordance with COVID-19 precautions) that would have the inscription 59th Electoral College, December 14, 2020. This mask would, in effect, be their identifying pass to enter the location where the Electoral College would meet.

It was obvious from the way the meeting was being arranged that there was genuine concern that there might be an effort to interfere with the proceedings. In fact, in Michigan, when the electoral college members met, there was a demonstration at the state capitol and the state police had to bar entry to the mob that assembled there. Hence, the location in Pennsylvania was a secret location. No visitors would be allowed to attend (it would be available on C-Span to watch the event), there would be a heavy police presence (and Marian did see police on rooftops and there were other police officers who were visibly present), and safety precautions were being taken. Fortunately, there were no problems and no effort to stop the meeting from occurring.

The meeting was scheduled to begin at 12:00 p.m. The agenda for the meeting was sent to the delegates.[50] Since most of us have never observed a meeting of the Electoral College, here is what happened at that meeting.

The Secretary of the Commonwealth of Pennsylvania, Kathy Boockvar, gave a short opening statement. There was a pledge of allegiance and an invocation. Secretary Boockvar then gave a longer speech. She started with the Founding Fathers:

> Pennsylvania is the birthplace of the U.S. Constitution and the Electoral College, which the framers of the Constitution created as a compromise between those who advocated for the direct election of the president by the people and those who advocated for the Congress to appoint the president. As a compromise, the decision was made that the people of the United States vote for 'electors' who, in turn, vote for the president and the vice president.

She reviewed the changes that have occurred since that beginning and the various constitutional amendments. 6.9 million people in Pennsylvania voted in the 2020 election. On this day, the electors will follow the tradition that started 231 years ago and cast their votes based on the outcome of that election.

Temporary officers were then appointed to serve just for this meeting. The Certificate of Ascertainment was accepted from the Governor. This document identifies the electors. Secretary Boockvar then read the names of the 20 electors and each one stood as their name was called.[51] Secretary Boockvar then declared: "Twenty Electors having answered to their names, we shall proceed with the business of the 59th Pennsylvania Electoral College".

The oath of office was administered to the electors by Justice Max Baer of the Pennsylvania Supreme Court. Each elector stood, raising their right hand, with their left hand on the Bible they had brought with them. They responded, "I do" to the following oath:

> Do you and each of you solemnly swear (or affirm) that you will support, obey and defend the Constitution of the United States and the Constitution of the Commonwealth of Pennsylvania and that you will discharge the duties of your office with fidelity?

The oath is interesting in several respects. The electors are going to vote for two national positions—the presidency and vice presidency—but their oath is to both the National Constitution and the State Constitution. The oath refers to the Constitution, rather than to the law. We know that the Constitution itself consists of not only the original document with its constitutional rules and principles but also the amendments, judicial interpretations, and customary rules with the force of law. In other words, if you look to the rule of recognition for the ascertainment of the law that is being defended, obeyed, and supported, the law consists of more than the original written Constitution.

When the oath refers to "fidelity," what does this mean? This is not a pledge to vote for the candidate who received the majority of the popular vote in the state. It is not even a pledge to vote for the candidates of the political party that selected the individuals to be electors. It is presumably fidelity to the Constitution and/or the broader concept of constitutional norms. It may even be extended to fidelity to the law. The question that is not resolved in the Constitution, the constitutional norms, or the law is whether "fidelity" means voting in accordance with the democratic process of voting for the candidate who wins the popular vote.

The next order of business of the meeting was to elect the president of the Electoral College. Nancy Mills of Allegheny County was accordingly nominated and elected and gave a short speech. The vice president of the Electoral College was then elected, and he made a brief speech. This was followed by the election of the other officers of the Electoral College: secretary, and parliamentarian.

The members of the Electoral College, following the traditional process for its meetings, proceeded with the voting for the president and vice president of the United States. The resolution for this action referred to the electors "in accordance with the provisions of the Constitution and the laws of the United States and the Commonwealth of Pennsylvania do now proceed to ballot for President of the United States". Note the slight change in language between this resolution and the oath of office, with this resolution referring to the law as well as the Constitution.

The resolution was adopted by voice vote of the electors. Three individuals, who were not electors, were then appointed to be the tellers for the vote. Each elector was instructed to write on their ballot the name of the individual for whom they were voting to be the president. The same procedure was then followed for the voting for the vice president. By roll call, each elector placed their ballots for president and vice president in the official ballot box. I should note here that the ballot box was the original one designed by Ben Franklin.

The tellers counted the ballots and prepared their written report. There were six alternate electors available, who were then thanked for being in attendance. Pennsylvania law has no legal rule for replacing faithless electors, so these alternate electors could act as electors only if one or more of the official electors did not attend the meeting.

The head teller announced that the electors had cast their 20 votes for Joseph R. Biden for president and Kamala D. Harris for vice president. The chair requested that the secretary record the vote in the written record of the proceedings. The six Certificates of Vote were then signed by each of the electors. I watched on C-Span as Marian went to the stage to sign her certificates.

Marian then offered the Resolution for the delivery of the signed documents:

> RESOLVED, that the President appoint one Elector to take charge and ensure that one package of all legally required documents be delivered to the President of the Senate of the United States in Washington, D.C.

The resolution was adopted, and the elector was appointed. The same procedure was followed for sending the documents to the Secretary of the Commonwealth of Pennsylvania, the National Archivist, and the Chief Judge of the District Court of the United States for the Middle District of Pennsylvania. It was also resolved that a copy of the proceedings be delivered to the Secretary of the Commonwealth.

Two electors were then appointed to settle the accounts and expenses of the College of Electors (the fee and expense payments to the electors are modest). The Pennsylvania statute also calls for the payment of $100 for the expenses of the Electoral College. A resolution was then adopted to publish the proceedings. The final resolutions were to express appreciation to all the participants in the meeting and to adjourn the meeting. The meeting took approximately one hour.

Marian proceeded by van to the garage to retrieve her car. The capitol police offered to accompany her from the parking garage to the Pennsylvania Turnpike, but she felt that would not be necessary. She encountered no hostile persons on her ride home.

2.9 The conspiracy to overturn the election

It was not known at the time of the electoral college meeting in Pennsylvania on December 14, 2020, that there was an organized campaign involving the seven battleground states to overturn the election results. The seven battleground states had 79 electoral college votes. Biden won those states by a margin of 311,257 votes out of 25.5 million ballots cast for president.

It was well known that Trump was and still is proclaiming that he was the winner in the election. His efforts in late 2020 to overturn the election results, however, seemed to be focused on lawsuits and not on an effort to avoid the peaceful transfer of power by virtually all conceivable means. These methods to overturn the election results were legal only if the law was distorted and highly questionable reasoning was employed. As I will explain in section 3.3, this was a coup in search of a legal theory.

Many of the details of the Trump/Eastman conspiracy are not known. Some of them may not be known for several years. The identity of the conspirators remains to be established. In sections 3.3, 3.11 and 3.12, I present what we know at the time of this writing. More will become known when all of John Eastman's email messages are reviewed and the trial discussed in sections 3.11 and 3.12 occurs. Most importantly, the legal theory of the conspirators is not based upon established law, and that is our primary interest.

3.
The Aftermath of the 2020 Election

3.1 The Trump lawsuits

Trump supporters filed 62 lawsuits challenging the results of the election. Most of the lawsuits were in six of the seven battleground states. There were no lawsuits in New Mexico except for a frivolous one filed to support the alternate electors.[52] The alternate electors signed fraudulent certificates which claimed that they were the electors because Trump had won the election in their state.

The cases were filed in both the state courts and the federal courts. One of John Eastman's theories is that the state legislatures could appoint the electors for Trump even though Trump did not win the popular election. They could do so on the basis that the election was fraudulent, even though they could not prove that it was. His legal theory behind this scheme is based upon the independent state legislative theory, which is that the state legislatures control the electoral process. This theory has never been accepted by a majority of the Justices of SCOTUS.

Trump lost 61 of the 62 lawsuits. Some cases were dismissed for lack of standing, some because the plaintiffs did not have a cause of action, and others based upon the plaintiffs not being able to prove that there was fraud. In none of the lawsuits were the plaintiffs able to come close to offering proof of fraud that would affect the outcome of the election in that state.

The Trump supporters had a small victory in just one case, but the outcome of the case did not affect who won the election. The court agreed with the Trump campaign that voters could not cure their ballots without providing proper identification. The ruling affected only a few voters.[53]

I have already discussed one of the Arizona lawsuits, *Gohmert v. Pence*.[54] The lawsuits challenging the vote in Wisconsin were also unsuccessful. There was an effort to recount the votes that had resulted in Biden winning in Wisconsin by more than 20,000 votes. The challenge was to only two of the Wisconsin counties (there are 70 other counties) which were the two with a large percentage of African American voters. A writ of certiorari to the U.S. Supreme Court was filed, but the Court declined to hear the case.[55]

Biden had defeated Trump by more than 80,000 votes in Pennsylvania. Only 10,000 ballots were being challenged in a case filed in the Pennsylvania courts, so even a decision for Trump in the case would not overturn the results of the election. This case was also unsuccessful. The Pennsylvania Supreme Court rejected appeals by the Republican Party of Pennsylvania that challenged the Court's order to election officials to count mail-in ballots that were postmarked by election day and received up to three days later.

Trump's supporters then filed a writ of certiorari with the U.S. Supreme Court to overturn the decision of the Pennsylvania Supreme Court. Six Justices voted not to hear the case. Three Justices dissented from that decision—Clarence Thomas, Samuel Alito, and Neal Gorsuch. Justice Thomas wrote a dissenting opinion based on the contention that state officials did not have the power to set election rules. The rules were made by election officials to facilitate voting because of the pandemic.

These changes in the election regulations favored mail-in ballots being cast, so that voters, because of concern about the COVID pandemic, would be able to avoid going into the election polling stations to vote in person. The Republican Party opposed the deadline extension. The Republican-controlled state legislature had set a strict deadline for mail-in voting, requiring that the ballots be received by 8:00 p.m. on election day. The Pennsylvania Supreme Court had extended that date not only because of the pandemic, but also to offset delays in the postal service.

Justice Thomas's dissent casts doubt upon the legitimacy of the 2020 election. After the election, it became clear that Justice Thomas's wife, Ginni Thomas, was very active in trying to convince state officials to accept John Eastman's theories about constitutional law and take steps to overturn the election results. Notwithstanding his wife's active involvement in the election conspiracy, Justice Thomas did not recuse himself from voting in the election cases. I discuss this issue, Justice Thomas not recusing himself, and its effect upon the growing disrespect for the U.S. Supreme Court, in *The Judge and the Incorrect Decision* (volume four).

The cases that I have mentioned are relatively moot because they do not affect the outcome of the election. The oddity in Justice Thomas's dissent in the Pennsylvania case is that he contends that the federal courts can overturn the state court's interpretation of its own constitution based on what it believes the legislature prefers. While this is what happened in *Bush v. Gore*, that decision is not consistent with the customary rules.

In Justice Thomas's dissent, he appears to accept Trump's claims of election fraud. He contends that SCOTUS must "override state courts that expand vote by mail pursuant to their state constitutions". The prevailing customary rule is that the state courts control election law in their states.[56] This case illustrates the confusing mix of federal law, state law, and local law that is illustrative of election law.

The U.S. Supreme Court rejected two other appeals filed by Trump's lawyers challenging the results in Pennsylvania and Wisconsin. This challenge was that the mail-in ballots in these two states were invalid. The Republican lawyers challenged 9,428 ballots in Pennsylvania out of 6.9 million votes. The attempt was to block a lower court ruling that the ballots be counted. The Supreme Court also rejected other cases brought by Trump lawyers challenging the results of the election in Pennsylvania, Michigan, Georgia, and Arizona.[57]

It is fair to declare that "[t]he American judiciary saved our democracy". In the four years of his presidency, Trump appointed 206 judges to the federal bench, including three to the Supreme Court and 54 to the 13 Federal Courts of Appeals. There were 62 post-election lawsuits. They were heard by approximately 90 judges. These 90 judges included 38 Republican appointees, and eight appointed by Trump himself. They heard these lawsuits and Trump won just one case.[59]

3.2 The counting of the electoral college votes

In accordance with the constitutional and statutory norms, the Congress met in joint session on January 6, 2021, for the counting of the electoral college votes. As explained in Sections 2.1 to 2.3 in this volume, Vice President Pence, as the presiding officer in the Senate, was responsible for announcing the results of each state in alphabetical order. Members of Congress could register objections to the results (one Senator and one House member would be required to lodge an objection). In the event of an objection, each of the Chambers of Congress would meet separately. A majority vote to accept the objection is required in both Chambers for the votes in a specific state to not be counted.

Some members of the House intended to register an objection to certifying the votes in several battleground states. If a single senator also objected to the certification, the entire body of the House and the Senate would then have to vote on the certification for the state in which there was an objection. Some of the Senate Republicans did not want to offend Trump and to accept the certification of the Biden electors in the battleground states. Senator Josh Hawley of Missouri, who had served as a law clerk to a Supreme Court Chief Justice, announced on December 30, 2020, that he would object to the certification of the votes in some states.

The first objection was to the counting of the votes from Arizona. The Senate rejected the challenge to the Arizona vote. The meeting in the joint session was suspended when a riot occurred, and the members of Congress departed the chamber to avoid the mob.

When the Congress reconvened on January 6, Senator Mike Lee gave the following description of the process:

> We each have to remember that we have sworn an oath to uphold, protect and defend this document. [He waved a copy of the Constitution]. The Vice President of the United States shall open the ballots and the votes shall be counted. It is these words that confine, define and constrain every scrap of authority that we have in the process. Our job is to open and then count. That's it. That's all there is.
>
> I have spent an enormous amount of time reaching out to state government officials in these states, but in none of the contested states— no, not even one—did I discover any indication that there was any chance that any state legislature, or secretary of state, or governor, or lieutenant governor, that had any intention to alter the slate of electors.
>
> Our job is to convene, to open the ballots, and to count them. That's it.[60]

When the Congress reconvened, there an objection to the Pennsylvania certification. The Senate rejected the challenge to the Pennsylvania electoral college vote by 92 to 7. The House reached the same result by vote of 282 to 138.

In summary, 145 Republican members of Congress (7 Senators and 138 House members) did not vote to accept the certificate of the Pennsylvania members of the Electoral College. Therefore, 145 members of Congress rejected the vote of the duly elected electors. They wanted to allow the vote of the alternate electors to be accepted, even though there was not then and there is not now any proof that there was fraud in the Pennsylvania election. Ultimately the vote of the alternate electors was ignored, and the Pennsylvania electoral college votes gave Joe Biden the presidency.

The scheme involving the alternate electors, even though ultimately unsuccessful, is still important because it illustrates a weakness in the electoral system. This strategy of organized alternate electors, coupled with the faithless elector possibility, jointly pose a real danger to the democratic system. Alternate electors and faithless electors are possible because of the way the votes are cast and the ambiguities in the process. In short, we need clear law, determinate applicable legal rules, rather than customary rules without the force of law, to dictate how the president is selected and to implement the peaceful transfer of power.

The reader may wonder what transpired after the counting of the votes. The House appointed a select committee, which I am calling the January 6 committee, to investigate what happened on January 6, 2021. The committee has issued its report. Based upon it, we can bring the story current regarding the alternate electors and John Eastman.

3.3 The January 6 committee

The House of Representatives created the House January 6 Select Committee to investigate the January 6 insurrection. The committee subpoenaed Jenna Ellis, a lawyer who worked on the Trump campaign with Rudolph Giuliani, to testify about the implementation of the scheme to deny Biden the presidency and retain Trump as the president. The subpoena indicates that she circulated two memos outlining such a program. These two memos are the Eastman memos.

The January 6 committee also subpoenaed the email messages written by John Eastman about the plan to overthrow the election results. Eastman filed a lawsuit claiming attorney/client privilege as his justification for not giving the committee approximately 100 messages. At the three-hour virtual court hearing before District Court Judge David O. Carter of the Central District of California Southern Division District Court, the oral argument concerned whether Eastman could claim the attorney/client privilege or whether the District Court might find that Eastman and President Trump conspired to violate federal law. If they did so conspire, the privilege would not apply. In addition, if the advice Eastman was giving was political rather than legal advice, Eastman might lose the case. Judge Carter might find that the law did not allow Vice President Pence to do what Eastman was requesting that he do.[61]

The January 6 committee contends that Eastman aided his client Trump in breaking the law in order to overturn the election results. Eastman's lawyer argued that Eastman's advice was based on his theory that the Electoral Count Act is unconstitutional. The committee's lawyer responded that, even if it were, Eastman could challenge it in court, but had to comply with the subpoena anyway: the Act should be considered constitutional until a court states otherwise.[62]

The January 6 committee produced an 845-page report. They referred Trump, Eastman, Rudy Giuliani, Jeffrey Clark, and Kenneth Chesebro to the Department of Justice for potential prosecution for their post-election activities and their role in the January 6 insurrection. Regarding Eastman's role, Greg Jacob, Pence's attorney, had testified that Eastman had acknowledged to him that his advice to Trump would violate the Electoral Count Act. Further, Trump had been told that it would be illegal for Pence to block Biden from becoming the president.

The committee pointed out that, when Eastman spoke at the "stop the steal" rally on January 6, he continued to claim that there was fraud in the election. He even pronounced a new wild conspiracy theory about secret folders in voting machines that were used to cast votes for Democrats.

In an opinion dated March 28, 2022, Judge Carter ruled that Dr. Eastman and President Trump conspired to overturn the results of the 2020 election. He described it as a "coup in search of a legal theory".[63] Judge Carter found that John Eastman, while he was a professor at Chapman University, worked with President Trump and his campaign in developing its legal and political strategy regarding the results of the November 3, 2020, election. Eastman used the Chapman University email account. Eastman turned over to the select committee some of his email messages. He withheld 111 messages that he claims are privileged, based on his acting as a lawyer when they were written.

Judge Carter concludes that Eastman met with state legislators to advise them that they had the authority to direct the "manner" of choosing presidential electors. On January 2, 2021, Eastman and President Trump conducted a briefing with several hundred state legislators urging them to decertify the Biden presidential electors. There were several other instances of efforts to influence state legislators and officials to disregard the popular vote in their states.

The two memoranda that Eastman wrote and distributed were reviewed in detail by Judge Carter. Judge Carter quotes Eastman's memos that state that the plan would work because the applicable rules were ambiguous.

Eastman claims that he was only stating his opinion as to the law and providing legal and political advice. This claim is shattered by the Court's conclusion of law:

> Ultimately, Dr. Eastman concluded that his argument was contrary to consistent historical practice, would likely be unanimously rejected by the U.S. Supreme Court, and violated the Electoral Count Act on four separate grounds.

Let's pause here for a moment. "Consistent historical practice" is a reference to the customary rules. Prediction of what the Supreme

Court will decide does not necessarily mean that the law is what the Supreme Court will declare it is before the decision is made.[64] The law, which is the pre-existing law before the case is decided, consists of the current legal rules. Regarding the Electoral Count Act, Eastman's contention is that the Act is unconstitutional, but Judge Carter correctly views it as constitutional until such time as a court decides that it is not.

Of the 111 documents in question in the lawsuit, 22 relate to Eastman's view of the Electoral Count Act and his suggestion that Vice President Pence reject or delay specific votes of electoral college members. It is significant that Eastman was proposing that Pence act without first seeking court review or support or approval at the joint session of the Congress. Eastman's only references to litigation related to suits brought to stop Pence from acting, suits like the *Gohmert* case. Eastman conceded that the action brought by Gohmert would be unsuccessful because, according to Eastman, his legal theories would be rejected by the Supreme Court by a 9 to 0 vote. Judge Carter holds that 21 of the 22 documents were not prepared in anticipation of litigation and should be available for the committee to review.

A lawyer should distinguish for his client whether he is telling the client what the law is or what he thinks the law should be. The client wants to know whether the contemplated action is consistent with the law. The lawyer should not advise the client to take an action that is contrary to the law, either because it could be a crime or, if there is civil litigation, the court is likely to reach the correct decision and the client would lose the case in most instances.

Of the documents before Judge Carter, 17 of them were prepared for distribution to members of Congress. These documents were not prepared in anticipation of litigation and are not protected by the attorney/client privilege. The District Court ordered that they be turned over to the January 6 committee. To the contrary, 13 of the documents were prepared for President Trump or his campaign attorneys or personal attorneys, and these documents need not be provided to the committee.

Some of the documents fall within the attorney/client privilege unless they are subject to the crime-fraud exception to the privilege. The crime-fraud exception applies if the client is seeking advice to aid in the commission of a crime or a fraud or the advice is in furtherance of the crime. The committee claims that these documents fall within the exception because they do relate to a crime. That crime being the obstruction or the attempted obstruction of an official proceeding, which in this case would be the counting of the electoral college votes.[65]

3.4 Eastman's legal advice

The State Bar of California is considering revoking Eastman's license to practice law (disbarment). It has sent to Eastman a Notice of Disciplinary Charges for obstructing the certification of the electoral college vote. The State Bar Association claims that Eastman's actions violate the State's Rules of Professional Conduct. The State Bar also contends that Eastman filed legal documents in two lawsuits that contained false and misleading statements that alleged election fraud without any evidence of such fraud.[66]

On June 19, 2023, a pretrial conference was held in the disbarment proceedings. There was a hearing in late June 2023 at which time the Bar Association presented its witnesses. One of the witnesses was Greg Jacob, Pence's lawyer, who was at the meeting at the White House on January 4, 2021. Jacob testified that Eastman's advice to Pence "brought our profession into disrepute".[67] It is estimated that the hearing will take approximately two weeks. Other Trump lawyers are also facing disciplinary proceedings from state bar associations.[68]

Eastman tried to convince Trump, Pence, and multiple state officials that Pence could, with or without the support of Congressmen, prevent Biden from being declared the winner of the 2020 presidential election:

That theory is at the heart of the state's case to punish Eastman on 11 professional charges, which include failure to support the laws and Constitution, seeking to mislead a court, misrepresentations to other Trump aides and the public, and moral turpitude.[69]

There are also ongoing investigations of Eastman's activities in federal and state investigations. Based upon testimony from the alternate electors (the fake Republican electors), the Department of Justice is looking into the activities of the Trump lawyers, including Eastman, in trying to overturn the results of the 2020 election. This testimony could include that the Republican electors were advised by Eastman and the other Trump lawyers to make false statements. It is also possible that the lawyers gave the fake electors misleading advice as part of a deliberate fraud designed to keep Trump in office.[70]

Eastman is also being investigated in Georgia by Fulton County district attorney Fani Willis, see section 3.12. In Georgia, Rudy Giuliani testified before the special Grand Jury. He talked to Georgia legislators three times after the election claiming that he had evidence of fraud in the election.[71]

The lesson for lawyers is that they must distinguish for their clients what is the law from what they think the law should be. Eastman failed to do so when he told his client what his client wanted to hear.

3.5 Judge Carter's decision in the *Eastman* case

In the first instance in American history in which a sitting president is accused of committing a crime by a federal judge, Judge Carter states that: "President Trump attempted to obstruct an official proceeding by launching a pressure campaign to convince Vice President Pence to disrupt the Joint Session on January 6". Since the Twelfth Amendment outlines the steps to elect the president, the January 6 Joint Session of Congress is clearly an official proceeding. While there is no authoritative source that is cited for this ruling, Judge Carter does refer to ten decisions at the District Court level (not in his District Court but in the District of Columbia District Court) declaring that the January 6 event qualifies as an official proceeding.

Eastman's entire theory is based upon the false claim by Donald Trump that fraud was involved in the 2020 presidential election. There were over 60 lawsuits in which there was an attempt to prove that there was fraud, and all these cases were unsuccessful due to lack of evidence of fraudulent behavior. Moreover, Eastman stepped outside the "bounds of normal legal practice" when he declared that "we're no longer playing by Queensbury rules". Some of the customary rules involved in this case are clearly part of the law.

Judge Carter rejects Eastman's contention that he is making a good faith interpretation of the Constitution when he asserts that the Electoral Count Act is unconstitutional. Just like a carpenter driving in a nail, Judge Carter strikes down this argument:

> Disagreeing with the law entitled President Trump to seek a remedy in court, not to disrupt a constitutionally mandated process. [Footnote omitted]. And President Trump knew how to pursue election claims in court—after filing and losing more than sixty suits, this plan was a last-ditch attempt to secure the Presidency by any means.

The peaceful transition of power is fundamental to our democracy. It is a constitutional principle and, as such, it is part of the law.[72] The phrase "peaceful transition of power" does not appear in the Constitution. It is not an enacted rule of law. I have contended that constitutional principles are an outlier. Principles, in general, are not part of the law. They are too general to be the equivalent of a rule of law. They do not function in the manner that rules do since they are too general to be applied. Constitutional principles are part of the written and unwritten Constitution and function as constitutional norms.

Judge Carter views the peaceful transfer of power after the presidential election to be a foundational principle and a part of the law. I assume that it becomes part of the law as a customary rule with the force of law. Starting with George Washington as the first president, every president except for Donald Trump has accepted that their successor would become the president. While the duty of the members of the Electoral College has evolved since the Constitution was drafted, the president is still elected by the Electoral College.

John Eastman knew that his legal theory was inconsistent with the law. He himself characterized the act that he wanted Vice President Pence to commit as only a "minor violation" of the Electoral Count Act. Eastman knew, according to Judge Carter, that his outcome-driven plan had to violate the law.

Before leaving this issue of Eastman's memos and his emails, Judge Carter was considering the emails subpoenaed by the January 6 committee. There is also another batch of emails that the committee did not subpoena. Eastman was a visiting professor at the Boulder campus of the University of Colorado during the 2020/2021 academic year. While there, he used the University of Colorado's email system to write other emails. The University of Colorado has made those emails available for public review.

This second batch of emails provides some insight into Eastman's interaction with the Pennsylvania legislators and the alternate Republican electors that he conspired with in an effort to deny Biden the electoral college votes from Pennsylvania. We now know that Eastman met with Pennsylvania legislators right after the election so that he could advise them about how to implement his strategy for overturning the election results.

More specifically, Eastman, shortly after November 3, 2020, went to Philadelphia to participate in an academic conference. While there, he met with Pennsylvania legislator Russ Diamond. Eastman tutored Diamond on how to challenge the election results in Pennsylvania. The emails from the University of Colorado email account also contain advice from Eastman to Diamond "on how to challenge his state's presidential electors". In the emails, Eastman offered edits to legislative resolutions and suggested ways in which Pennsylvania lawmakers could seat an alternate set of electors after Joe Biden won the state—and with it the presidency—in the 2020 election.[73]

Eastman also advised Representative Diamond that there was "ample evidence of sufficient anomalies and illegal votes to have turned the election from Trump to Biden".[74] In an email, Diamond introduces Eastman to other legislators. Diamond claims that Eastman has established how "to decertify presidential electors without ANY evidence of retail 'voter fraud'".[75] In fact, there was no evidence of voter fraud in Pennsylvania and all the lawsuits challenging Pennsylvania's election were unsuccessful.

In another email from Eastman to Diamond, Eastman provides an even more devious methodology for subverting the results of the election. This strategy involves declaring that the mail-in ballots are illegitimate. This would reduce Biden's vote count and could give Trump more votes than Biden. Eastman advises:

> Then, having done that math, you'd be left with a significant Trump lead that would bolster the argument for the Legislature adopting a slate of Trump electors—perfectly within your authority to do anyway, but now bolstered by the untainted popular vote. That would help provide some cover.

This would allow the legislature to reject the Biden electors certified by the governor and to certify the Trump electors instead.[76]

Finally, the January 6 committee also wants at least 12 of the alternate electors to appear before the committee and explain why they certified that they were the duly elected and qualified electors. They knew that their candidate, Trump, had lost the election in their states. As mentioned earlier, in five of the states, they misrepresented their status. In Pennsylvania and New Mexico, they claimed to be electors only if the lawsuits were successful.[77]

Before we leave this subject of the presidential election, let's take one more detour into the issue of the faithless elector. This will allow, once again, for distinguishing customary rules with the force of law from customary rules that lack the force of law. The customary rule that members of the Electoral College must vote for the candidate who won the popular vote in their state may, in the circumstances that I will describe, be a customary rule *with* the force of law. It may, also, be the subject of a state statute and become part of the law because of that enactment. Absent a relevant state statute, the individual faithless elector does not violate the law when he votes for a candidate other than the candidate who won the popular election if his vote does not affect the outcome of the election. I return to this issue in section 3.10.

3.6 The faithless electors

I am considering in this section the central issues concerning the election of POTUS. Simply put, the question is whether a member of the Electoral College may exercise independent judgment on who should get his electoral college vote. In other words, is the member of the Electoral College legally required to vote in accordance with the popular vote in the state that appointed him to the Electoral College?[78]

Eastman's strategy is a return to the time when the Founding Fathers were considering the issue. Many of the citizens at that time were illiterate. Many were uneducated. Many were ill-informed about events outside of their community. Accurate news about what was happening on a national basis was not readily available. Political parties were not anticipated and not regarded as desirable. Forming a democracy was a new idea without historical experience to guide the colonists. And the democracy that they formed was not egalitarian in nature but a democracy of the landholding white elite, excluding females, slaves, and former slaves, and those who did not own property.

Moreover, the whole idea of a national government, a joint government of the separate and distinct colonies, did not have full support of the entire populace. This endeavor was an experiment. The men, and it was only men, who wrote the Constitution were brilliant and rational with a wide view of the world and a clear idea of what they were doing. They were well educated in philosophy and history. But many of the decisions they made, like the question of dealing with slavery, were compromises, designed to achieve the widest acceptance and the ultimate ratification of the Constitution they were writing.

Since the Constitution was adopted, much has changed. The landscape we have now is a multidimensional composite of horizontal and vertical (like east/west and north/south) relationships. As we have considered above, the legal rules that have been developed in the United States are derived from the Constitution, amendments to the Constitution, federal statutes and precedents, state statutes and precedents, local rules and customs with the force of law. The legal system also includes local customs without the force of law. The issue of the faithless elector has roots within this network of rules, including the customary rules.

States are primarily in control of the electoral college system. 32 states have statutes that bind electors in voting as members of the Electoral College. In only 15 states, the statutes permit the political parties to replace a faithless elector. In some states, the statutes allow the state to levy a fine on the faithless elector, though his vote is submitted to Congress. Congress generally does not reject the vote of a faithless elector when it completes its final tally of the votes.

Different states have different norms on electoral processes, such as mail-in voting, drop-in boxes, checking of signatures, showing identification, hours for voting, days for voting, when votes may be counted, and so forth. The Texas legislature has not adopted binding laws about faithless electors even though there were two faithless electors in Texas in 2016.[79] In fact, there were seven faithless electors in the 2016 election. In summary, electors are free to vote for the candidate of their choice regardless of the popular vote in some states while in others they are constrained.

To return to the faithless elector, there are three cases we can consider that shed light on the issue of the faithless elector. Our first precedent is *Ray v. Blair.*[80] This case involves the 1952 presidential election. Even though the selection of electors is controlled by state law, the U.S. Supreme Court agreed to hear the case because it involved a federal election.

In 1952, the statute in Alabama provided that the executive committee of the political party had the duty of determining who would be the party's candidates for the Electoral College. Ben F. Ray was the Chairman of the Alabama Executive Committee of the Democratic Party. Edmund Blair was qualified to be an elector and he wanted to be an elector for the Democratic Party. Ray refused to certify him as an elector. Ray did so because Blair refused to sign a pledge that he would support the endorsed Democratic Party candidates for the presidency and vice presidency.

While the Alabama state statute did not stipulate that an elector had to agree to sign a pledge, the statute granted to the executive committees of the political parties the right to establish the criteria for being an elector for their party. The Democratic Party required that the elector sign the pledge.

Blair filed a lawsuit requesting that the court order Ray to accept him as an elector. The Alabama Supreme Court ruled in favor of Blair. It held that the Twelfth Amendment to the Constitution allowed electors to exercise discretion in deciding for whom they would vote. The U.S. Supreme Court decided to take the case.

The U.S. Supreme Court reversed the decision of the Alabama Supreme Court. The U.S. Supreme Court found that states may exclude or may allow political parties to exclude potential electors if they refuse to sign a pledge. The Supreme Court did not decide what happens if the elector signs the pledge but does not honor it in casting his vote. In other words, the consequences of the faithless elector signing the pledge but not honoring it is not an issue in this case. The decision did not resolve the issue of whether a state could penalize a faithless elector.

The second and third cases were consolidated into one decision entitled *Chiafalo v. Washington*. The cases concern Washington and Colorado faithless electors in the 2016 presidential election. The electors involved in the two cases are subject to their respective state statutes.[81] This unanimous decision (9 to 0) answers the question left hanging in *Ray v. Blair*—can a state penalize its electors if they do not honor their pledge to vote for the candidate who wins the popular vote?

The Supreme Court ruled that states do have the authority to require that electors honor their pledge in presidential elections. In the Washington situation, faithless electors were fined $1,000 for not voting for the nominees of their party. In the Colorado version, *Colorado Department of State v. Bacca*, the Colorado statute provided for the removal and replacement of an elector who does not vote for the presidential candidate who won the popular vote in the state.[82] The Supreme Court rejected the argument that electors have discretion to vote for their candidate of choice pursuant to the Twelfth Amendment to the U.S. Constitution. As in the *Washington* case, this was a unanimous decision, though this one was 8 to 0 because Justice Sotomayor recused herself. The *Colorado* decision was a per curiam decision that followed the reasoning in the *Washington* case.

In the 2016 election, Trump should have received 306 electoral college votes, but two faithless electors did not vote for him, so he received 304. There were other faithless electors in states that Clinton won. In Washington, where Clinton won the popular vote, four of the twelve electors did not vote for her. They were each fined $1,000, and three of those four electors challenged the legality of the fines being imposed. It is unknown whether any of the four ever paid the fine.

In the *Washington* case, the votes of the faithless electors were counted, and the fines were imposed. In the *Colorado* case, the Supreme Court held that the faithless electors could be replaced if they refused to honor their pledge. The Supreme Court did not decide that the vote of a faithless elector could be disregarded if there was no applicable state statute. The Supreme Court also did not decide that an elector had to cast their vote in accordance with the popular vote in the state.

The requirement that the elector vote consistently with the popular vote in the state remains a customary rule without the force of law if there is no applicable state statute. I contend below that there is an exception to the customary rule without the force of law as applied to electors if the cumulative vote of the faithless electors affects the outcome of the election.

3.7 The Wisconsin lawsuit

In the *Gohmert* case, the plaintiffs were Congressman Gohmert and the Arizona alternate electors. They were attempting to force Vice President Pence to decertify the duly elected Arizona electors. In the converse of that case, the duly elected Wisconsin electors, on May 17, 2022, sued the alternate Wisconsin electors in Wisconsin state court.[83] The plaintiffs are two Wisconsin Democratic electors and Wisconsin voters.

The defendants are ten Republican politicians who attempted to cast ballots for Trump. They were part of the coordinated effort by the Trump forces in the seven battleground states to get alternate electors certified. There are two additional defendants. They are Kenneth Chesebro, a Boston lawyer, and Jim Troupis. Both were Trump's lawyers in Wisconsin. I mentioned these two lawyers in section 2.1 because they wrote two memos in November 2020 that preceded the Eastman memos.

Their two memos suggested the strategy that I described as the Pence Card in section 2.2. The plaintiffs refer to the two memos in their complaint. The plaintiffs claim that the defendants engaged in an unlawful civil conspiracy. More specifically, the plaintiffs assert that the defendants: "caused permanent and irreparable damage to the country's political institutions generally, and representative government in Wisconsin specifically".[84]

The complaint continues:

By spreading false allegations of widespread fraud, the scheme undermined—and continues to undermine—Wisconsin voters' faith in the integrity of their electors, and citizens' belief in the legitimacy of government's authority.[85]

The plaintiffs are requesting declaratory relief in the form of a court order that the defendants acted unlawfully and the banning of the defendants from serving as presidential electors in any future election. The plaintiffs are also seeking compensatory damages in the amount of $400,000 ($20,000 from each defendant alternate elector) and punitive damages of up to $2,000,000 ($200,000 from each of the same defendants).

The Republican alternate electors met in Madison, the State Capitol, at the same time as the Biden electors. Biden won in Wisconsin by almost 20,000 votes. The defendants filed preliminary objections to the complaint, which were dismissed by the trial judge. As of August 2023, the trial has not yet occurred.[86]

3.8 Looking to the 2024 presidential election

There is a massive movement underway to restrict voting rights in many states, especially in the seven battleground states of the 2020 election. Pennsylvania is one of three states in which the secretary of state, who oversees the election process in the state, is appointed by the governor. This not only illustrates the differences in state laws concerning the national election, but it also makes the election of the governor in Pennsylvania in 2022 supremely important. At the present time, after the 2022 election, the Pennsylvania state House is controlled by the Democrats and the state Senate by the Republicans.

The Republican candidate for governor in Pennsylvania in 2022, Doug Mastriano, is a fervent supporter of former president Donald Trump. A state senator, he organized a hearing in the Pennsylvania Senate a few weeks after the 2020 election to consider Trump's claim that the election was fraudulent. He was also actively involved in the Pennsylvania alternate elector effort that I discuss in section 2.6. He was the point person selected by the Trump supporters for their efforts to overturn the election results in Pennsylvania. He asserted that the election was fraudulent, and that Biden had not been elected, even though Biden won Pennsylvania by more than 80,000 votes.

Mastriano is a proponent of the Eastman legal theory that state legislatures have the authority to override the results of the popular election and to select their own group of electoral college members. He was at the U.S. Capitol on January 6, 2021, and was an organizer of the events that occurred there. He paid for buses to bring members of the group that assembled at the Capitol to challenge the counting of the votes. If he had been elected governor in 2022, he would have selected the secretary of state who would be the state's highest election official when the 2024 presidential election is conducted in Pennsylvania.[87]

As governor, Mastriano would be the person who certifies who the electors are in the certificate of ascertainment. He would certify the votes of the electors. He, and his secretary of state, would control the 2024 presidential election. He announced that he would name a secretary of state who would assist him in overturning the election results.

In an article published in *The Guardian* on May 20, 2022, Sam Levine quotes Mastriano's statements about what he would do if elected as governor. Mastriano has embraced the possibility of getting to overturn an election, saying he already has a secretary of state picked out (he has declined to say who).

Mastriano said: "I get to appoint the secretary of state, who is delegated from me the power to make the corrections to elections, the voting logs and everything. I could decertify every machine in the state with the stroke of a pen."[88]

In addition to decertifying the election machines, Mastriano claims that he can reconstitute the voting lists:

> Mastriano has also said he might 'reset' voter registration in Pennsylvania and 'start all over', something that would probably violate federal law. He has pledged to eliminate the state's contract with 'compromised voting machine companies', even though there's no evidence any machines were compromised in 2020. He wants to end no-excuse mail-in voting, which passed the state legislature with Republican support.[89]

The discussion about the 2020 election and the 2024 election underscores the threat to the American democracy that exists in the ambiguities in the electoral system for electing the president. From the jurisprudential point of view, the overlapping legal systems demonstrate the complexity that Hart's concept of the law does not capture. In short, as I discuss in the subsequent chapters, Hart's version of the rule of recognition has to be stretched or expanded to encompass the complexities inherent in the overlapping, sometimes inconsistent, and frequently complicated legal systems in the U.S.

3.9 The overlapping legal systems

The electoral process for electing POTUS includes the constitutional norms, the federal statutes and precedents, the state statutes and precedents, the customary rules with the force of law, and local rules and regulations. As examples of the local rules and regulations, in the 67 counties in Pennsylvania, each county has its own policies for drop boxes and mail-in ballots. State law and federal law is silent on the logistical details that regulate the voting process in the individual counties.

The county boards of elections comprise the officials ultimately responsible for election administration at the county level. The members of the county boards are elected directly by the voters in home-rule counties (counties which have their own charters). In home-rule counties, the boards are made up of members of the county's legislative body. In the counties that are not home-rule counties, which is most of them, the boards are made up of the county commissioners. Philadelphia, the largest city in the state, has its own system.

The county boards establish the guidelines for the county, hire the staff, sort and process the mail-in ballots, compute, canvass and certify the election results, watch out for fraud, and conduct recounts of the votes. Some of the members of the county boards are election deniers, which is the term used for those individuals who deny the results of the 2020 presidential election.

For examples of the variety of regulations, consider the following:

The Pennsylvania Supreme Court initially decided that counties should not count ballots with incorrectly dated or undated outer envelopes (even though the ballots had arrived within the designated time period for being counted). The Supreme Court reaffirmed that undated mail-in ballots should not be counted, but the Court left it to the individual counties to decide exactly which ballots to count. Each county established its own procedure for handling the ballots that were undated or incorrectly dated.

The Supreme Court then decided that counties may engage in ballot curing, giving voters the opportunity to fix their mail-in ballots that have flaws, but it did not require that counties do so. Ballot curing is permitted in 12 counties. If a ballot has a missing date or signature, nine counties specifically prohibit a voter from coming to the county election office to fix the problem. Eight counties contact voters to inform them about fatal defects in their mail-in ballots and six of them publish lists of voters who have sent in ballots with defects. These lists are also given in some counties to third-party organizations, such as local political parties, so that they may independently contact voters. Seven counties, including Chester County, contact voters with flawed mail-in ballots to direct them to the county election office.

The availability of drop boxes for mail-in ballots (I use this term for ballots that are delivered to a ballot box by voters who are concerned that mailing the ballots may not be prudent because of delays in the postal services) varies widely among the counties. There are 24-hour drop boxes for mail-in ballots in 27 counties. Of the 27 counties that did offer drop boxes, 15 of them only had one available. The counties that offer multiple drop boxes tend to be the more populated counties. Chester County, where I live, has 13 drop boxes. Drop boxes are not available in 40 counties. Most of these counties are in rural areas.

The Election Code in Pennsylvania declares that each voting precinct should have 100 to 1,200 voters. The Code does not specify how a county should determine the exact number. While the state has recommendations on how many voters should be assigned to a precinct, 62 counties exceed the recommendation. There are 9,155 voting precincts in Pennsylvania, and one-quarter of them exceed the recommended 1,200 voters: some of the precincts exceed 3,600 voters.

The availability of minutes of the meetings of county election boards varies, so that almost 40 do not post them online. Four make them available upon request at the county election office.[90]

Local election regulations affect how individual voters are able to vote. The regulations may make it difficult for voters to cast their vote. Therefore to understand the electoral process one has to consider, not only the federal and state norms, but also the specific regulations at the local level.

3.10 Saving democracy

Here is the question that is central to the discussion in this chapter. Assume that the Democratic candidate for president wins the popular vote in a battleground state in 2024. If the state has a Republican governor and a Republican secretary of state and they appoint a group of alternate electors other than those offered by the Democratic presidential candidate and the Democratic Party in that state, would this act be authorized and binding? In short, would it be a lawful act? Would it be consistent with the legal norms that govern the election of the president of the United States?

According to the rule of recognition about what is the law, there are no enacted norms that determine the answer to this question. Therefore, we are left with customary norms. The customary norm is that the electors vote according to the popular vote. There have been, however, faithless electors, who have voted for their candidate of choice and not for the candidate who won the popular vote in their state. Their votes have, in general, been counted as they voted. This would seem to indicate that the customary rule that a member of the Electoral College must cast his vote as an elector for the candidate who won the popular vote in his state is a customary rule that lacks the force of law.

There is a crucial point to make regarding the faithless electors. There has never been an election in the history of the United States in which the faithless electors have altered the outcome of the election in which they were serving as electors. If the faithless electors or alternate electors (electors other than those representing the winning candidate) vote to override the will of the electorate and change who the president would be, they would, I believe, violate the law. They would violate the customary norm which has the force of law that is central to American democracy, the rule of law and the peaceful transition of presidential power. The faithless electors cannot legally change the outcome of the election.

There is undoubtedly a customary norm that the chosen electors cast their vote for the president in accordance with the popular vote in their state. The question is whether this is a customary rule with the force of law or a customary rule without the force of law. You could conclude it is the latter because, in the past, the votes of faithless electors have been counted as the faithless electors have voted. But to have a functioning democracy or even, as we have in America, a quasi-democracy, there must be a peaceful transition of power. The winner of the electoral college votes that should be cast in accordance with the popular vote in the states of which they are electors must result in voting for the candidate who should win the election actually doing so and becoming president.

Ultimately, if the winning candidate was not acknowledged to be the president and no credible fraud in the election occurred, I cannot conceive of the U.S. Supreme Court not ensuring that the results of the election be honored. The members of the Supreme Court, and the federal and state legislators, and the governors, secretaries of state, and the vice president have all taken oaths to support the Constitution. The Constitution requires that the winner of the election, in accordance with the electoral college system and the written and unwritten Constitution, becomes the president. Just as in all other contests, the rules need not definitely declare that the winner is the winner.

The legal theory that the winner of the electoral college votes must become the president is based upon the customary norm with the force of law that provides that the winner of the election must be acknowledged to be the president. That is central to the concept of the reason for having an election. I consider the legal significance of this customary norm with the force of law in sections 4.7 and 4.8.

3.11 The DOJ indictment

This section concerns Donald Trump's third indictment. His first indictment is in the state courts in New York and concerns the payment of hush money to Stormy Daniels. Trump is charged with 34 felony counts for falsifying business records. The events giving rise to this offense occurred prior to the 2020 election.

The second indictment is in the federal courts, and it concerns Trump's mishandling of classified documents, lying to federal authorities, displaying the documents to individuals who lacked security clearance, and attempting to destroy evidence. These events happened after his term as president had ended.

The indictment that I want to discuss provides issues relevant to legal philosophy and is the most important of the three cases. Trump was indicted on July 28, 2023, for four counts of federal crimes for activities that he was involved in while he was the sitting 45th President. These crimes occurred after the November 3, 2020, presidential election. They are primarily concerned with Trump's false claims of election fraud, his efforts to overturn the results of the election, and the riot that occurred on January 6, 2021. The riot was the culmination of his effort to delay the certification of Joe Biden having won the election.

It is no surprise that Trump would contend that fraud had occurred in the 2020 election. He had previously made claims of election fraud before he himself became a candidate in 2015. After he announced his candidacy in Trump Tower and even more specifically after the election on November 3, 2020, he proclaimed many times that the election would be and was rigged. In fact, on February 1, 2016, after Trump had lost the Iowa primary to Senator Ted Cruz, and before his private airplane left the airport in Iowa, Trump called the chairman of the Iowa Republican Party. He complained that Cruz had not won a fair election and that there should be an investigation to determine how Cruz had cheated before the official announcement that he, Trump, had not won the election in Iowa.[91]

Trump repeated his claims of election fraud after the November 3, 2020, election. He claimed that he had won the election before all the votes were counted. When the television pundits declared that Biden had won the election, Trump claimed that there was fraud. To this day, he has not conceded the election to Biden, and he has not publicly withdrawn his claims of election fraud or his declaration that he in fact won the election.

He continued to claim that the election was fraudulent notwithstanding the failure of his supporters to prove outcome-determinative fraudulent events in the 62 lawsuits challenging the election results. No significant fraud was found in multiple recounts. Subsequent to investigations from various agencies, including the Department of Justice, there is still no evidence of substantial fraud. As the indictment clearly states, Trump was told by his own appointees and supporters on multiple occasions that there was no fraud, and he lost the election. Trump cannot accept that he was the loser in the election.

Consequently, it is not surprising in light of Trump's activities after the election that he has been charged with four counts related to his efforts to prevent the peaceful transfer of power after he lost the election. Three counts are for conspiracy to commit federal crimes and the fourth count is for obstruction of an official proceeding. To obtain a conviction for conspiracy, the government will have to prove that there was a plan (an agreement between two or more individuals), that the plan was to commit acts that would be criminal acts if consummated, and that specific acts to implement the plan are undertaken. All of this has to be proven at the trial.

Before the trial begins, there will be pre-trial motions filed by the defense raising legal issues about whether there was a crime, challenging the legal basis for the indictment, and other preliminary legal issues that should be resolved before there is a trial. The pretrial motions will be resolved at the trial court level. There usually are no appeals from the trial court's decisions on these issues before the trial. There will then be a trial. If Trump is acquitted, the case is over and there is no potential appeal. If the jury is a hung jury (its decision has to be unanimous), the prosecution will have to decide if they want to try again to get a conviction or they may decide to end the case. If the jury convicts Trump of one or more of the crimes with which he is charged, he can, and he likely will, appeal the case to the Court of Appeals.

The Court of Appeals will rule on the legal issues raised at the trial, such as whether the judge made an error in her charge to the jury. The conviction will be reversed only if there is an error at the trial or the judge erred in allowing the trial to proceed (appellate review of her decision on the pretrial motions). If the conviction is affirmed by the Court of Appeals, Trump will almost undoubtedly file a petition for writ of certiorari to the Supreme Court.

It is very difficult without knowing what will happen at the trial and on the appeal to predict whether the Supreme Court will hear the case. Four Justices have to vote to hear the case. In the typical case, it would be unlikely that the Supreme Court would grant the writ and decide the appeal. This is not, of course, the typical case.

Here is my first question about this indictment. Can Trump's defense be that he believes and always believed, that there was election fraud (even though he could not prove it) and that he in fact won the election? To assert this defense, however, it would probably be necessary for Trump to be a witness at the trial. I do not expect that he will be a witness, so I conclude that he will be unable to prevail with this defense based upon what he believed was true. This is a defense that cannot be easily established without him testifying.

Moreover, to assert the defense of Trump not being able to accept that he lost the election is to invent a variant of a mental impairment defense. Trump maintains that he is a "stable genius," and he has declared so on many occasions. He would not allow his attorneys to offer a form of mental deficiency defense. He was told many times that there was no outcome-determinative fraud in the election.

The indictment, in No. 83, indicates that Trump knew that he lost the election. On January 3, Trump met with the Chairman of the Joint Chiefs of Staff and others. When he was told that inauguration day was only 17 days away, Trump said: "Yeah, you are right, it's too late for us. We're going to give that to the other guy".

I do not anticipate that whether there was fraud in the election will even be an issue in the trial based upon this indictment. No other candidates in the 2020 election are contending that they lost the election because there was fraud. When Trump claimed that there was fraud, and local officials were asked if there was fraud, the local election officials generally responded that they did not know of any significant fraud.

The strength of the electoral system in the U.S. is that it is locally controlled. Most of the election officials in Republican controlled states are Republicans. Virtually none of them has maintained that their local election was fraudulent. In fact, as I explain below, the indictment raises the issue of whether the individuals who agreed to be alternate electors in the battleground states were lied to in order to induce them to become electors. Many of them did not believe that there was provable fraud in the election.

Many of Trump's supporters are claiming that Trump cannot be convicted of these crimes because he has the right of freedom of speech. This defense is not likely to be successful because, as the indictment states, he is not being charged with having claimed either that there was fraud in the election or that he was the winner in the election. He is being charged with having committed criminal acts in furtherance of his claims of election fraud. It is not what he said that is the crime, but what he did to prevent the peaceful transfer of power.

It is an important aspect of the charges in the indictment that there is an element of fraud on the part of Trump that is being charged. The claim that the election was fraudulent, while knowing that there is no credible proof of sufficient fraudulent voter activity to have affected the outcome of the election, is itself a false and, therefore, fraudulent statement.

Trump and the co-conspirators tried to get the Department of Justice involved in a sham investigation of their election fraud claim. A letter was drafted by Jeffrey Clark that could be sent from the Department of Justice to state legislators claiming that the DOJ had discovered election fraud in their state. The letter was never sent, but the act of drafting the letter was an act in furtherance of the conspiracy.

The conspiracy also included the pressuring of Vice President Pence to undertake various acts to overturn the election results or to delay the counting of the votes. I discussed these strategies when I reviewed the memos written by John Eastman. This pressure was asserted prior to and during the riot. The riot itself was the result of Trump's incitement of the January 6 invasion of the Capitol in an effort to halt the counting of the electoral college votes. The indictment presents what I called "The Pence Card" as culminating in the January 6 mob attacking the Capitol when "the Defendant attempted to use a crowd of supporters that had gathered in Washington, D.C. to pressure the Vice President to fraudulently alter the election results." (No. 86 in the indictment).

In addition, the alternate electors claiming to be the duly elected electors and signing certificates stating such is also a fraudulent act. Regarding the alternate electors, it is also significant that the indictment frames their actions as having been the result of yet another fraud. This fraud was the result of claims made by Trump and his co-conspirators that the certificates would be used only if Trump prevailed in his election contest, claiming election fraud in their state.

There was, for example, a conference call on December 12, 2020, to Pennsylvania Republican potential electors. Biden had won the election in Pennsylvania. Giuliani told the alternate electors that the certificates were to be used only on a contingency basis. The elector certificates would be submitted to Washington only if Trump prevailed in his litigation contesting the Pennsylvania election result.

The Pennsylvania alternate electors requested an opinion letter from a national law firm that is certified to be accurate by a Pennsylvania lawyer. They received, instead, a memo from Kenneth Chesebro, one of the unnamed co-conspirators in the indictment, stating that the plan in Pennsylvania is "dicey". It was this response that led to the Pennsylvania certificate being modified with insertion of a disclaimer. The alternate electors in Pennsylvania agreed to proceed only if language constituting a disclaimer was inserted in the certificate. But they were cautioned to not inform alternate electors in other states about this modification in the certificate.

Of the seven battleground states, only in Pennsylvania and New Mexico was the disclaimer in the certificate included. In the five other battleground states, this limitation in the certificates was absent and the certificates proclaimed that the signatories were the legitimate electors. Trump, Giuliani, and others misled these Republican alternate electors. The 16 Republican electors in Michigan have been charged with defrauding the State of Michigan. Their defense will probably be that they were lied to by Trump, the defendant in the indictment, and his co-conspirators.

Defense attorneys for the alternate electors in Georgia stated in a court filing in May 2023 that at least eight of the 16 alternate electors in Georgia accepted immunity in the Georgia potential litigation. It appears, therefore, that this will be an element in the Georgia litigation that I will discuss below.

Regarding the alternate electors, it does not appear that the Department of Justice has finished its investigation concerning them. A new batch of subpoenas has been served in multiple states. It is possible that some of the alternate electors will be witnesses in the trial on this indictment.

Trump's defense is most likely to be that he was acting on advice of counsel. It appears that the prosecutors are anticipating this defense. In the indictment, six individuals are depicted as co-conspirators. They are not identified in the indictment. The only defendant in the indictment is Trump. By not including other defendants, the prosecution is keeping Trump as the central figure in the trial. The trial will be a shorter trial with just one defendant, and it will be easier to present the evidence without having to contend with issues other than the crimes committed by Trump.

Trump is the central figure in each of the charges. It is ultimately his plan to overturn the results of the election that is driving the events forward. The trial will focus on his activities to spread the lie that the election was fraudulent, his attempt to get states not to certify the election results, his promoting the program for alternate electors, and, ultimately, putting pressure on Vice President Pence to take the actions proposed by John Eastman in his memos. It is Trump who is continually driving this program forward.

Five of the six co-conspirators are attorneys (the sixth one, identified as a campaign official, may also be an attorney). There is a consensus among the journalists about the identity of the first five co-conspirators. We have already met some of these individuals in the prior sections in the first three chapters.

Kenneth Chesebro is one of the two attorneys who wrote memos related to the election in Wisconsin. He is probably Co-conspirator 5, who is described as an attorney who devised and implemented the plan of the alternate electors. In his second memo, he expands the scheme of having alternate electors to five states in addition to Wisconsin.

The reasoning in these memos was adopted and expanded upon in John Eastman's two memos. He is probably Co-conspirator 2, who is described as an attorney who devised the scheme to and attempted to get Vice President Mike Pence to obstruct the certification of the electors.

The best known of Trump's attorneys and the most active in public appearances claiming election fraud is Rudy Giuliani. He is probably Co-conspirator 1, who is described as an attorney who spread the lies.

Co-conspirator 3 is probably Sidney Powell, who is an attorney who was active in the litigation claiming election fraud. In the indictment, she is described as an attorney who Trump embraced, and he publicly amplified her claim of election fraud, even though he called her "crazy".

The most likely candidate for Co-conspirator 4 is Jeffrey Clark. He is described as a Department of Justice official (he is also an attorney) who attempted to get the Department of Justice to open sham crime investigations and influence state legislators "with knowingly false claims of election fraud".

Co-conspirator 6 is described as a political consultant who helped implement the plan of the alternate electors. There is speculation about who this might be. I identify the most likely candidate in the endnotes.

Based upon the format of this indictment, we should consider why the indictment refers to these individuals as co-conspirators and what will their role in the trial be. The co-conspirators are not indicted, but they are also not described as unindicted co-conspirators. It is possible that they will be indicted. Does the prosecution intend to call them as witnesses? If they are not called by the prosecution, will the defense call them?

The typical indictment is a short document that informs the defendant what the crimes are that will be prosecuted. It generally does not provide evidence nor list potential witnesses. In this instance, the indictment is 45 pages long, with 130 statements (and subsections to some of them). It is a talking indictment. In some of the statements, the actual words that will be offered into evidence are presented in quotation marks. This indicates that the quoted statements appear in a written document or in a recording or video.

It is quite possible, and maybe even likely, that one or more of the co-conspirators is going to receive, or has received, immunity from prosecution for agreeing voluntarily to testify for the prosecution. If this is the case, they could state that Trump knew that he had lost the election and that his efforts after the election were directed toward overturning the results of the election.

Here are some examples from the indictment of what the prosecutors might offer into evidence. Trump declared that 36,000 non-citizens had voted in Arizona. He claimed that election workers in Detroit had counted phony ballots. He repeated these claims in meetings with the Michigan Speaker of the House and Minority Leader of the Michigan Senate.

Trump also claimed that the vote count in Philadelphia, Pennsylvania was fraudulent. As a result of these false claims, Al Schmidt, the Philadelphia City Commissioner, and his family later received death threats.

Eastman and Trump called the national Republican Party Chairwoman and discussed with her the alternate elector strategy. They told her that the false certificates would be used only if the litigation claiming voter fraud was successful. They repeated this to campaign officials in the battleground states in order to get the alternate electors to sign the false certificates claiming that they were the legitimate electors.

Trump, at the rally on January 6, notwithstanding the caution being exercised by the Pennsylvania legislature, mischaracterizes their response:

> After the Defendant falsely stated that the Pennsylvania legislature wanted 'to recertify their votes. They want to recertify. But the only way that can happen is if Mike Pence agrees to send it back.' The crowd began to shout, 'Send it back.'" (No. 104b in the indictment).

Here is an example from No. 62 in the indictment about the strategy that the conspirators were using with the potential alternate electors. On December 13, Co-conspirator 5 and Co-conspirator 1 exchanged an email memo that they would use the certificates of the fake electors even if the litigation did not succeed. It is likely that the prosecutors have a copy of the memo to introduce into evidence.

Giuliani could be called as a witness and asked what his source was for making the statement that dead people had voted in Georgia. He called the Michigan House Speaker to request that hearings be held and that the electors be decertified because there was fraud in their election. He sent a text message to the Michigan Senate Majority Leader claiming that the legal electors were illegitimate because of election fraud in Detroit. Trump repeated the claims of fraud in Detroit on January 6.

There were several meetings that Giuliani attended with Republican leaders in Pennsylvania during which he, according to the indictment, "falsely claimed that Pennsylvania had issued 1.8 million absentee ballots and received 2.5 million in return". He was told that this was not true, but he continued to repeat the false claim. On December 31 and January 3, Trump claimed that there were 250,000 more votes than voters in Pennsylvania. The DOJ informed him that this was not true, but he repeated the claim on January 6.

Sidney Powell claimed that there was fraud in the Georgia election. Trump repeated her claims even though he had declared that she sounded like she was "crazy". She repeated the claims in an unsuccessful lawsuit. Trump signed the verification for the lawsuit swearing that the facts alleged in the lawsuit were true, even though he knew that they were not.

Trump's attorney, John Lauro, stated on the night of the arraignment in a television interview that Trump was attempting only to delay the certification. This he claimed would be an effective defense. In fact, since he is Trump's attorney, this statement could be introduced into evidence even if Trump does not testify. It is proof of Trump's intention to delay the certification of the electoral college vote, which is a criminal offense. Bear in mind that it is highly unlikely, virtually inconceivable, that Trump will be a witness.

There can be little doubt that the counting of the electoral college votes is an official function. In accordance with constitutional and statutory norms, the counting of the votes was scheduled for January 6. Undoubtedly, the prosecution will put into evidence the videos of the riot that occurred on January 6. I am being kind by calling it a riot. It could also be described as an insurrection. But, and this is very important, Trump is not being charged with causing an insurrection. If he were so charged and convicted of this offense, his ability to run as a candidate in the 2024 election would be questionable. This is based upon the language of the Fourteenth Amendment to the U.S. Constitution. The January 6 committee in its report referred various crimes to the Department of Justice to be considered for prosecution. This indictment does not accept that recommendation regarding this specific crime.

Our next issue to consider is whether Trump is likely to be convicted of any or all of these crimes. Three of the charges in the four counts in this indictment are for conspiracies. The fourth is the crime of denying people the right to vote, which is based upon the provisions of the Ku Klux Klan (KKK) Acts.

Trump is being charged with violation of one of the KKK Acts. Three statutes were adopted after the Civil War. The South Carolina Governor Robert K. Scott told President Ulysses S. Grant in 1870 that white supremacists were murdering recently enslaved African Americans for exercising their voting rights. Groups like the Ku Klux Klan wanted to keep the Republican Party, with its black voter base, from winning local elections.

The three statutes were designed to give the federal government additional power, including the power to send troops to ensure fair elections. It became a crime to prevent people from voting. The Acts were also known as the Enforcement Acts and are still considered to be valid. They have been applied to acts of police brutality, vote buying, and a Klan member who burned a cross on the lawn of a Latino couple.

I have discussed the 1876 election. Before this election, we had a civil war that ended in 1865. As part of the effort of punishing the states that had withdrawn from the nation, and to eradicate the aftermath of slavery having existed in those states, the Constitution was amended. Reconstruction in the Southern states commenced. There was organized and passionate resistance to cultural realignment in the society in the confederate states. Slavery was now prohibited, but freedom for the former slaves was not implemented. In fact, there was strong resistance to the change in their status.

The resolution of the 1876 election dispute resulted in the disembowelment of the reconstruction effort and the beginning of the Jim Crow era. The drive for racial equality diminished. The barriers to the former slaves entering civil society were established. I discuss how the law has been ineffective in the elimination of racial discrimination in chapter seven.

The indictment has charged Trump with a violation of Section 241 of Title 18 of the U.S. Criminal Code, which is part of the first Enforcement Act passed in 1870. More specifically, the charge is that Trump and his co-conspirators sought to destroy trust in a fair election process and "pursued unlawful means of discounting legitimate votes and subverting the election results".

Now it is more than 150 years after the statute was adopted, and Trump is being charged with violating this statute. The statute is being utilized to realize its original purpose of protecting the right to vote. Trump is challenging the voting areas in which African Americans live, such as in Milwaukee, Atlanta, Detroit, and Philadelphia or Hispanic areas in Arizona. It is in the predominantly African American areas or Hispanic areas where Trump concentrates his claims that voter fraud occurred. There is an element of poetic justice in the charge of violating the KKK Acts.

I discuss in chapter seven the difficulty of obtaining jury verdicts to convict white supremacists of murder in the lynching of African

Americans. Juries in the South would usually not convict the white male defendants and they were the jurors in these cases (this is called jury nullification). Trump will be before a jury of his peers in the District of Columbia, a jury that almost certainly will include African American jurors.

In addition to a jury that will have minority representation, the judge on the election indictment case, Tanya Chutkan, has the reputation of being a no-nonsense judge. She has imposed stiff sentences on defendants convicted of participating in the January 6 riot. She has declared in one of her decisions that "Presidents are not kings". Many of the January 6 defendants have argued that they were only following the instructions of the President. Now, it is the former president who is on trial for having invited them to "stop the steal", or, perhaps more accurately, implement the steal. If you are going to prosecute the rioters, which is ongoing, you should also pursue the organizers, the instigators, and the enablers.

After reading the indictment and being familiar with the evidence gathered by the January 6 committee, some of which will be part of the record in this case, it appears very possible that Trump will be convicted by a District of Columbia jury. Bear in mind that it is difficult to predict jury verdicts. Also, the jury has to reach a unanimous verdict. It will only take one recalcitrant juror to avoid a conviction. But the January 6 defendants have been convicted and, from the point of view of ultimate responsibility, Trump is more guilty than they are.

It is also ironic that the star witness at the trial is likely to be former Vice President Mike Pence. I mentioned in section 2.1 that Pence is the unlikely hero of this book. For the 48 months of the Trump presidency, Pence was a lap dog sleeping on the sofa in the oval office during important meetings. He was in the room, but he was irrelevant. For the 30 months after the protest, Pence, ignoring the threat to himself and his family, did not condemn the events of January 6.

Now, he is talking at last. He did not testify before the January 6 committee, and he did not disclose that he had contemporaneous notes prepared during and immediately after his meetings and discussions with Trump. It is important that they were contemporaneous because that will ensure that they will be able to be introduced at the trial as an exception to the hearsay rules. Pence will be the star witness.

So, the next question you might ask is what impact, if any, would a jury conviction have on Trump's candidacy in the 2024 presidential election? Here are the things that you should understand about this issue. Trump is not the first president to be charged with committing a crime. Richard Nixon also committed a crime, and his fate was resolved by a presidential pardon. Trump is the first former president to be tried for felony offenses after his term in office.

There have been other individuals who were charged with crimes and who were candidates for the presidency. So, convictions for the crimes in this indictment would not bar Trump from being a candidate. Suppose that he is convicted by the jury. There will undoubtedly be an appeal. I anticipate that the appeal would not be resolved by the highest court in the land before the 2024 election. Trump could, then, be elected to be the next president.

If Trump is the next president, he could serve as such even while these cases were pending during his presidency. In short, none of the 78 felonies that he is accused of having committed would prevent him from being the president. In any event, in accordance with current DOJ policy, there will not be ongoing litigation against a sitting president.

It is also possible that Trump, if he becomes President Trump, will pardon himself. This has never happened (a president pardoning himself). If he did pardon himself, who could challenge it and how would it be challenged? These are interesting questions. He could also allow the Twenty-Fifth Amendment to be invoked, and his vice president could become the acting president, and he could pardon

Trump. After being pardoned, Trump could resume being president.

If Trump is convicted, it is inconceivable to me that he would ever be sentenced to serve in a prison. He is legally entitled to lifetime protection by the Secret Service. It would be impossible for them to perform this duty while he is in prison. He might be sentenced to house confinement.

There have been additional charges against Trump filed this year. Fani Willis, the District Attorney of Fulton County, Georgia, was asked if she would abandon her investigation into Trump's efforts to overturn the election results in Georgia. She replied that, as the district attorney, it is her job to investigate crimes committed in Georgia. If she finds that a crime has been committed, it is her duty to prosecute. She did so as this book was going to print, see the inserted section 3.12 below.

Willis's reaction to the question is a good example of a customary rule without the force of law, which will be the subject of the next chapter. There would have been no legal way to force her to proceed with prosecution of a crime if she decided not to do so. Any effort to prevent her from prosecuting would also not be likely to be successful. She has prosecutorial discretion.

The case filed in Georgia, is a RICO (Racketeer Influenced and Corrupt Organizations Act) case. Approximately 20 states have state RICO statutes modeled after the federal statute, and Georgia is one of them. The Georgia statute, in fact, is more detailed than the federal statute. The federal statute lists 36 crimes that can be brought in federal court. The Georgia statute adds 30 additional crimes. The Georgia statute, unlike the federal statute, includes making false statements as part of the criminal effort to be part of a potential racketeering crime.

So, sink deep in your seat. This could be a long ride living through the worst constitutional crisis since the Civil War.

3.12 The Georgia indictment

The Georgia indictment is very different from the indictment discussed in the preceding section (which I call "the indictment" or "the DOJ indictment" or "the federal indictment"). The DOJ indictment is focused on Trump's efforts to stay in office. It is like a shot from a sniper's rifle, very much aimed at a specific target and designed to hit just that target. Hitting Trump, the specific target, will be the central theme in that trial.

In contrast to the DOJ indictment, the Georgia indictment is like shooting with a shotgun toward a crowd of potential targets. It proclaims and describes a massive, coordinated plot to steal the election. The Georgia indictment is more detailed and twice as long as the DOJ indictment; 97 pages compared to 45 pages. There are 41 counts in the Georgia indictment compared to 4 counts in the DOJ indictment. Instead of a single defendant, the Georgia indictment refers to 19 named defendants, and 30 unnamed individuals. In other words, there are multiple unnamed potential additional defendants who are likely to be witnesses in the trial.

There are conspiracies alleged in both indictments. The conspiracies are three counts of the four counts in the DOJ indictment. The Georgia indictment is so detailed that I can only provide a sketch of its structure. I will start with the most important differences in the two indictments.

The Georgia indictment is filed in state court while the DOJ indictment is filed in federal court. In accordance with the policy of the DOJ, if Trump becomes the president, the prosecution will be put on hold during his term in office. The Georgia District Attorney is not required to pause her prosecution during Trump's potential tenure as the president. In addition, the Georgia legal system offers a speedy trial to defendants, which I will return to below.

An equally important distinction is that Trump, if he becomes president again, could potentially give himself a pardon for the federal crimes. Alternatively, he could maneuver a pardon from his vice-president acting as president during a real or contrived Twenty-Fifth Amendment temporary hiatus in his presidency. The vice president acting as the president could pardon Trump. Trump could then reassume the presidency. Trump will have no power to pardon himself or arrange for his pardon from the vice president for the Georgia crimes.

Another very important difference is that the Georgia indictment is focused on a RICO crime. "RICO" refers to the Racketeer Influenced and Corrupt Organizations Act. The Georgia indictment charges Trump with violation of the Georgia RICO statute. His co-conspirators, the named 18 additional defendants, are also charged with violation of the Georgia RICO statute. As I already mentioned, there are unnamed individuals in the Georgia indictment who are also potential co-conspirators and who may also ultimately become defendants.

The charge of a RICO violation calls for a very different type of trial. I tried only one RICO case in my career as a trial lawyer and it was a trial unlike any other case. Let me explain why the RICO charge is so important.

My guestimate is that the trial based on the federal indictment in Washington, D.C. will take six to eight weeks. If Trump is convicted, there will undoubtedly be an appeal to the Court of Appeals. If he loses in the Court of Appeals, he will file a petition for writ of certiorari in SCOTUS, which may accept the case for review. I think the likelihood of the case being accepted by SCOTUS is less than 50%.

The Georgia trial, I would estimate, will take six to nine months. Once again, if Trump is convicted, there will be an appeal through the Georgia judicial appellate system. If the Georgia Supreme Court confirms the conviction, Trump will, once again, file a petition for writ of certiorari to SCOTUS. I think the likelihood of that case being accepted is less than 15%.

The final decision in the federal case will not be decided before the 2024 election. If Trump wins the election, the case against him will probably never reach a conclusion. The Georgia case, however, will not be subject to a similar delay. The final decision regarding Trump will be made in 2025, and, if not then, almost certainly in 2026. Therefore, the risk to Trump is much greater in the Georgia case than in the federal case.

The RICO charge in Georgia also presents a heightened risk because of the nature of a RICO case. A RICO case allows the prosecution to charge various crimes committed by different people by establishing that they formed an enterprise. An enterprise demonstrates that the group of individuals decided to act together in order to achieve a goal that involves commission of a crime or crimes. The prosecution may present evidence to connect a series of crimes that have a relationship with each other based upon common objectives.

A RICO enterprise is similar to a conspiracy, but it allows for a series of conspiracies, like a conspiracy on steroids. It allows for one conspiracy to piggyback upon another conspiracy. For example, the presentation of the evidence in the Georgia RICO trial can include repeating any evidence that the DOJ presents in its federal trial on its indictment. RICO opens a wide door because it defines racketeering in an extremely broad manner. It includes offenses that do not usually result in criminal charges.

The Georgia indictment, for example, has charges for perjury regarding testimony presented to the Grand Jury. It also has charges for impersonating a police officer, forgery, filing false documents, improperly influencing witnesses, computer theft and computer trespass, election fraud, invasion of privacy and defrauding the State of Georgia. This indictment not only refers to the alternate electors in Georgia but to the alternate electors in the other battleground states. It, therefore, goes beyond crimes committed in Fulton County and also includes crimes committed elsewhere in Georgia and in other states.

The indictment in the Georgia case has 41 counts. Count 1 is the RICO count which refers to events that occurred between November 4, 2020, and September 15, 2022. The racketeering activity of the enterprise was the implementation of a plan to change the outcome of the 2020 presidential election. All 19 defendants are alleged to have been involved in the racketeering activity or in the conspiracy to implement the plan of the enterprise.

The explosion of the RICO bomb covers a much larger geographical area than the federal indictment and involves many more persons. Testimony concerning the RICO charge alone may include the 161 acts recited in the Georgia indictment (some of the acts having several sub-actions). This will be a long trial. And this is just the RICO charge. There are 40 other charges in the Georgia indictment that may require additional testimony, though some of it will be included within the RICO portion of the trial.

In the RICO case I tried, there were five defendants with four lawyers representing them. To get ready for the trial, you had not only to prepare your client to testify, but you had to consider what the other defendants would say. With five co-conspirators, there could be five different versions of the facts. Some might support your client's version, and some might contradict it. The crosscurrents of five defendants, each wanting to protect himself, with each considering potentially seeking immunity for testifying against the others, is very challenging. Bear in mind that, with 19 defendants in the Georgia trial, every witness may be subject to potentially 19 lawyers cross-examining him (lawyers for 18 other defendants and the prosecuting attorney).

The discussion so far presupposes that there will be one trial with 19 defendants. There may, instead, be a series of trials. One or more of the defendants may file a motion for a speedy trial. Georgia procedural law requires a speedy trial if the defendant requests it. There are some advantages to a defendant if the trial occurs within a few months of the indictment. If there will be a series of trials, the prosecution will be less prepared for the first trial than for the subsequent trials, the witnesses will be more nervous (and they will be better prepared the second and third time that they testify), and the trial will be focused on just those counts involving that defendant.

From page 13 of the Georgia indictment to page 72 is just the RICO count. There are another 40 counts in addition to Count 1. Count 41, the last of the counts, is on page 98. I will provide just a few examples to allow the reader to get some sense of what the evidence will be.

Rudy Giuliani, one of the 18 co-conspirators, is charged in 13 counts. John Eastman is charged in 9 counts. Mark Meadows, the White House Chief of Staff, is charged in 2 counts. Each of the 40 counts applies to some of the defendants, with the RICO count including all of them. Let's look at a few acts listed in the Georgia indictment referring to two lawyers.

I discussed Kenneth Chesebro in sections 2.1, 3.7 and 3.11. He wrote two memos at the beginning stages of the enterprise. After writing those two memos, he remained active in subsequent events. Here is one of the acts in the Georgia indictment:

Act 61:

On or about the 11th day of December 2020, KENNETH JOHN CHESEBRO sent an e-mail with attached documents to MICHAEL A. ROMAN, unindicted co-conspirator Individual 5, whose identity is known to the Grand Jury, and others. The documents were to be used by Trump presidential elector nominees in Georgia for the purpose of casting electoral votes for DONALD JOHN TRUMP on December 14, 2020, despite the fact that DONALD JOHN TRUMP lost the November 3, 2020, presidential election in Georgia. This was an overt act in furtherance of the conspiracy.

This act and several other acts prove that the Trump Campaign orchestrated the alternate elector program. The setting up of the slates of the alternate electors in the seven battleground states was an organized event. They, the alternate electors, while acting independently in their respective state capitols, were acting jointly in the criminal enterprise. Many of the Georgia alternate electors have accepted immunity, presumably in exchange for their testimony in the trial.

In the context of a RICO trial, the prosecutor may present testimony from many alternate electors from several or all of the battleground states. There are 84 alternate electors from seven battleground states who are potential witnesses.

We know that members of the Trump team lied to some of the alternate electors, urging the alternate elector candidates to sign the false certificates and send them to the National Archivist, the Congress, and the other officials. Signing the false certificates and filing them with the appropriate authorities as though they were genuine (and the signatories were the true electors) is the criminal enterprise in action, and the evidence of the commission of this crime will be compelling.

In the Georgia indictment, the activities of Chesebro in the formulation of the enterprise strategy and its implementation are detailed. I anticipate that much of the testimony in his trial will relate to the efforts to avoid the peaceful transfer of power after the 2020 election. It could start with the memoranda that he prepared and continue with the efforts to pressure Pence, the January 6 insurrection, and many other activities of the enterprise.

In messages and memoranda that Chesebro distributed, he declares that the program he suggests represents a "bold controversial strategy". He mentions that the rules could make assembling alternate slates "very problematic" in Nevada and "somewhat dicey" in Michigan and Pennsylvania. Without the cover of taking the case to the Supreme Court, he admits that the strategy could appear "treasonous".

In addition, I do not believe that Chesebro's potential defense that he was acting in accordance with his honest and forthright interpretation of the Constitution and election law will be credible. As an experienced attorney, he knows the difference between giving legal advice based on what the law is, rather than a theory about what the law should be. He recognizes the difference, and his opinion about what the law should be does not justify claiming that his statement of what the law is represents an accurate statement.

There is one primary reason why his testimony will not be credible. He was at the Capitol during the riot on January 6, 2021, and he was not there to help protect the Capitol and support the peaceful transfer of power. His advice, and his actions based upon his legal theory, will not be convincing.

Sidney Powell is another lawyer associated with the Trump effort to overturn the results of the election. She appears in seven counts. Here is an example, according to the Georgia indictment, of her role in an important part of the efforts of the enterprise.

> Act 90:
>
> On or about the 18th day of December 2020, DONALD JOHN TRUMP met with RUDOLPH WILLIAM LOUIS GIULIANI, SIDNEY KATHERINE POWELL, unindicted co-conspirator Individual 20, whose identity is known to the Grand Jury, and others in the White House. The individuals present at the meeting discussed certain strategies and theories intended to influence the outcome of the November 3, 2020, presidential election, including seizing voting equipment and appointing SIDNEY KATHERINE POWELL, as special counsel with broad authority to investigate allegations of voter fraud in Georgia and elsewhere. This was an act in furtherance of the conspiracy.
>
> Act 91:
>
> On or about the 21st day of December 2020, SIDNEY KATHERINE POWELL sent an e-mail to the Chief Operations Officer of SullivanStriclker LLC and instructed him that she and unindicted co-conspirators Individual 6, Individual 21, and

Individual 22, whose identities are known to the Grand Jury, were to immediately "receive a copy of all data" obtained by SullivanStrickler LLC from Dominion Voting Systems in Michigan. This was an overt act in furtherance of the conspiracy.

The case against Sidney Powell is especially strong, and I view her as a likely candidate ultimately to plead guilty. SullivanStrickler is a forensic data firm in Fulton County. Sidney Powell on December 6, 2020, signed the contract with them to analyze the voting tabulations in several states. On January 7, 2021, SullivanStrickler was given access to the voting equipment and copies of voting data from the election system in Coffee County, Georgia. There is surveillance footage showing entry by their representatives into the elections office where the data breach took place.

Other Acts in the Georgia indictment, like this data breach in Coffee County, relate to the distribution of voting data. This might include how individual voters voted in what is supposed to be a private act. This is obviously an invasion of privacy and is clearly a criminal act (conspiracy to commit computer invasion of privacy). In addition to the RICO count, Powell has also been charged with conspiracy to commit election fraud, conspiracy to commit computer trespass, conspiracy to commit computer theft, and conspiracy to defraud the state. All of these crimes are easy to prove. They are all clear violations of Georgia law. And Coffee County is not the only place where Sidney Powell was involved in election tampering.

Powell was authorized by Trump himself and Rudy Giuliani to commit these crimes. In Act 159 in the Georgia indictment, Powell is charged with making false statements on May 7, 2022, to the January 6 Committee. She testified "that she 'didn't' have any role in really setting up 'efforts to access voting machines in Coffee County, Georgia or Antrim, Michigan'". She also testified:

She was aware there was an 'effort by some people' to get access to voting machines in Georgia but that she did not 'know what happened with that' and did not 'remember whether that was Rudy or other folks.'

Yet, Powell signed the contract with SullivanStrickler, and she met with Rudy Giuliani and Donald Trump in the White House to plan for the voting machine breach. This example illustrates why the RICO count allows for a broad approach to offering testimony about multiple events that are related to the enterprise.

Powell may testify trying to explain why she participated in these acts or why these acts should not be considered to be crimes. This defense will be unconvincing. She will be convicted of the crimes and be potentially sentenced to serve time in prison. Trump, even if he is elected to another term as the president, will not be able to pardon her for these violations of the Georgia statutes. The "Individuals" named in Acts 90 and 91 will probably be witnesses in her trial. Powell is likely to be a witness in the trials of the other co-conspirators.

It is the distinct possibility, and the likelihood, that some of the indicted co-conspirators in the Georgia trial, and some of the "Individuals" who are not named but are known to the Grand Jury (and, therefore, to the prosecution), will be the key witnesses. I predict that a number of the indicted co-conspirators in the Georgia trial will plead guilty and will testify against the other participants in the enterprise. This is the primary reason why the Georgia trial poses a higher risk to Trump than the Washington, D.C. trial.

Trump's strongest potential defense is that he was acting pursuant to the advice of his lawyers. Some of these lawyers will eventually be the key witnesses in his RICO trial. And they will throw him under the bus, just as he would if it was advantageous to him to do so. The RICO trial sets the table for the sharks to feed on each other.

The only credible interpretation of the Constitution is that the winner of the election becomes the president. If I say to you, "let's race to the front door", it is implicit in the concept of a race that the one who gets to the front door first is the winner. I do not have to say that getting there first means you win. When the Founding Fathers decided that the president should be elected, they did not have to state that the person who received the most votes would win the election. Since Trump and his supporters were not able to prove fraud, Biden won the election. No other result is logically conceivable.

One final observation. It is unlikely that the trial based on the DOJ indictment will be televised. It is likely that the Georgia trial will be televised. It is difficult to speculate how this will affect the outcome of the two or more trials. It will undoubtedly make the Georgia trial more significant than the DOJ trial regarding its impact on how the election system in the United States functions, and the future of the American experiment in maintaining a democracy.

3.13 Complexity in the law

In Appendix A of *The Judge and the Philosopher*, I review the law of zoning to demonstrate the complexity in the law and the legal system. In the first three chapters in this volume, I have looked at the law regarding the election of the president as another example of the complexity of the multiple overlapping legal systems of the law at the federal, state, and local levels. This analysis is not inconsistent with Hart's rule of recognition. The rule of recognition is based upon the social fact of general consensus about what is the law. That social fact exists. I am pointing out the complexities of that social fact.

Much of the electoral system for electing the president is subject to customary norms. Some of these customary norms have the force of law and some do not. While Hart included customary norms within the law, he does not explain their role and he does not distinguish the two types of customary norms. In expanding upon Hart's version of the rule of recognition, our next task is to describe customary norms and to establish that some customary norms, even though they are not enacted, have the force of law. This will then lead to an expanded description of the rule of recognition that accommodates the complexity that exists in the law in our current Anglo-American legal world.

4.
Customary Legal Norms

"Conventions are indeed part and parcel of constitutional law. With the widening of the scope of conventions, there has come the realization that dividing law between law and convention is by no means clear. Nor can the observation of rules of a conventional character be always, or even usually, explained by reference to the ultimate sanction of law enforced in courts of justice." *A.V. Dicey* [92]

A.V. Dicey (Albert Venn Dicey), an English Whig jurist and constitutional theorist during the late nineteenth and early twentieth centuries, maintained that customs related to foundational issues may be part of the law even though they are not enacted nor enforced by the courts.

4.1 Custom and the rule of recognition

Hart views the rule of recognition as a social fact that lays the foundation for the law, so that it is a defining feature of the law in addition to being fundamental to the legal system. It is the basic rule that sets the foundation for the legal system not necessarily in a canonical fashion but like a custom or a convention. The rule of recognition in Hart's original version of it, classifies the law as part of the structure of the legal system.[93] The rule of recognition provides "only the general conditions which correct legal decisions must satisfy in modern systems of law."[94] Note Hart's reference to the correct decision.

In Hart's expanded version of the pedigree theory, the rule of recognition "may supply tests not to the factual content of laws but to their conformity with substantive moral values or principles".[95] Established judicial practice may accept such tests as relevant, though judges may disagree as to what the test requires in a specific case. Judges may also disagree about whether the moral test is satisfied, and the rule of recognition may not resolve such disagreement. But Hart insists that there is enough certainty and acceptance by all concerned individuals to support his concept of the rule of recognition as the qualifying determinate test of the law.

Hart's explanation still does not answer the fundamental question in this chapter, which is whether a custom may become a legal rule without there being an enactment by either legislation or declaration in a judicial decision that the custom is a law or part of a law. Because Hart is attempting to present a concept of law that will be descriptive of a vast variety of legal systems, it is difficult for him to explain how a custom becomes part of the legal system considering the great variability in legal systems and in legal cultures.

He recognizes custom as the social fact forming the basis for the rule of recognition. But Hart insists upon some enactment, some action by an authorized agent, that is consistent with the pedigree theory for custom to be recognized as part of the pre-existing law and to be viewed as authoritative. He does not accept the concept of the self-executing customary norm. Acceptance of the self-executing customary norm as part of the rule of recognition is a significant addition to Hart's entire conceptual framework. This is a possible modification of Hart's rule of recognition. At a minimum, it stretches it.

My contention is that Hart's original version of the rule of recognition should be expanded. I maintain that there are legal rules that have not been enacted as such by a law-making authority. The opposite is also true. There may be actions taken by authorities who are empowered to make laws, but their actions may not in fact create legal rules. Eg. Every judicial decision is not necessarily a precedent.

In fact, to go even further, there may be legal rules that are by their terms unenforceable; legal rules that do not provide a method for enforcement, and legal rules that provide the authority for enforcement but the agency having the authority has not adopted regulations to be enforced. There are also several other situations to be considered later that stretch Hart's explanation of how the law works and his description of the rule of recognition.

Finally, there are at least two different types of customary norms. There are customary norms that have the force of law and customary norms that do not have the force of law. To determine what is law, and which customary norms would be included in the law, the distinction between the two types of customary norms must be considered. A customary norm with the force of law is part of the law, even if no court has ever declared it to be so. A customary norm that does not have the force of law becomes part of the law only if it is enacted in some manner, either by a court, a legislature or some other individual or agency which has the authority to create legal rules. Both types of customary norms are social facts, but only the former version should be acknowledged by the rule of recognition to be part of the law.

I presented examples of these two different types of customary norms in chapters 1 to 3 when discussing the norms related to the election of the U.S. president. Just as there are customary norms that have the force of law and customary norms that do not have the force of law, there are judicial decisions that are precedents and judicial decisions that are not precedents. I discuss decisions that are not precedents below.

4.2 Self-executing customary norms

As distinct from customary norms that lack the force of law but are part of the legal culture, customary norms that have the force of law may be considered to be part of the law. They are converted from common usage into legal norms when people believe that they have a legal obligation imposed by the norm and not just a moral duty or a concern for courteous behavior.[96] The legally binding custom should be distinguished from a practice that might be observed in a community that does not rise to the level of a legally binding custom.

Hundreds of years ago, it was the general belief in England that the judge-made common law was itself a customary regime.[97] Blackstone stated that the common law is the expression of the "general customs" of the entire citizenry.[98] These customs are doctrines that are not in any written statute or ordinance but are the subject of immemorial usage. To establish a general rule of common usage, it is necessary to show that a practice is universally observed and has been observed for a long period of time.

Traditional legal norms may also include what Blackstone referred to as "local customs," such as servitudes over land that were held by an inchoate group of residents of a particular locality.[99] To establish a local custom, there are seven factors: continued, peaceable, reasonable, certain, compulsory usage from time immemorial and consistency with all other local customs. This view of customary law has been the subject of recent judicial decisions, as I explain below.

Customs may clearly be incorporated into legal rules. A good example of this is in the Uniform Commercial Code (UCC). Karl Llewellyn, one of the leading American Legal Realists, was one of the principal drafters of the UCC. Usage of trade is a controlling concept in the format of this potential statute that has received wide acceptance in the United States.[100] Industry practices are considered in the UCC to be the applicable standard of compliance with the UCC. There are many other examples of custom being incorporated into statutes.

In addition to customs being incorporated into legislation, custom may be trumped by statutes or by judicial decisions. If this occurs, the custom is, from a legal point of view, nullified. It will have no legal effect in justifying behavior prohibited by an enacted legal norm (established by statute or precedent). For example, in some segments of the population in the United States, it is customary to have multiple wives, but a statute and a judicial decision prohibiting bigamy will trump that custom.

4.3 Custom may trump statutes or judicial decisions

An interesting question is whether custom can under any circumstances ever trump a statutory provision or a judicial decision. Most legal positivists would argue that this is impossible in a mature legal system. In the United States, in some of the states, such as Hawaii, one could argue that precedents establish that customary norms may override the general common law.[101] There is a recognized legal right based upon custom in Hawaii that the public has the right to walk on the beaches because the beaches are regarded as being owned by the public. A similar theory may prevail in Oregon in the form of a public easement in the dry sandy area of the beaches in the state. In fact, it could be argued that this customary right in Oregon may even prevail over a judicial decision based upon constitutional principles.

In *Lucas v. South Carolina Coastal Council*, the United States Supreme Court found that a legal rule that required that the owner of real property allow the general public walking on the beach to cross his property was a taking without just compensation. This is based upon the constitutional law of the U.S. (it is an inverse or de facto condemnation).[102]

Lucas bought two vacant beachfront lots in 1986 for $975,000. South Carolina had a Beachfront Management Act that prevented Lucas from building a house on the two lots. Lucas claimed that the restrictions on the use of the property constituted a regulatory taking of his property without just compensation. The trial court agreed with Lucas and awarded him $1,232,387.50 as just compensation for the taking. The Supreme Court of South Carolina reversed that decision. The U.S. Supreme Court reversed that court and reinstated the lower court decision.

One year after the *Lucas* decision, in the case of *Stevens v. City of Cannon Beach*, the Oregon Supreme Court dismissed an inverse condemnation claim that was similar to the claim in the *Lucas* case.[103] The Oregon court found that the public always had a right based upon the doctrine of custom to use the dry sandy area of Oregon's beaches. While Stevens, the landowner in this case, is regarded as having a "bundle of legal rights" as the property owner of the beachfront property, these rights do not include the right to exclude the public from the ocean shores in Oregon.

It is the doctrine of custom that is the basis for determining what rights are in the landowner's bundle of legal rights under Oregon's real property law. Oregon law, in effect, recognizes an easement in the public to use the ocean shore beaches based upon custom. It could be argued that, based upon this Oregon case, the doctrine of custom related to the beach area constitutes a state property law that can prevail over the U.S. Supreme Court's pronouncement of a constitutional right.[104] It has also been suggested that the Oregon legislature should adopt a statute recognizing the public's easement because its present statutes do not clearly do so.

This Oregon case raises an additional question, which is whether the legal rule that is established by custom can be self-executing. In other words, can there be a legal rule established by custom without an enactment or acknowledgement of that rule by either legislation or judicial decision? A second question could be whether a legal positivist would accept the possibility of a self-executing customary legal rule, even though the customary rule is not in any way posited?

To put this first question into an historical context, bear in mind that in *Swift v. Tyson*, the U.S. Supreme Court declared that the law consists of statutes and customs, but not legal rules established by precedent.[105] Then, in *Black & White Taxicab*, Justice Holmes in his dissenting opinion questioned whether there could be federal common law without reference to some act by which this federal common law was created.[106]

Justice Holmes's approach found its way into the majority opinion of the Supreme Court in *Erie Railroad Co. v. Tompkins* when Justice Brandeis appeared to accept that federal common law does not exist without some definite authority behind it.[107] Justice Brandeis's view, however, does not mean that a custom cannot give rise to a legal norm without a legislative or judicial law-creating act.

It is the approach of the Supreme Court in the *Erie* case that should have been followed by the Supreme Court in deciding whether to overrule *Roe v. Wade*. The sound reasoning process in *Erie* with its consideration of the consequences of its decision was ignored when *Roe v. Wade* was overruled. This is discussed in volume 4 of this series of books.

Even if there is clear proof of a custom as an objective practice within a relevant community, and a subjective acceptance of the custom being of value as a norm that is considered by the citizenry to be obligatory, Hart would sometimes not consider the custom to be law. The custom, according to most Hartian scholars, should not be accepted as a legal norm if it is not recognized as such within a judicial decision or by incorporation into a statute. In other words, Hart ultimately contends, according to this interpretation of his legal philosophy, that a custom cannot be self-executing because its status as a legal norm is dependent upon a law-creating act. Freedom to walk on the beach in Oregon, however, appears to be a legal right established by custom without any enactment of a legal rule establishing that right.

4.4 Other uses of custom

Even if a customary norm is not self-executing, custom may still play a major role in a modern legal system in many ways. Customary norms are internalized, just like moral norms. A long-standing custom, such as public use of a beach, may become part of the "background principles" of real property law, so that a private individual who owns the beach does not acquire the right to exclusive use of the beach. In other words, there is no private right to build on the beach and thereby exclude the public.

Interpretation of the terms in a legal norm may be influenced by custom, so that, for example, the cruel and unusual punishment clause in the U.S. Constitution has a customary base that controls what the clause means.[108] The red line between law-application and law-creation is often blurred. Sometimes, a custom may influence the content of law when a statute or a precedent directly or indirectly incorporates a custom into the law. The custom may also control how a legal norm is enforced after it is enacted. Custom may, therefore, impact the administration of the law even without formal recognition.

Even if a custom is not enforced in some formal manner by a legal actor or in some informal manner by citizens honoring the custom as though it is obligatory, the custom can still have a legal effect in controlling behavior or influencing legal actors. The speed limit may be 55 M.P.H. but custom may preclude enforcement between 55 and 60 M.P.H. If it is generally accepted that there will be no prosecution for driving at speeds below 60 M.P.H., even though the posted speed limit is 55 M.P.H., this is a customary norm that may be viewed as a real rule. Therefore, there may be customary norms that are also real rules. I discuss real rules after considering other situations that may modify our understanding of the rule of recognition.

4.5 Structural customary norms

A customary norm that I would not consider to be a real rule because it relates to the structure of the legal system is the rule of non-contradiction. This rule is necessary in order to maintain the internal coherence of the legal system. It is not generally referenced in a statute and is, instead, part of the legal culture. The rule of non-contradiction controls how the rules work. The law must be systematized to ensure that it is non-contradictory. An individual cannot be required to do something that it is illegal to do.

Another fundamental structural norm is that acts that are not prohibited by law are permitted.[109] Based upon this customary norm, when interpreting a zoning ordinance, we assume that the list of prohibited acts in a specific district sets the boundaries for what one cannot do. The underlying rule, while not always stated this way specifically, is that one may do anything that is not prohibited.

4.6 Legal positivists and custom

Custom may or may not be regarded as a legal norm according to the legal positivist's version of the pedigree theory. Therefore, legal positivists may or may not include customary norms within the pre-existing law. Even if customary norms are not part of the law, they are certainly part of the legal system. Consequently, for the legal positivists, determination of the correct decision, which is based upon the application of the pre-existing law, may or may not consider custom in arriving at the correct decision.

The theory of creative positivism would accept the inclusion of customary norms in determining whether a decision is a just decision or a wise decision. Custom, therefore, may float into the evaluation of the judicial decision by it having an impact on whether the decision is the just decision or the wise decision.

In addition to the customary norms being relevant to the just decision and the wise decision, I maintain that self-executing customary norms with the force of law should be regarded as part of the pre-existing law for determining whether a judicial decision is the correct decision. To apply the customary norm, however, you must first decide if it has the force of law.

4.7 A hypothetical example of a customary norm as part of the correct decision

Before I leave the subject of custom, I want to offer some support for the theory that custom may create a legal norm in a self-executing manner without its having been incorporated into a statute or precedent. Allow me to offer a hypothetical example.

Joe Blackletter goes to the Trattoria San Nicola on Wednesday for dinner. After eating dinner, he leaves a note in the form of an IOU note (a promissory note or a bill like the document in *Swift v. Tyson*) promising to pay the bill of the restaurant with a 25% gratuity on Friday. He includes his name, address, email address and telephone numbers (business, home and mobile) in the IOU note which he then signs. The waiter sees him leaving and summons Vito, the owner of the restaurant. Vito bars Joe's exit and declares that he must pay before leaving. The waiter calls the police. The patrol officer arrives and he arrests Joe for disorderly conduct.

At the hearing on Monday before Judge Green, Joe, who is a lawyer, claims in his defense that he has researched the statutes, ordinances, rules, regulations and published judicial decisions. None of them mentions anything about when and how you should pay your bill when dining in a restaurant. Joe argues that there is no reference in the law to an obligation to pay for your meal before leaving the restaurant. He testifies that he did, in fact, return to the restaurant on Friday and make the payment he outlined in his note. He argues that his behavior should be viewed as not being a violation of the disorderly conduct ordinance.

Joe further testifies that there is no notice in the restaurant menu that one must pay before leaving the restaurant, that there is no sign in the restaurant giving him notice that he must pay before leaving and that no one mentioned to him when he ordered his meal or before he was leaving the restaurant that payment was required before he departed. He also claims that he always pays his bills each week on Friday and that is the procedure he follows with his doctor, dentist, accountant, the lady who cleans his house and his office employees. And in his legal practice he does not require that his clients pay his bill before they leave his office.

Judge Green finds that Joe is guilty of disorderly conduct and fines him $100 and orders him to never repeat his action when dining in a restaurant. The judge claims that there is a custom within the community of paying for your meal before leaving the restaurant and that this is a self-executing customary rule that has the force of law.

I believe that Judge Green has made a correct, just and wise decision. It makes little difference whether the basis for the decision is that paying for meals before leaving the restaurant is a legally binding custom or that it is not, in itself, a legally binding norm but forms the basis for the finding that Joe's behavior is a violation of the disorderly conduct ordinance due to established custom. Regardless of which approach is taken, it is still reasonable to conclude that Judge Green's decision is correct.[110] Therefore, I would assert that this reasoning leads to the conclusion that a custom may be self-executing and, therefore, a custom can be a legally binding norm.[111]

I distinguish the payment of the bill from the payment of the tip, though both are subject to customary rules. Payment of the bill is a customary rule with the force of law, while payment of the gratuity is a customary rule that lacks the force of law. The payment of the tip is a voluntary act even though it is the subject of a customary rule. There is no legal obligation to pay the gratuity. It is this distinction between the customary rule that is legally obligatory and the customary rule that is not so that I rely upon in section 3.10 in describing the legal structure of the electoral college system for electing the U.S. president.

This hypothetical example is offered to demonstrate how a customary norm may affect a judicial decision. It may form the basis for the correct decision by representing the application of a norm of the pre-existing law. The customary norm may also be relevant to evaluating the judicial decision in order to decide if it is a just decision and a wise decision. Accepting customary norms in evaluating judicial decisions is not inconsistent with Hart's rule of recognition.

Applying customary norms to make judicial decisions as part of the rule of adjudication may not be consistent with Hart's version of the rule of recognition. Creative positivism does not view the rule of recognition as superior to the rule of adjudication. Therefore, in my creative positivist version of the secondary rules, the rule of adjudication may declare that a customary norm is part of the law. After the decision doing so is made, the rule of recognition will also accept the customary norm that the rule of adjudication used in making the judicial decision.

Accepting customary norms as part of the law may also be viewed as a tertiary rule, along with the other tertiary rules that are part of creative positivism. Accepting the rule of adjudication and the rule of change as being on the same level as (and not inferior to) the rule of recognition represents an expansion of Hart's version of the rule of recognition.

4.8 Customary norms and the secondary rules

Ultimately, the rule of recognition is neither valid nor invalid. It just forms the basis for determining legal validity for all other rules of the legal system. It is a customary norm that is accepted as the basis for legitimizing all other aspects of the legal system and the institutions that qualify as legal agencies for law applying and/or law creating. In his postscript, Hart extends his legal philosophy and contends that the rule of recognition is a form of judicial customary rule. As such, it could be regarded as a customary legal rule.[112]

The rule of recognition, then, would be binding in the same way, with the same underlying understanding, that allows customary rules to have the force of law. The customary norms with the force of law are valid based upon the rule of recognition, which means that they are accepted as law without reference to other legal rules created by statutes or precedents. Customary norms may be part of the legal culture and they may also be part of the law like other legal norms.

When an individual makes a legally binding promise in accordance with the power-conferring primary rule allowing for contracts to be legally enforceable, the obligation is self-created (the promisor imposes it upon herself). This is similar to customary norms that are self-imposed, though they are not self-created. Adherence to the requirements of customary norms and expectations of behavior in conformity with such norms is generally the result of social pressure. As I have explained, customary norms may also be the subject of official recognition and for that reason they are law.

Not all promises are legally binding promises. For example, I may promise not to see a movie unless you accompany me. When I forget or disregard my promise, there is no legal mechanism by which you can enforce the promise or require me to suffer a sanction for not following through with honoring my promise. Similarly, there can be customs that do not rise to the status of customary legal norms, like a man standing up when a woman approaches his table. There are other customs that are obligatory customary norms, like paying for your meal after you consume it and before you depart from the restaurant, which could be regarded as a customary norm with the force of law.

Hart's internal point of view is also applicable to the law enforcing officials. We say that judges have the obligation to apply the law. Do we mean by this that the judge ought to apply the law? Does this mean that the judge must apply the law? Or is it just that the judge is authorized to apply the law?

If the obligation means that the judge is authorized to apply the law but not that she is required to apply the law or is restricted in some way from not applying the law, then we may conclude that the judge may be legally permitted to disregard applying the law. She may be acting legally, within the scope of her authority, to make the just decision or the wise decision, even though, by doing so, she is not making the correct decision. This decision will likely be an authoritative decision, which means that it will be a precedent. It will also be binding which means that it will obligate the parties. If the decision is both authoritative and binding, surely it follows that she had the authority to make the decision. She is, in other words, authorized by the rule of adjudication and the rule of change to make the decision. By definition, she has changed the law because she did not make the correct decision.

As I explain below, the secondary rule of adjudication, acting in conjunction with the rule of recognition, provides a combination of legal rules and customary rules that identify who is a judge, specify when he is acting as a judge, and stipulate how cases should be decided. In fact, I view these constraints on judges as a tertiary rule if this set of procedural rules is not regarded as part of the rule of adjudication in coordination with the rule of recognition. Moreover, in addition to the rules that control judicial decision-making, there are similar sets of legal and customary rules that relate to law-applying by other officials. These officials, such as police officers, zoning officers and other administrative officials, are not considered to be judges.

Creative positivism does not conflict with Hart's description of the legal system. Hart acknowledges that the primary rules are not uniformly obeyed. This is also true of the rule of recognition. The rule of recognition presents the test for validity and is the basis for law ascertainment. But the rule of change and the rule of adjudication can allow for the decision of a court to be authorized, authoritative and binding even if the decision conflicts with the law-ascertaining and law-applying function called for by the rule of recognition.

This analysis presupposes that the rule of change is not subordinate to the rule of recognition. The judge changes the law by creating a new legal norm, even though he is not thereby deciding the case in accordance with the rule of recognition. He is not applying the pre-existing law. His decision is nonetheless valid pursuant to the rule of recognition because he is authorized to create new law pursuant to the rule of change. After the new legal rule is created, the rule of recognition acknowledges that it is law.

Customary rules to a large extent tell us what is supposed to be law. But there can be situations that are difficult to place in one category or another (law or non-law). These confusing situations cannot be easily encompassed within Hart's version of the rule of recognition. Moreover, as the discussion in chapters 1 to 3 illustrates regarding the election of POTUS, the multiple legal systems in the U.S adds to the confusion that stretches Hart's rule of recognition.

Which individuals, or which institution decides how elections are conducted is a recurrent question that has already been touched upon. The Constitution provides for state legislatures to be the final authority to create the rules governing federal elections, such as the election of POTUS.[113] Does this mean that state courts may not intervene in the state legislative decisions? Does this preclude federal courts from doing so? Who has the final word on which rules will govern federal elections? Such questions concern the rule of recognition.

In the next chapter, I discuss the issue of decisions being made that have legal consequences, despite it not being clear that the decisions are consistent with Hart's rule of recognition. We will accept these decisions as authorized and binding upon the parties involved in the case, even though the decisions may not be classifiable as authoritative. These decisions may be judicial decisions or decisions made by another type of governmental official acting within the scope of their authority. The decisions may or may not be consistent with the rule of recognition regarding both law-ascertainment and law-application.

If the decisions are not authoritative, they will not constitute an enactment of a legal rule. Therefore, the legal rule that was applied to make the decision may not qualify as an enactment or the positing of a legal rule. The decision, and the legal rule applied to make the decision, may not become part of the pre-existing law for the next decision. The question that arises is whether that type of decision, once it has been made, can be regarded as being consistent with the rule of recognition.

We will now explore those situations that challenge Hart's rule of recognition to illustrate how they may be viewed as supplementing, modifying, and even requiring reconstruction of Hart's rule of recognition.

5.
Expanding the Rule of Recognition

The issue that I am addressing in this chapter is how the rule of recognition works in a series of situations in which the law is uncertain. Hart's version of the rule of recognition is a social fact which presupposes that there is general consensus among legal officials about what the law is. I do not mean by "uncertain" that there is no agreement upon the relevant legal rule. These are situations in which the lack of clarity is not based upon finding the law. I am assuming that these are situations in which we are relatively in agreement about law-ascertainment and law-application. The question we are considering is how to reconcile these situations with the rule of recognition.

5.1 The same state law in two jurisdictions

Even though we may talk about the law of contracts in the United States, there is no uniform set of legal rules governing contracts everywhere in the U.S. Every jurisdiction has its own unique set of legal rules. These rules apply in that jurisdiction and the network of legal rules in that jurisdiction is not authoritative in any other jurisdiction.[114] In that sense, every jurisdiction is unique, and the rule of recognition does not provide for the same legal rules in every jurisdiction. This is

The Judge and the President

true—the rule of recognition does not provide for the same legal rules in two very similar jurisdictions—even if the two jurisdictions are, in a broader sense, part of the same legal system (the legal system of a single state).

Here is one example illustrating the difference in the law in two similar jurisdictions. Tower Health is a non-profit corporation that owns six hospitals and other health facilities in the Philadelphia suburbs. Three of the hospitals are in Chester County, Pennsylvania (Phoenixville, Brandywine and Jennersville). Their status as tax-exempt non-profit facilities was challenged in the Court of Common Pleas of Chester County. This court, in a decision by Judge Jeffrey Sommer, held that the Tower Health hospitals are not tax-exempt, even though they are non-profit and, as such, are subject to payment of real estate taxes.[115]

In an earlier case, decided a few days before the Chester County case and involving the very same issue, but heard in Montgomery County in reference to Tower Health's Pottstown Hospital, Judge Jeffrey S. Saltz reached the opposite conclusion. In this case, the court held that Tower Health's Pottstown Hospital is tax-exempt.[116] There is no relevant factual difference among the four hospitals. In both courts, the same Pennsylvania law was reviewed and applied.

It should be obvious from this example that there is a difference in interpretation of Pennsylvania law in Chester County and Montgomery County. For every judge in Montgomery County, the law is the interpretation by Judge Saltz, the interpretation of which is binding for each of these judges. The Montgomery County decision, however, is not authoritative in Chester County. In Chester County, the same Pennsylvania state law has been interpreted to reach a different conclusion. The Chester County decision is not authoritative in Montgomery County, and it binds only the Chester County judges and not the Montgomery County judges. Montgomery County and Chester County are adjacent to each other and are two of the 67 counties in Pennsylvania. In the United States, there are more than 3,000 counties, each of which has its own legal system.[117]

Here are the questions. Are the Tower Health hospitals tax exempt according to the law in Pennsylvania? When the relevant state statute is ascertained pursuant to the rule of recognition, is there a difference between the law in Montgomery County and the law in Chester County, even though there is no relevant difference in the facts in the two counties? The two judges that heard these two cases are at the same level in the judicial hierarchy. It necessarily follows that the rule of recognition provides a different answer to the question of the tax-exempt status of Tower Health hospitals in two adjacent counties in Pennsylvania. Law-ascertainment is not the same in these two counties, even though the same statute is authoritative in both counties.

Only one of the two Court of Common Pleas decisions will ultimately be the correct decision when both cases are appealed. An appellate court will make a definitive decision as to how the Pennsylvania law should be interpreted. One of these two decisions is, consequently, an incorrect decision and it will be reversed on appeal, while the other decision is affirmed. If there is no appeal filed in the two cases, the two decisions are final and are authoritative in their respective counties. Let me repeat, the rule of recognition provides a different result in the two counties even though the same law, the same legal rule, is being applied in the two counties to the same corporate entity. From the point of view of Tower Health, it is tax exempt in one jurisdiction and not tax exempt in the next-door jurisdiction.

Moreover, the legal systems in the two counties are part of the same state-wide legal system, which is from an analytical point of view another legal system at a different level than the county legal systems. The state-wide legal system is subject, then, to its own rule of recognition. The state legal system is, in turn, separate from the federal legal system, which has its own rule of recognition. Looking at these two legal systems—the state legal system and the federal legal system—

provides a different form of potential complexity. Let me provide an example for this situation.

5.2 State law and federal law

Two states, Pennsylvania and Texas, have issued contrasting COVID-19 restrictions related to wearing of masks. In Pennsylvania, the legal rule as established by the Pennsylvania Department of Health is that schools must require that students wear masks. This rule was initially held to be valid in the state trial court. The appellate court in Pennsylvania reversed the decision and found the requirement to be invalid.[118] Therefore, the state of the law in Pennsylvania as based upon this decision is that school districts may adopt their own regulations regarding the wearing of masks.

The boundaries of school districts are not the same as the boundaries of counties. There may be several school districts in a county. There may be school districts that cross county lines and are in multiple counties. Each school district in Pennsylvania may adopt its own rules and regulations.

There are some interesting aspects of this appellate decision that are worth noting. While the argument was made that the order of the Department of Health was advisory in nature, the Commonwealth Court held that the order was a binding regulation. The order had the force of law because it is viewed as a rule that affects all school districts in the state. Later in this chapter, I discuss whether an order that lacks a remedy for violation of the order (which is the case with this rule) should be viewed as a legal rule.

Another point that the Commonwealth Court made is that the order is invalid because the Department of Health failed to follow the standard rule-making procedure. Consequently, the order of the Department of Health was invalid from the day it was announced. This raises the question of whether this order of the Department of Health could be the law prior to the decision of the Commonwealth Court. In other words, does the rule of recognition include the possibility that an enactment may be invalid from the day the rule is promulgated, and, if so, does the rule of recognition acknowledge its invalidity? Is the mandate we are discussing law or non-law prior to the decision of the Commonwealth Court?

In Texas, in contrast to Pennsylvania, the rule established by the Governor's executive order is that no school district may require that masks be worn. This executive order has also been held to be invalid. This time, the decision was made in the federal courts. The executive order prohibiting school districts from requiring masks is invalid based upon federal law. This federal law, the Americans with Disabilities Act, is the same federal law that is applicable in Pennsylvania.[120] The claim in this Texas case is that COVID-19 poses a greater risk for children with special health needs than it does for other children. The restriction on schools requiring masks could exacerbate the problems experienced by vulnerable children as a result of COVID-19.

Therefore, in Texas, based upon federal law, the rule prohibiting school districts from requiring masks is a nullity. So, school districts in Texas may legally require masks. In Pennsylvania, the state requirement that school districts must require masks is invalid, leaving the decision to the individual school districts. The result in both states is the same—the individual school districts have the authority to decide upon the wearing of masks. In other words, in both states, the requirement that masks be worn is a school district by school district decision. Therefore, one could suggest that each school district is a separate jurisdiction with its own distinct rules. This does not mean, however, that the law is the same in Texas as in Pennsylvania (though the federal law, as mentioned, may be the same).

Even though the outcome of the two cases is the same (school districts make the decision about whether masks are required), this does not mean that the law as determined by the rule of recognition is the same in Texas and Pennsylvania. Not only will state law potentially not be the same, but federal law may also be different in the two states. The same result in Texas and Pennsylvania is not based upon the same legal rules.

The decision in the Pennsylvania appellate court is authoritative in Pennsylvania but has no legal significance in Texas. The decision in the federal court in Texas, while it relates to the federal law that applies in Pennsylvania, is not considered to be a binding precedent in the circuit in which Pennsylvania is located. It is the same federal law, but it is subject to potentially different interpretations in the two circuits, even though they are part of the same federal legal system.

In other words, just like Pennsylvania law in Montgomery County and Chester County, federal law in the Fifth Circuit may be different from federal law in the Third Circuit. These two circuits potentially have rules of recognition that may generate different legal rules. Is there an effect upon the concept of the rule of recognition if there are different legal rules on the issue of masks in the Third and the Fifth Circuits? Is the law as ascertained in the two circuits potentially different, even though it is the same federal law being applied?

Pennsylvania law, while it is subject to federal standards, is obviously not necessarily the same as the federal law as ascertained by the Court of Appeals in the Fifth Circuit in which Texas is located. In both cases, the regulation adopted by the state government has been declared to be invalid. The Pennsylvania decision is not authoritative in Texas or in any other state. Since Pennsylvania is in a different circuit than Texas, while the federal law is the same federal law, the Fifth Circuit decision is not binding on the Pennsylvania courts, nor is it binding in the Third Circuit Court of Appeals in the federal system in Pennsylvania.

These four cases, the two involving the tax-exempt status of the Tower Health hospitals and the two involving the wearing of masks, demonstrate that the legal culture in Pennsylvania and Texas contains or acknowledges customary rules that govern which enactments are authoritative and binding. These customary rules control how the rule of recognition in a particular jurisdiction will function in performing the task of law-ascertainment, which in turn will determine law-application. There is general agreement about these customary rules which promotes their effectiveness in allowing us to discuss what is the law in a specific jurisdiction as of a particular time.

5.3 Laws which by their terms are non-reviewable

I have introduced the distinction between law and non-law in section 4.1.[121] The example that I would offer of a law that is, in terms of its practical effect, a non-law is the mandate provision in The Patient Protection and Affordable Care Act (often referred to as "ACA" or "Obamacare"), adopted in 2010. The mandate provision required most citizens to obtain minimum health insurance coverage and imposed a penalty on those who did not do so. This provision was amended by Congress to provide for a penalty of $0 for failure to carry the required healthcare insurance.[122] The District Court held that the penalty was unconstitutional. Since the mandate could not be severed from the Act, the Act itself was also unconstitutional.

The Fifth Circuit Court of Appeals agreed that the penalty was unconstitutional. It reversed the District Court, however, on the severability issue and did not find the entire statute to be unconstitutional. Since this penalty is not really a penalty, when the ACA was challenged, the Supreme Court reversed the Court of Appeals and held that the challengers lacked standing because there was no real relief that could be granted. The plaintiffs suffered no injury because there was no penalty. Since the penalty is zero, there is no potential or actual governmental conduct that could cause harm to the plaintiffs. The law, while still a law on the books, was not enforceable.[123]

A similar situation to the law that operates like a non-law are the decisions that are made by legal agencies that are similarly not subject to being challenged. Verdicts of juries are not subject to review by the trial court or the appellate court if no error has been made in the trial. The jury verdict is not a precedent for future trials. A conviction of one defendant for an act that he committed with associates does not bind the next jury when they consider the guilt or innocence of the other persons who participated in the same act. When a conspirator is found to be guilty, this does not mean that co-conspirators are also guilty.

The U.S. Supreme Court decides which cases it will accept. For a case to be heard, four justices must accept the case. The reasons for why a case is accepted or rejected are not disclosed. The decision is final and binding and not subject to review. The memoranda prepared by the law clerks for the justices of the cases for potential review are not made available to the public. The act of accepting or not accepting a case is a legal act by legal actors, but, since there is no way to challenge the act, and no reasons are given for the act, the decisions to deny hearing a case lack some of the characteristics of other types of legal actions.

The situation in which legal actions are taken by legal actors with the authority to take the legal action but no reasons are offered for the actions gives rise to the question of how we will determine whether the decision is a correct decision. You could study all the cases accepted by the Supreme Court for review and all the cases not accepted and create a matrix of the similarities in each of the groups of cases. This could be useful information, but it would not provide the information one would need to determine whether a decision to accept or not accept a case for review is correct. The study would identify consistencies, inconsistencies and variables. In order to determine the correct decision, however, you need more than the variants.

We do not know whether there are rules that individual justices view as self-binding rules in deciding whether to accept a case for review. If there is no obligation to follow rules, there is no basis for finding the correct decision. All that one could discover is potential consistencies and inconsistencies. In fact, the variety of variables would probably be too overwhelming to provide insight into when or why a case is accepted for review. There is no way to know if law has been ascertained and applied.[124]

5.4 Non-legal acts that are enforced by legal actors

The example that I use for non-legal acts becoming legally enforceable are the rules of homeowners' associations (HOAs).[125] When I call these acts "non-legal," I am not implying that they are illegal. I am referring to the authority of the HOA that adopts the regulations. Violations of these regulations are not acts prohibited by law. They are acts prohibited by the rules of an agency that has legal authority to adopt rules but no legal authority to enforce them except by requesting and obtaining the supportive action of a legal agency. For example, the HOA can file a lien against a member's property. But the HOA needs the Recorder of Deeds or another clerk of the judicial system to place the lien on record. To enforce its regulations, the HOA needs a legal agency to act; it itself is not a legal agency with authority to enforce its regulations of its own volition.

A similar situation is a congressional committee issuing a subpoena to compel a witness to appear before the committee. The committee, and even the Congress, does not have authority to take legal action itself in the form of imposing a sanction against the uncooperative witness. It needs another governmental agency, in this case the Department of Justice, to bring an action in the courts.

It may surprise the reader to learn that individual lawyers may obtain subpoenas to serve upon witnesses (they will generally retain a constable or a professional process server to deliver the subpoena). Obviously, the lawyer herself has no legal authority to impose a sanction for refusing to honor the subpoena. She also needs to request the courts to enforce the subpoena.

5.5 Lack of standing

Lack of standing is a little different from non-law. It refers to whether the person filing the lawsuit and asserting the claim (the plaintiff) is legally entitled to be heard. The result of the non-standing ruling is that this plaintiff lacks the legal capacity to obtain relief on his claim. In other words, this plaintiff does not have a cause of action. There is no law available to this individual even though other potential plaintiffs may be able to assert the claim.

The case of *Conway v. Cutler Group* may be useful to explain this point.[126] In Pennsylvania law, there is an implied warranty of habitability established by judicial decision. If a builder constructs a house with defects, and sells the house to a purchaser, the purchaser has a cause of action allowing the purchaser to obtain compensation from the builder in order to remedy the defects in the house. Therefore, the purchaser from Cutler Group, which built the house, has a cause of action for the defects in the house. The cause of action is based upon the judicially created implied warranty of habitability which the courts will assume is within every contract to sell the house from the builder to the first purchaser of the house.

In the *Conway* case, this first purchaser, in this case, sold the house to the Conway family. The Conway family, who did not purchase the house from the builder, does not have a cause of action against the builder. They lack standing to bring the claim. They are not a beneficiary of the implied warranty of habitability which applies only to the initial purchaser. Consequently, they are not entitled to judicial relief because they do not have a cause of action.

Another type of lack of standing case is *Lightcap v. Wrightstown Township* which denied standing to a non-resident to challenge exclusionary zoning.[127] Only a resident, a developer or a landowner can do so. The individuals who are denied standing because they are non-residents are prevented from challenging the practices that prevent them from becoming residents.

Lack of standing has the effect of closing the courthouse doors to those who are adversely affected by the laws that they want to challenge. While the rules that are applied to deny standing are available pursuant to the rule of recognition, the effect of applying these rules is to deny judicial relief. Therefore, it could be argued that applying the legal rules derived from the rule of recognition denies potential legal rights. This seems contradictory. If you have a legal right but are unable to obtain relief, do you really have a legal right?

5.6 Judicial decisions that are not precedents

Non-published judicial decisions are decisions by judges deciding cases that will not become precedents because they are not published. This issue of non-published judicial opinions is consistent with the rule of recognition because the opinion that is non-published is a reasoned opinion. You can determine from the opinion whether law has been ascertained and applied, even though the opinion does not reinforce the pre-existing law or create new law. An example of non-publication of a judicial decision is *Gohmert v. Pence*.[128] This decision also involves the issue of standing to bring the case.

For one example, the clearest case of a judicial decision that is not a precedent occurs when the court declares that the decision is authoritative only for the case being considered. The decision is limited to the parties before the court and binds only those individuals. A similar result occurs when the decision is limited to the exact facts presented in the case being heard by the court.

An example with a potential similar result occurs in the case of *In re Elias V.*[129] A 13-year-old boy named Elias was accused of sexual assault upon a three-year-old neighbor. Under questionable circumstances, Elias confessed to a detective who had interviewed him at school. He was found guilty in the California trial court, and he went on to appeal on the grounds that his confession was involuntary.

The California Court of Appeals reversed the conviction and agreed that the confession should not have been admitted into evidence. The Court of Appeals reviewed the facts in great detail and surveyed many precedents and texts regarding confessions by minors. The most controversial aspect of the opinion of the Court of Appeals is its finding that, even if a statement was given freely, it will be deemed to be involuntary unless there is some corroboration of the suspect's guilt or some "internal indicia" of the statement's credibility.

There is a practice within some of the American legal systems that allows courts to choose not to publish their opinions. In fact, more decisions are unpublished in the federal judicial system than are published in the law reports. Some of the federal circuits allow unpublished opinions to be cited (if cited, a copy of the unpublished opinion must be filed with the court as an appendix to the brief. Other circuits do not permit the citing of unpublished opinions because the court that decided not to have the opinion published is thereby denying that opinion the status of being a precedent. The rules in the federal system are discussed in section 2.5.

In the California judicial system, as in the federal system, there are rules that govern publishing and depublishing. The opinion in *Elias V* is a published opinion. The California Attorney General's Office decided not to seek depublication of the case. Therefore, the case could be a precedent and may be cited as such.

This is not, however, the end of the *Elias V* case. In California, even after the Attorney General decides not to pursue an appeal, others may seek to limit the precedential nature of the decision because they disagree with it. They may file in the California Supreme Court a petition to depublish an opinion to render it devoid of precedential value. They may seek a judicial declaration that the legal rule applied to decide one case is not law for the next. Prosecutors in two California counties not involved in the *Elias V* case wrote letters to the California Supreme Court asking that the *Elias V* decision be depublished.

The judges in the Court of Appeals then responded to the letters of the prosecutors by a letter of their own to the California Supreme Court in which they objected to depublication of their decision. The Supreme Court took some time to consider not only the issue of depublication but whether they should treat the depublication controversy as an occasion to consider the underlying case as though it had been appealed (even though it had not been appealed). The Supreme Court decided to rule against the prosecutors in their depublication request.

Consequently, but only barely so, the *Elias V* decision remains an authoritative precedent. The *Elias V* case may proceed to trial, but the confession will not be admissible in it. I am using this case to illustrate two aspects of the judicial process that are important to notice.

First, if the depublication had occurred, then no legal rule would exist that would be based upon the opinion in the *Elias V* case. The case would not be a precedent and it could not be cited in the California courts as having established an authoritative rule. Therefore, the reasoning in the case, and the legal rule announced in the case, would apply only in the *Elias V* case and not to any other legal matter. It would be a ruling that would be applicable only to that one set of facts and to the parties in that specific case. It is important to distinguish authoritativeness from validity. Authoritativeness is related to whether it is a precedent and not to whether it is a valid decision.

Second, the entire concept of non-publication of opinions results in decisions that lack precedential value. They are not decisions that give rise to legal rules, though the individual cases are subject to legal rulings. These legal rulings, however, apply only to the litigants in the individual case. They create, then, what Hans Kelsen, an Austrian legal philosopher who taught in the U.S., called individual norms. They have no value beyond their application in a single case.

The point that I am stressing must be more clearly stated. In addition to court-enacted procedural rules, there are customary rules that govern the process of authoritativeness and the binding nature of decisions in the common law. Customary rules establish the basis for determining the precedential value of prior decisions, for allowing for stare decisis to apply to these decisions, all within the concept of what Stanley Fish called the legal culture. These are customary rules or conventions that control how the law works. These customary rules may become enacted rules when they are formally adopted by courts or included in legislation.

Customary norms are not created through the exercise of legal authority. The rule of recognition could be viewed, however, as validating norms which are derived from customs and for allowing, in coordination with the rule of adjudication, such norms to be part of the law-ascertainment and law-application process. In fact, one could conclude that Hart's secondary rules are themselves customary norms.

The bottom line is that the court, when deciding that a case should be a published decision, is declaring that the legal rule applied in the case is part of the law. If the judge decides that the decision should not be published, he is refusing to include within the law the legal rule applied by the court in making the decision. He is restricting the case to its facts and to its litigants.

This decision to publish or not to publish is a clear example of the exercising of judicial discretion determining what shall be law and what shall not be law (except as it is applied to the parties in the case). Therefore, the rule of recognition does not declare what is the law. The judge making the decision to publish or not to publish decides what is the law. The rule of recognition acknowledges the judge's decision.

Since umpires do not have authority to create baseball rules, no umpire decides whether his ruling will be authoritative. A judge may decide to restrict his ruling to the parties in the case or request that his decision will be non-published. The customary rules relating to judicial discretion empower the judge to decide if he is creating law.

6.

Additional Situations that Require Reconsideration of the Rule of Recognition

6.1 Situations without judicial remedies

There are constitutional, statutory and judicially created rules, as well as customary rules, that define the jurisdiction of courts. The federal courts will not hear cases that they are not authorized to consider. The rules for jurisdiction in the federal courts are beyond the scope of this book. Like the plaintiffs lacking standing, there is only a slight distinction between the cases in which the court decides that it lacks jurisdiction and a similar barrier to adjudication which is that the court has jurisdiction, but the court decides that the case is non-justiciable.

Creative positivism contends that the court must decide every case that is brought to the court. This statement is true, and it is not true. It is not true in the cases in which the court simply refuses to decide the case. The court decides that the matter is non-justiciable. This is like the doctor telling you that there is no treatment that he can offer you for your illness. You will just have to let the disease take its course.

In the non-justiciable case, the court declares that it will not hear the case and, therefore, not render a decision in the case. In other words, the case involves human activities for which the court and, therefore, the law does not provide relief. The matter at issue will have to be resolved by some other agency or remain unresolved. The court does not have, or declines to accept, jurisdiction of the case. There is, in a sense, no case.

The statement that each case must be decided is an accurate description of the court's response to the case before it because the decision to not make a decision is itself a decision. The court is deciding not to decide. The law is that there is no law that allows for the claimant to have the court hear this type of complaint.

I do not view this situation of non-justiciability as a gap in the law. The law, however, does not control every aspect of human activity. If the woman you proposed to will not marry you, the judge will not order her to do so. You will just have to live your life knowing that the judicial system is not open for business to relieve your disappointment.

This situation of non-justiciability is also not within Hart's concept of open texture because the court is able to refer to settled law in order to establish that there is no law that would provide relief to the plaintiff. The plaintiff does not have a cause of action. The plaintiff may not be asserting a claim upon which the court will act. For example, the Court of Common Pleas and the Pennsylvania Supreme Court decided in the *Conway* case that Conway did not have a cause of action.[130]

There are precedents for non-justiciability, and I will discuss a few. There are also statutory constraints on jurisdiction and even constitutional barriers to obtaining judicial relief in certain types of cases. It is not that there is no law—the law is that there is just no law that gives the plaintiff a cause of action that the court will hear. Non-justiciability is a feature of all legal systems. The doors of the courthouse are not open for every type of case.

6.2 Non-justiciability in the English courts
The leading case on non-justiciability in England is *Buttes Gas and Oil Co. v. Hammer*.[131] The case involves a dispute over the rights to oil

discovered at a site in the Mideast. The facts in the case are complex, there are multiple parties (the two companies mainly involved are both California companies), parties that are successors to other parties, and the United Kingdom is a tangential party along with some other countries (for example, the Trucial States, which is a precursor to the United Arab Emirates). I am not going to discuss the facts or the background for the case. There are also some earlier cases between these same parties involving the same issues.

The importance of the *Buttes* case is that the House of Lords decides that the commercial dispute is non-justiciable because the case involves a political question. Lord Wilberforce gives the opinion for the House of Lords and the other four Lords join in his opinion. The basic question in the case is whether the English courts will adjudicate cases involving the transactions of foreign sovereign states.

Lord Wilberforce reviews the history of political questions being considered by the English courts in discussing the precedents starting with a 17th century decision. He concludes that the *Buttes* case does not raise issues "upon which a municipal court can pass".[132]

Let's look at another case in the United Kingdom. In one of the most controversial political questions in the past 100 years, the Supreme Courts in England and Scotland (High Court of England and Wales, and Inner House of the Court of Sessions in Scotland, respectively) have considered the following question: Was the advice of the Prime Minister to the Queen that Parliament should be prorogued from between September 9, 2019, and September 12, 2019, until October 24, 2019 lawful? What would be the legal consequences if it were not? "Proroguing" is discontinuing a session of a legislative body (such as Parliament) without dissolving it.

The High Court of England had decided that the matter was non-justiciable, while the Court of Sessions in Scotland had decided that it was justiciable. On September 24, 2019, in an opinion read by Justice Lady Hale, the Supreme Court of the House of Lords decided that the

Supreme Court had jurisdiction to decide upon the existence and limits of the prorogation power. More importantly for the subject we are considering, the Supreme Court decided that the issue was justiciable.[133]

The Supreme Court, in deciding that the action was unlawful, does not directly refer to the customary rules that are applicable. There is no reference in the opinion to any statutes or precedents. The Supreme Court's reasoning has to be based upon the customary rules for why cases would be justiciable and the customary rule for the lawful exercise of the prorogation power. The holding of the Supreme Court is that prorogation for five weeks, rather than the customary four or five days, is unlawful. There is no enacted law that is applied. Therefore, I conclude that the Supreme Court must be applying a customary rule with the force of law.

6.3 Non-justiciability in the American courts

Earlier versions of the *Buttes* case had been filed in the United States courts and the Court of Appeals for the Fifth Circuit had also declined to hear the case. The reasoning of the Court of Appeals is that, in order to decide the case, the Court of Appeals would have to determine which nation had territorial sovereignty. Territorial disputes are generally considered to be issues of national significance, which are politically delicate. The U.S. Supreme Court denied the petition for certiorari and declined to hear the case.

There are several types of cases in which the U.S. courts will generally find that they involve non-justiciable issues: the court will not issue an advisory opinion; there must be an actual case or controversy between the parties; the action must be ripe, which means that there is an injury or the real threat of an injury; the case must not be moot, which means that the threat of the injury has not ended; and the case must not involve a political question.

The issue of a political question is the most interesting reason for a case to be found to be non-justiciable. The courts often hear cases involving political questions, such as voter denial or election fraud. The issue in the leading case about justiciability in the United States, *Baker v. Carr*, involved the drawing of legislative district maps, which the U.S. Supreme Court decided was a justiciable matter.[134]

Political questions may also involve matters such as: those in which another branch of government other than the judiciary has constitutional authority to resolve the matter; there are no judicial standards for resolving the matter (in other words, if there is a gap, the court will decide not to hear the case which negates the argument that there was a gap; an impossibility of deciding a matter without an initial policy determination of a kind clearly not suitable for judicial discretion; the court is unable to decide the case without expressing lack of respect for coordinate branches of government; an unusual need for unquestioning adherence to a political decision already made; or a potentiality of embarrassment from multifarious pronouncements by various departments on one question. The reasoning in *Baker v. Carr* is based upon statutory and constitutional provisions and prior case law. The problem of drawing unfair legislative districts has been so pervasive in the U.S. that it has a name, to wit, "gerrymandering". Gerrymandering is manipulating the boundaries of electoral districts to favor one party, class or race. The legislative maps are drawn to give one political party an advantage or to ensure that sitting legislators retain their seats by establishing favorable districts in which they can run for reelection.

The Supreme Court goes back and forth on this issue. There have been many decisions since the *Baker* case concerning gerrymandering and this remains a topic for litigation to the present day. More than 50 years after the decision in *Baker v. Carr*, the U.S. Supreme Court decided *Rucho v. Cannon*, and it went the opposite way declaring that the gerrymandering issue is non-justiciable.[135] Gerrymandering remains a common practice, and it is fair to state that the courts have not been very effective in controlling the effects of gerrymandering. In part, the reluctance of the courts to become too involved in the drawing of legislative district maps is based upon the lack of clear standards for drawing the district lines.

Consequently, it was a pleasant surprise when the current Supreme Court in its 2022-23 term decided an important legislative district case entitled *Moore v. Harper*.[136] In section 1.4, I raised the issue of the independent state legislature theory. The independent state legislature theory is the concept that state legislatures have the ultimate authority to set election rules. In addition, state courts would have little authority to oversee the state rules.

There was substantial nervousness that the current Supreme Court, with its 6 to 3 conservative majority, would accept this theory. This might place at risk the 2024 presidential election by allowing state legislatures to disregard the popular vote in their state and legitimize alternate electors (electors who would not vote for the winner of the popular election).[137] For the present, however, the *Harper* decision has diminished the likelihood of the independent state legislature theory being the law.

From the perspective of how the complexity of multiple legal systems affects Hart's rule of recognition, the procedural development of the drawing of the congressional district lines and those of the State House and State Senate in North Carolina provides an interesting set of facts. After the 2020 census, the North Carolina legislature adopted the maps for the aforementioned legislative districts, and it appears obvious that their maps are an excellent example of partisan gerrymandering. This is the conclusion of the trial court when the maps were challenged. The trial court, however, following the reasoning in the *Rucho* case, ruled that the issue is non-justiciable.

The Supreme Court of North Carolina reversed the trial court decision and held that the issue is justiciable (*Harper I*).[138] After the

U.S. Supreme Court (SCOTUS) agreed to hear the appeal of *Harper I*, the trial court accepted a revised map and the North Carolina Supreme Court then overruled *Harper I* and decided *Harper II*.[139] Notwithstanding the argument that the case had now become moot, SCOTUS decided that it had jurisdiction to hear the case.

After SCOTUS agreed to hear the case, the North Carolina Supreme Court affirmed the decision of the trial court accepting the revised map, withdrew the opinion in *Harper II* and overruled *Harper I*. SCOTUS in *Moore v. Harper* decided that it had jurisdiction to hear the case, even though, on the surface at least, the case appeared to be moot. The latest revised district map would no longer be effective. Even more importantly, the independent state legislature theory is discarded, and partisan gerrymandering is, once again, subject to judicial review.[140]

By a 6 to 3 vote, the majority opinion makes it clear that the elections clause does not place the final authority in state legislatures to establish the rules regarding federal elections. State courts have the power of judicial review in deciding if the rules of the state legislature are constitutional based upon the State Constitution. SCOTUS has the authority to decide if the state court's interpretation of state law violates federal law. Joining in Chief Justice Roberts' majority opinion are Justices Kavanaugh and Barrett (three of the conservative wing of the Court), and Justices Kagan, Jackson and Sotomayor (the three liberal Justices on the Court).

SCOTUS holds that the North Carolina Supreme Court had authority to decide the case (the issue is justiciable). The case is sent back to the trial court to draw new maps. Consequently, SCOTUS empowers the state courts to assert their authority to exercise judicial review. But it not only establishes state court authority, but it also reaffirms federal court authority also to exercise judicial review of the partisan gerrymandering issue. State courts may not read state law in a way that circumvents federal constitutional law.

There are three jurisprudential issues that make the *Harper* case very interesting. Hart's rule of recognition finds it difficult to state what the law is in the situation in which the validity of the law must satisfy multiple standards of both state and federal constitutions. Chief Justice Roberts, in the majority opinion, points out the complexity involved in this situation:

> The questions presented in this area are complex and content specific. We hold only that state courts may not transgress the ordinary bounds of judicial review such that they arrogate to themselves the power vested in state legislatures to regulate federal elections.[141]

My second point concerns the reference to the "ordinary bounds of judicial review" which must be a reference to the customary rules with the force of law. These "ordinary bounds" do not appear in any written constitutional provision. Hence, SCOTUS is acknowledging that there are customary rules with the force of law in the unwritten Constitution.

Chief Justice Roberts in my third jurisprudential issue makes a similar observation in the following statement: "We have long looked to 'settled and established practice' to interpret the Constitution".[142] "Settled and established practice" is not only a reference to the customary rules with the force of law, but it may also be read as an acknowledgement that the real rules, which I introduce in chapter eight, play an important role in constitutional interpretation.

6.4 Laws that provide for regulatory authority that is not exercised

Let me start by mentioning what we are not considering in this section. This is not an area of non-law because there are laws that relate to the activity in question. This is also not an area of non-enforcement of the law, like non-enforcement of the jaywalking laws. Non-enforcement or selective enforcement or enforcement of a variant of the written law will be considered in chapter eight about real rules. The situation being discussed in this section involves a different subject than non-law and non-enforcement of the law.

In the situation that I am considering in this section, there is legal authority to regulate the conduct in question. The individual or entity that has the authority to regulate elects not to do so, while other potential regulators are precluded from acting regarding the activity. My example will involve very hazardous and dangerous pipelines that are operating without adequate supervision. I will focus on the siting of the pipelines as the specific issue that is not controlled by the agencies that have legal authority to regulate the activity in question. The siting of the pipelines refers to the decision about where the pipelines may be located, especially in reference to how close they may be placed near homes, schools, libraries, factories, and other land uses.[143]

There is legal authority to create rules that would be applicable and enforceable as conditions to the license being issued to the pipeline company. This authority to regulate the activities of the pipeline company, however, is not exercised by the legal agencies that issue the license. These legal agencies have the legal authority to adopt regulations that relate to this licensee or to all licensees. Therefore, the rule of recognition tells us where to look for legal authority to regulate. There is no procedure, however, in the legal system (other than additional legislation, which cannot be compelled) for forcing the legal agency to exercise its authority to enact regulations or conditions to the licenses that relate specifically to reducing or avoiding the danger associated with the pipelines being installed close to homes, and other vulnerable facilities.[144]

Pipelines carry fossil and synthetic fuels across the United States.[145] The pipelines are generally underground and carry a large percentage of the petroleum and other sources of fuel that is consumed within the U.S and exported. While the pipelines mainly carry fuels, they may also carry other chemical products. Underground pipelines are more efficient and safer than transportation of fuel via railroads and trucks. The fuels may be in a gas or liquid state and liquids may become gases and gases may become liquids.

The potential regulators of the pipeline industry include federal, state, and local governments.[146] The local governments include counties and municipalities. If the pipeline crosses state boundaries, it may be viewed as a national public utility. The federal government may then regulate the pipeline company in granting it a license to operate. It may establish regulations related to the operation of the pipelines. There are federal regulations covering many aspects of construction and operation of the pipelines and they are very detailed. These regulations are enforced by several different federal agencies and cover interstate pipelines and some aspects of intrastate pipelines.[147]

Inside a particular state, the state government has the authority to regulate the construction and operation of the intrastate pipelines. The state government may, in turn, delegate some of its authority to a statewide agency and to local governments to monitor construction activity and the operation of the pipelines in their jurisdiction. Each of these levels of government may, in theory, provide standards for the regulation of the pipelines, including the siting of pipelines.

There are different types of pipelines. There are transmission (or trunk) pipelines and distribution pipelines (both main and service). For example, my house is heated by a natural gas pipeline that is located under the street in front of my house. The lateral to my house is connected to the distribution pipeline in the street. While there are risk factors associated with the distribution pipeline, they are minimal. The issue that I want to discuss concerns transmission pipelines.

Transmission pipelines are the transit mechanism for gases and liquids from the source of the energy to a terminal, from which they may be transferred to a distribution pipeline or a port to be transported overseas. Those with which we are here concerned are transmission pipelines primaly for fuel products that will be shipped overseas.

The case involving pipelines that I am going to discuss is *Flynn, et al. v. Sunoco Pipeline, L.P.*[148] Some of the information that I will refer to comes from the Opinion dated April 9, 2021, written by Administrative Law Judge Elizabeth H. Barnes. Administrative law judges in the Pennsylvania public utility system write initial decisions which they submit to the Pennsylvania Public Utility Commission (PUC). The PUC is the regulatory agency which makes the actual decision in accordance with the Pennsylvania Public Utility Code.[149]

The Public Utility Code is the system in Pennsylvania for the regulation of utilities. It is a regulatory system "with a crazy quilt of local regulations."[150] Most importantly regarding why I am discussing this case and the regulatory system that it presents, is to consider the decision-making process involving where the pipelines may be installed. These are underground pipelines that are installed within easements that are obtained by the pipeline companies from the landowners who own the land through which the pipeline will pass. The pipeline companies purchase the easements, or they use their eminent domain authority to condemn land for the easements.[151]

It is important to note that the municipalities and counties in which the pipelines will be installed are generally preempted from regulating public utilities as part of this regulatory system. In Pennsylvania, the PUC is solely responsible for regulating utilities and the Public Utility Code is the supreme law.[152]

The PUC is the primary forum for problems relating to the pipelines. According to ALJ Barnes, the pipelines involved in the case we are considering impose serious risks:

> The PUC has the authority to enforce the federal safety regulations in relating to siting requirements. The pipelines have been sited within high population areas and thousands of people are exposed to the dangers resulting from a rupture of a pipeline. State and federal law allow pipelines to be sited in such areas.[153]

The question then is what are the dangers that ALJ Barnes is referring to that are inherent in the siting of pipelines in locations with dense populations? To answer this question, we must look at the history of how the decisions are made about where pipelines should be located. We need to study what controls there are, if they exist, regarding locating the pipelines in high population areas based upon the current federal and state regulations.

The first pipeline involved in this controversy is an 8" pipeline originally installed in the 1930s for transporting petroleum. This pipeline is called Mariner East 1 (ME1) and it was abandoned in 2013. In 2014, the PUC authorized Sunoco, the owner of the pipeline, to use the old existing pipeline located in easements obtained 90 years ago to transport natural gas liquids.

In the same existing easements, the PUC also agreed that Sunoco could install a new 20" pipeline called Mariner East 2 (ME2). The PUC also allowed Sunoco to construct a new 16" pipeline called Mariner East 2X.[154] All three pipelines are used to transport natural gas liquids. Approximately one-third of these pipelines are in high population areas.

While there is a small risk involved with the original petroleum pipeline, the three new pipelines constitute a significant risk because they carry hazardous volatile liquids (HVLs) which are much more dangerous than petroleum or natural gas. HVLs are liquids in the pipeline that are transformed to vapor upon release and slump towards the ground and stay there. At the time of ALJ Barnes' opinion being published, there had been many reported accidents in the pipelines for HVLs in less than ten years of construction and use of the pipelines.[155]

The HVLs, upon release, are odorless, colorless, and tasteless. The pipelines have no early warning system that there has been a rupture causing a release. When a release occurs in a high population area near a school, other public facilities, and homes, nearby persons must depart from the vicinity. They must walk uphill, upwind and avoid ignition sources. Ignition sources include cellular phones and using an automobile. Some people cannot proceed on foot because they are disabled. Some must cross the pipeline to evacuate. Some school children must proceed through locked gates. How far one must go to be at a safe distance varies in each location.[156]

The ALJ found that the pipeline company had not adequately described the hazards, that there is no adequate early warning audible system and that it is not clear how an individual would be informed of the emergency.[157] Moreover, and this increases the risk of a catastrophic event, the emergency plans prepared by Sunoco are confidential and cannot be disclosed to the public. If there is a release from one of these pipelines, the only notice is an explosion or a police officer coming to your door and ordering you to evacuate your home or business or school or library. The ordinary citizen is left with an unclearly defined risk and without an established available plan as to what he or she should do if the risk occurs.

Faced with this potential life-threatening emergency, citizens, governmental agents and HOAs filed complaints with the PUC. They requested that the PUC order Sunoco to install early warning systems, disclose emergency plans, place controls eliminating or reducing the risks inherent in the pipeline systems, provide training for first responders, and, ultimately, withdraw the licenses to install the pipelines and order Sunoco to cease operating the pipelines. These complainants wanted the PUC to exercise its regulatory authority because the municipalities and the counties are preempted from adopting regulations. These preemption provisions in the regulatory system preclude the local governmental agencies from controlling where the pipelines are installed and how close they are to houses and institutional facilities like schools and libraries.[158]

Pipelines carrying HVLs are very dangerous. As ALJ Barnes found in her lengthy opinion, the danger to nearby persons if there is a rupture is that there can be a release that results in a vapor cloud caused by the rupture. The vapor cloud can ignite if it encounters an ignition source which will result in an explosion. The ignition source can be an automobile or any electric device. Another ignition source can be the use of a cell phone.[159]

In addition to the possibility of an explosion, ALJ Barnes explains that there is another equally dangerous risk associated with the vapor cloud. There is the possibility of asphyxiation from the displacement of oxygen which is consumed by the fast-growing vapor cloud. Another significant risk is the result of HVLs flowing through the old 8" pipelines than were originally constructed for petroleum, which was the original use of the pipelines.

If the rupture occurs in the night, the risk increases significantly. During the daylight hours, the vapor cloud could be visible. In the nighttime, however, the vapor cloud cannot be seen. This increases the fright that occurs from a risk that is not visible. And the risk is increased by the lack of an early warning system. There are no legal rules requiring the installation of an early warning system. If the homeowner is sleeping, they find out about the risk when a first responder knocks on their door. They must evacuate immediately during the night, and they cannot use their automobile or even their cell phone.

While the pipeline company did establish a public awareness plan, ALJ Barnes finds that the plan is inadequate to reduce public anxiety about the risks associated with the possibility of a rupture in the pipeline. Without an early warning system, there would be no way for the public to be rapidly informed of the existence of a dangerous situation. Moreover, when the danger erupts, the public does not know what to do in response to the danger, even if they are aware that it exists. Here are ALJ Barnes' conclusions of law:

Any requirement to add odorants, dye, or to employ an early warning system must be done by regulation and is outside the authority of the Commission [the PUC] proceeding.[160]

Furthermore:

> ...the requested relief of adding odorant and/or dye to the products in the ME [Mariner East] pipelines is not available as a form of relief in this complaint proceeding, but rather is a subject for the regulatory rulemaking process.[161]

In other words, the activity being challenged is not controlled by regulations that could have been adopted by the regulatory agency that has the authority to regulate the activity.

The complainants did not receive the relief they were requesting. Moreover, there exists no legal mechanism by which the complainants can force the PUC to exercise its regulatory authority to adopt the regulations that would protect the public or diminish the risks that they are facing. While the regulatory authority exists, the law does not include any way to force the regulatory agency to adopt the necessary regulations without a legislative mandate that requires that they do so. And the law does not contain a legal mechanism to force the legislature to adopt a statute that will provide the protection that this situation demands.

Perhaps, the solution, then, is to not permit the pipeline companies to locate their pipelines in areas where they present the risks associated with the Mariner pipelines. The law, however, allows for the pipelines to be located where the pipeline companies have placed them. "Locating the Mariner East pipelines in Chester and Delaware Counties in high consequence areas are permitted as a matter of law."[162] High consequence areas include urbanized areas with a highly concentrated population. Locating pipelines in such areas does not violate any regulation or law and is, in fact, lawful.

State and federal law allows for pipelines to be sited in high consequence areas, even though doing so exposes thousands of people to the dangers resulting from the rupture of a pipeline.[163] The PUC has the authority to adopt regulations controlling the locating of pipelines in high consequence areas, but the PUC has not adopted such regulations. In contrast to the lack of such regulations for pipelines, high voltage electric lines are subject to PUC siting oversight, even though they pose fewer risks than the pipelines.[164]

The complainants also questioned whether it is reasonable and safe to allow Sunoco to place valves controlling the pressure in the pipelines at approximately eight miles apart. The ALJ concludes that this spacing does not violate any PUC regulations. It does violate, however, engineering practices of the pipeline industry.[165] While the PUC may consider those practices, there is no codification or incorporation of them within the regulations. Therefore, the siting of the valves does not violate the law. The engineering practices are customary rules without the force of law.

The customary rules, however, could be incorporated into regulations. This is another example of a serious risk being placed upon the residents and other persons who happen to be living or working near the pipelines. It is another instance of the regulatory agency failing to enact regulations to protect the public. The law is that there is no law regulating some of the activities of the pipeline companies.

The question that I am raising by consideration of the pipeline siting issue is whether the rule of recognition provides insight into how to describe this situation. This is not a question of a gap in the law because the law does exist in that it grants regulatory authority over the pipelines in question to the PUC (in addition to the authority in the federal agencies that regulate pipelines). Here, regulatory authority exists but it has not been exercised. There is no mechanism in the law to force the PUC to regulate the siting of the pipelines and the valves controlling the pressure in the pipelines.[166]

The situation posed by the lack of regulation of the siting of pipelines is different from the situation when there is no law related to the activity in question. To clarify this distinction, consider the provision in the First Amendment to the U.S. Constitution that provides that there may be no law restraining the free exercise of religious rights. This is not an area of non-law because there is a law and, in this instance, a super law; a law that can be changed only if there is another constitutional amendment. Somewhere between the situation where there is a law that prohibits a law to the contrary and no law on the subject is the instance where there is a law on the subject that provides authority for regulations to be adopted (authority to create legal norms) but the regulations have not been adopted. When there is authority to adopt regulations, that is the law, even though no laws (legal rules) have been enacted by the agency which has the authority.

A variant of this distinction is when there is a law that prohibits there being a law, but it is not a super law that prohibits it. An example of a super law is the First Amendment to the U.S. Constitution that declares that there may be no law prohibiting the free exercise of religion. In this instance, the law can only be changed by adoption of a constitutional amendment. The law with the preemption prohibition in the pipeline situation may be amended by a statutory change. The preemption of local control over the siting of pipelines (the preemption of local regulations) could be changed by amending the statute. There could then be regulation and the municipalities could regulate when the PUC is not doing so. Again, this requires legislative action.

The rule of recognition tells us that, regarding the siting of pipelines, there is law that allows for regulations to be adopted. There are, however, no such regulations. Therefore, without statutory revision, there is no enacted law and no legal mechanism, other than potential future regulation, or a change in the approach of the PUC, to provide relief to the individuals living near the pipelines.

In a lawsuit involving these pipelines, a township in which the pipelines are located adopted regulations concerning pipelines in its zoning ordinance. The pipelines violated the zoning ordinance. The

Court of Common Pleas, a trial level court, rejected the claim that the pipelines were in violation of the zoning ordinance. The Commonwealth Court, an intermediate appellate court, affirmed the decision of the trial court. The township zoning ordinance is preempted by PUC authority. Municipalities have no authority to regulate the siting of pipelines. Regarding the PUC authority, the Commonwealth Court declared: "While it may be true that the PUC has no regulations covering pipeline siting, that is irrelevant."[167] Only the PUC can regulate land use concerning pipeline siting. And the PUC has elected not to regulate.

In another lawsuit involving pipelines, but not the pipelines we have been discussing, the lack of local control of the siting of the pipelines is readily apparent. This case also illustrates the distinction between customary rules with the force of law and customary rules without the force of law. In July 2020, the Environmental Protection Agency (EPA) changed the rules which gave states and eligible tribes some power over interstate pipelines, coal terminals, and other federally licensed projects. The change made it impossible for states to block projects for any reason other than the project causing direct pollution of waterways in the state.

The change in the rules by the EPA provoked two coalitions of environmental groups and tribes and several states controlled by Democrats to file a lawsuit requesting that the change in rules be vacated. The District Court agreed with the plaintiffs. The defendant industry groups and several states that supported the new rule appealed to the Ninth Circuit Court of Appeals.

While the appeal in the Court of Appeals was pending, the defendants filed an application for a stay of the District Court Order that had reversed the EPA change in the rules. The District Court Order was stayed by a 5 to 4 vote of the Supreme Court. The Supreme Court may stay a decision under review in a Court of Appeals "only in extraordinary circumstances" and "upon the weightiest considerations." To get a stay, an appellant must establish that there will be an irreparable injury caused if the stay is not granted.

The majority of five in the Supreme Court gave no reasons for granting the stay.[168] Justice Kagan, with three other Justices joining in the opinion, filed a dissenting opinion. The application was filed on the emergency docket. This is called the shadow docket because the cases are decided without the customary briefs being filed, oral argument being held, and opinions being written explaining the reasons for the decision.[169]

Justice Kagan, in the dissenting opinion, contended that the appellants had not established irreparable harm. The stay is inconsistent with the ordinary procedures of judicial review and administration of the judicial system. The stay is a disruption of the normal order (the customary rules that govern judicial procedures). The appellants did not identify a single project that a state had prevented after the District Court's decision. No project is threatened, or likely to be threatened, before the appellate process concludes. In short, the customary rules have not been followed.

The takeaway from this decision is that the customary rules were not viewed as having the force of law by a majority of the Supreme Court Justices. The majority used the emergency docket for a situation that, according to the four dissenters, was not an emergency. The customary rules, therefore, did not have the force of law.

Returning to the Mariner pipelines, there is the very real possibility of a vapor cloud next to a house requiring that the inhabitants vacate their house with all due speed to walk upwind to an unspecified safe distance and wait for the emergency to recede. This is consistent with the law as determined by the rule of recognition. For the affected citizens who are living everyday with this unnecessary risk, the law, such as it is, is inadequate. There is law, and there is regulatory authority, but the citizens who are the victims of this law do not have the legal right to protection from this terrible risk.

6.5 Violations of the law without recourse

When there is a very real problem but there is no mechanism to solve the problem, such as the siting of the pipelines, there is in a sense no recourse for resolution of the problem. Yet, there is law because there is a regulatory scheme but there are no regulations related to the issue. The examples in this section are similar because there are laws. Built into the laws, however, is the lack of a remedy for their violation.

I discuss in section 5.2 Pennsylvania Governor Tom Wolf's emergency proclamation in response to the COVID-19 crisis. The emergency proclamation requires that masks be worn. There is, however, no penalty if you decline to do so. This is a law without recourse. It is different from a law that is not enforced because, in this case, the law lacks an enforcement mechanism. The result, however, is the same. There is a law that is a duty-imposing law, as distinct from a power-conferring law, that imposes a duty with no penalty for avoidance of honoring the duty.

Another example that I also mentioned previously is the $0 penalty in the Affordable Care Act for not following the mandate that you provide for medical insurance. Here, one could argue that there is a penalty, but if the fine is zero dollars and there is no other sanction, it is a law without recourse for violation of the law.

Executive orders, such as those issued by the U.S. President, offer another example of quasi-laws. When President Trump issued an executive order to move the U.S. Embassy in Israel from Tel Aviv to Jerusalem, this had real consequences for the geopolitics of the Israeli/Palestinian conflict.[170] Yet, it is a kind of law that does not easily fit within Hart's structure of types of laws. For Hart, the primary norms are either power-conferring or duty-imposing. This type of law is similar to the laws without recourse in the sense that it may not be challenged in a judicial proceeding. This executive order is also not challengeable. Like this executive order, the $0 penalty and no penalty for not wearing a mask do not fit easily within Hart's primary rules.

Even more difficult to fit into Hart's rule of recognition are official statements like the one issued by President Biden recognizing the genocide committed against the Armenian population by the Turkish military and quasi-military forces.[171] This also had real political consequences, but it did not require any activity by anyone or by any political agency. It is also neither power-conferring nor duty-imposing.

Here is another example of a law that lacks enforcement provisions, and this example is slightly different because it is an actual statute with specific duties built into the statute. The statute is the Presidential Records Act.[172] There are statutes requiring governmental agencies to preserve their records, but these statues specifically exclude the president. President Franklin D. Roosevelt, in 1941, opened his presidential library and eventually donated his papers to it. Congress, in 1955, passed the Congressional Libraries Act, which encouraged presidents, but did not require them, to donate their records to libraries. President Richard Nixon attempted to destroy his tapes which were crucial to the Watergate investigation, and this led to a statute applying specifically to his records. Congress later adopted the Presidential Records Act ("PRA") in 1978 to resolve the issue of presidents destroying their records.

The problem with the PRA is that it lacks an enforcement mechanism. The PRA "requires" presidents to preserve their records while they are in office and to give them to the National Archives when they leave office. The oversight authority of the National Archivist is limited. The president is given discretionary authority to determine what materials should be preserved. There is no penalty or enforcement mechanism in the statute.

Former President Donald Trump is notorious for his common practice of destroying important presidential papers, removing records from the White House, placing documents in the toilet, and tearing and discarding documents which then had to be assembled and taped to be preserved.

Regarding President Trump's routine practice of ignoring the PRA, the authors of a recent article explained: "Today, the most persistent PRA problems stem from the lack of enforcement mechanisms and the statute's reliance on a president who acts in good faith."[173] More specifically, the authors point out the following:

> The result is that, as things stand, a president can largely evade any meaningful accountability for violations of the PRA while in office by either not issuing PRA guidelines, or (like the Trump administration did) issuing facially valid guidelines, and, in either case, flagrantly destroying records and declining to self-report such destruction to the archivist.[174]

Former President Trump's situation involves more than the PRA. He actually moved presidential records, including classified documents, to his various homes and golf courses. He also displayed the documents to individuals who lacked security clearance to see them. Some of these documents had the highest security clearance required to be viewed and could only be viewed within certain locations subject to various restrictions. He has not been indicted for violation of the PRA, because the PRA, while it is duty-imposing, provides for no penalty for its violation.

The federal indictment of former President Trump is very detailed. It refers to five occasions when Trump, as a presidential candidate in 2016, stated that classified documents have to be protected and classification rules have to be enforced. As President, he made similar statements. The indictment includes photos of boxes containing documents in the ballroom, bathroom, shower, business center, storage room and Lake Room at Mar-a-Lago. There are also photos of documents that had spilled out of the boxes and were on the floor.

Trump was personally involved in going through boxes before some were given to federal officials. He and his assistant lied to the FBI about the documents. The boxes contained 197 classified documents. He did not provide the documents even after a subpoena was served upon him. Trump's attorney signed a false affidavit stating that all the documents had been provided. The FBI searched Trump's property and found 102 classified documents in Trump's office and storage room. Six of the documents are marked "top secret".

Trump has claimed that he can declassify documents by declaring that he is doing so, or by just thinking about doing so. Therefore, he contends that these documents have been declassified. There are statutory procedures, however, for declassification, and they were not followed. Moreover, Trump has acknowledged that he cannot, as a former president, declassify documents.[175]

Trump has also contended that the PRA authorized him to decide which documents he could retain. This argument is contrary to the terms of the PRA, the purpose of which is to induce presidents to preserve their records and provide them to governmental agencies. The depository will make them available for researchers to examine. In some cases, they do not become available for many years. The fact that the PRA does not contain a penalty for its violation does not immunize the violator.

While Trump is not indicted for violation of the PRA, he is indicted for obstruction of justice, withholding documents and records, corruptly concealing a document or record, concealing a document in a federal investigation, a scheme to conceal documents, false statements and representations, and conspiracy to commit a crime(s). He is also charged with directing employees to delete security camera footage showing the removal of documents. These are all criminal offenses. They are duty-imposing rules with penalties. The PRA is a duty-imposing rule with no sanction. The issue that I am raising is how the PRA fits within Hart's rule of recognition.

These examples are different from the crimes referred to in Trump's indictment. They are violations of the law without recourse. They may fit within the rule of recognition as being related to and part of the legal system. They are laws, but they do not neatly fit within Hart's two types of primary rules. There is conduct that is prohibited, but compliance is dependent upon voluntary willingness to act in accordance with the statutory terms.

6.6 Providing legal advice

Before I consider racial discrimination and the real rules that may be different from the paper rules, let me pause to reflect upon the providing of legal advice as it is affected by some of the issues already discussed. The legal rule in the *Gohmert* case has no legal force beyond its historical interest.[176] It is an historical fact with no authoritative status in later cases. It may or it may not be persuasive. It lacks legal teeth; the legal rule applied in the case has no bite after the case is deprived of precedential value because the decision is a non-published decision.

Non-publication of a decision is like the law in the pipeline case that provides regulatory authority but no regulations. In the pipeline case, the regulations regarding siting of pipelines have not been adopted. No potential plaintiff could rely upon the possibility of the failure to adhere to reasonable safety regulations that have not been promulgated. There is, in effect, when a pipeline is placed near a home, no law to be applied to prohibit the conduct.

The homeowner may have a claim for negligence against the pipeline company if there is a rupture in the pipeline that causes damages. But, just like the fines imposed upon the pipeline company, this would just be a business expense. The law relating to the risks created by the pipeline, as far as the regulation of pipelines is concerned, has not been violated. No crime has been committed when the pipeline is closer to the house than would be reasonable considering the hazardous condition created by the pipeline. There is no way by application of current law that the company installing the pipeline can be forced to move their pipeline a safe distance from the homes and other facilities that are now right next to the pipelines.[177]

Before we discuss the real rules, we will take a slight detour and discuss racial discrimination in chapter seven. In chapter eight, I consider the real rules, some of which will also be customary rules without the force of law.

7.
Litigation Regarding Racial Discrimination

T he history of the law involving racial discrimination in America provides additional examples of many of the issues that I have been discussing. It also illustrates problems unique to the effort to eliminate racial discrimination in the U.S.. Many of the methods used to abolish racial discrimination have been ineffective. I believe that a majority of Americans support the efforts to eliminate racial discrimination and to provide equal opportunity and equal justice. Most citizens desire that all individuals have a reasonable quality of life. Yet, we have been unable to realize these goals.

7.1 Civil rights laws

One of the difficulties with the civil rights laws is that some of the provisions do not allow for lawsuits by individuals (private causes of action) to challenge discriminatory effects. As we looked at in other types of lawsuits, cases challenging racial discriminations sometimes encounter the problem of lack of standing. In other situations, state action is required as the basis for the lawsuit and the discriminatory act being challenged may not involve a state actor. In other cases, there are state or federal agencies available for hearing claims of discrimination and the action must first be filed with the agency. This allows for an initial investigation, and the claimant is required to exhaust his administrative remedy before a lawsuit may be filed in the courts.

There are time limits to all lawsuits being filed, called statutes of limitations. The time frame for allowing lawsuits varies. The cost of litigation is also a limiting factor. The burden of proof in these lawsuits is often an obstacle because it is difficult to establish that the action is based upon racial factors. The claimant has the burden of convincing the court or jury that intentional discrimination was involved in the action that is being challenged. Also, as will become obvious when we consider housing discrimination, institutional and systemic bias is difficult to address through legal means.

Let us start with looking at a case that would qualify as ethnic discrimination rather than racial discrimination. Alabama amended its Constitution in 1990 to make English the official state language. Driver license examinations are only in English. A lawsuit challenging this restriction on behalf of non-English speaking citizens claimed that this law had the effect of discriminating against them. This was unsuccessful because the court held that there is no private cause of action for this form of discrimination. In other words, there is no private remedy available.[178] Justice Stevens filed a dissenting opinion. Even if this was a correct decision, he contended that the Supreme Court should have answered the question differently on the merits of the claim. In other words, the Justices should have made a just and wise decision. Instead, no relief was provided.

While the civil rights statutes have resulted in regulations prohibiting certain discriminatory acts, private citizens may be precluded from bringing actions. For example, the citizens of Chester, Pennsylvania claimed that there are too many waste facilities in African American neighborhoods in the City of Chester. They requested that some of these facilities be placed in white neighborhoods in Delaware County, Pennsylvania (Chester is located in Delaware County).

The District Court found that there was no private cause of action.[179] The Court of Appeals reversed the District Court and found for the plaintiffs.[180] The Supreme Court reversed the Court of Appeals and held that there is no private cause of action.[181]

In short, there are laws establishing civil rights, but these laws do not always provide for causes of action for the right holders. The rule of recognition, therefore, acknowledges that there is a legal rule providing for a legal right to be free from discriminatory activity, but it also acknowledges the lack of a cause of action. This is another example of a right without a remedy.

7.2 Education

Another situation that I will not pursue at length that falls within the minefield of non-law and laws without remedies involves racial discrimination in education. *Brown v. Board of Education* is the foundational case for integrated educational facilities. It overruled a well-established precedent. The Supreme Court made the wise decision that "separate but equal" schools are racially discriminatory. Schools are required to be integrated.[182] Segregated schools were not in fact equal in 1954 and remain unequal.

After the *Brown* decision, racial segregation in public schools is unconstitutional. Efforts were made to desegregate schools after the decision, by court orders, busing programs, and other policies. During the 1960s and 1970s, racial segregation in public schools decreased. Since then, there has been a different trend and racial segregation is increasing.

Notwithstanding that landmark judicial decision, the schools in the U.S. are still not, in general, integrated because of housing patterns that result in segregated residential neighborhoods. Everyone agrees that neighborhood schools are more desirable than bussing children to other neighborhoods, but neighborhood schools will not be integrated if housing is not integrated. Moreover, school district boundaries are sometimes drawn to foster schools with high concentrations of low income and minority students.

The efforts to increase desegregation have not worked. In 1968, 77% of African American students in the U.S. attended majority non-white schools. In 2019, that figure was at 81%. A recent report concluded that "school segregation is now more severe than in the late 1960's".[183] Another study found that half of the public schools that had 90% or more students of color (Black and Hispanic students) also had a student population that was 90% or more from low-income households.[184]

The conclusion is obvious: "School integration is intrinsically tied to the racial gaps in housing and income. The end of court-ordered integration in 1991 led to the reemergence of color lines in school districts."[185] As I explain in the next section, this conclusion was anticipated many years ago.

7.3 Zoning

After the decision of the U.S. Supreme Court in *Brown v. Board of Education*, one of the most controversial issues in my lifetime has been how to achieve educational integration considering the extensive residential segregation that exists in the U.S. I discuss zoning law in Appendix A of *The Judge and the Philosopher*. Zoning law serves a variety of purposes, but one of the effects of zoning law is its impact upon racial segregation.

Very few persons accept bussing of young children for one hour in each direction as a suitable solution for integration of the elementary schools. Pennsylvania Governor Milton Shapp decided to attempt to promote housing integration, which, if it could be achieved, would allow for children to attend integrated neighborhood schools. I was engaged to file a test case.

The case I filed involved the Commonwealth of Pennsylvania suing Bucks County, a beautiful suburban county next to Philadelphia, as a place in which we could attempt to promote integrated housing. I filed the lawsuit in 1972. The plaintiffs were the Commonwealth of Pennsylvania, Bucks County Interfaith Housing Corporation, Suburban Action Institute, and several individuals who were representatives of the class of persons who supported the effort to achieve the construction of residential housing within Bucks County that would be integrated housing (they were both residents of Bucks County and non-residents who wanted to live in Bucks County). The defendants were the County of Bucks, the County Commissioners, the Bucks County Planning Commission and all 54 of the municipalities in Bucks County.

The complaint stated that during the period from 1950 to the filing of the complaint in 1972 the county had experienced substantial growth in the number of housing units, residents, and job opportunities. During this same period, however, because of pernicious zoning ordinances and practices and housing policies within the municipalities in the county, the percentage of housing opportunities for low-income and moderate-income persons had decreased. Individual municipalities desired the more expensive housing rather than more affordable housing (affordable to low-income and moderate-income persons). The result of this widespread practice was increasing denial of housing opportunities for minority and other low-income persons.

The plaintiffs argued that this widespread practice had the inevitable result of denying housing opportunities to African Americans and Hispanic Americans and that the practice was unconstitutional. The relief sought was that the court order the county agencies to adopt a plan for integrated housing within the county and to allocate the required number of units to each municipality. By doing so, each municipality would take its fair share and no municipality would be flooded with more than its fair share of the less-expensive housing units.

The defendants filed preliminary objections to the complaint. The trial court found in favor of the defendants.[186] The plaintiffs appealed to the Commonwealth Court, which is an intermediate appellate court in Pennsylvania. The Commonwealth Court affirmed the decision of the trial court.[187] The Supreme Court of Pennsylvania and the U.S. Supreme Court denied applications requesting that they accept an appeal of the Commonwealth Court decision.[188]

The Commonwealth Court issued a per curiam opinion and based its decision upon the opinion of the trial court. The trial court found that the case was non-justiciable. Judge James S. Bowman of the Commonwealth Court wrote a short concurring opinion. He maintained that the courts should exercise judicial restraint and not interfere with municipal zoning. Judge Harry A. Kramer of the Commonwealth Court wrote a dissenting opinion.

According to Judge Kramer, the case is justiciable. He agrees that the courts should not become involved in matters that are purely political: "Courts should never take on the job of legislating, even when the legislative branch refuses to or fails to act".[189] Rather than entering the order requested by the plaintiffs of the allocation of the required number of units among the 54 municipalities, Judge Kramer points out that the plaintiffs had also requested alternative relief in the form of the court declaring that the intentional exclusionary zoning legislation of the municipalities was invalid and leaving the question of the appropriate relief for later consideration.

Judge Kramer then declares that the Court "may take jurisdiction to determine the constitutional validity of all of the zoning ordinances of Bucks County."[190] Therefore, he argues that "the issue of whether exclusionary zoning ordinances were intentionally designed in violation of the plaintiffs' constitutional rights is a justiciable issue."[191]

Since Judge Kramer is not speaking for the Commonwealth Court, the ultimate outcome of this case is that the Commonwealth Court has decided that this type of case is non-justiciable. Even though this case is non-justiciable, however, the ruling in the case is still authorized, authoritative and binding, notwithstanding that the decision may be correct or incorrect, just or unjust, wise or unwise.

Zoning ordinances often exclude housing for lower income persons. While builders could challenge such restrictions, the persons who are being excluded from living in the neighborhood where the housing that they could afford could have been built are denied standing to challenge the zoning laws that prevent the building of such housing.[192]

7.4 Redlining

Redlining, the practice of not selling houses or giving mortgages to African Americans in white neighborhoods, was a common practice in the twentieth century, and it continues to the present time.[193] The term comes from the practice of banks using red markers on maps to identify neighborhoods deemed to be undesirable for granting mortgages to minority applicants for the mortgages. These neighborhoods are characterized as "high risk" based on racial demographics. While redlining has been illegal since 1968, the practice persists to this day.

Not only did redlining deny housing opportunities that in turn resulted in segregated neighborhoods, but this practice also denies minority individuals the ability to build equity in the houses that they could have owned. The effect, therefore, is not only the denial of the opportunity to own a house, but the resulting impossibility of building credit and equity to create net worth to become members of the middle class rather than the lower class.

Zoning practices, housing and financing discrimination, and segregated schools are all interrelated. Zoning practices concentrate low-income housing in specific areas, and these areas then become the victim of redlining practices. The burden of poverty feeds the perpetuation of social and economic disparities. School district boundaries then deny educational opportunities because the schools in the minority neighborhoods are inferior to those in the affluent areas.

Section 7.5 Voting

Even though the Fifteenth Amendment prohibits restrictions based upon race affecting the right to vote, we do not have equal voting rights in the United States.[194] Racial discrimination has an impact upon the right to vote. Consider the case of *Shelby County v. Holder* to illustrate how voting rights are denied.[195]

This case is another example of a statute that provides for specific action to be taken but there is no possible enforcement mechanism. The Voting Rights Act of 1965 was enacted to address racial discrimination in voting.[196] Section 4(b) specifies jurisdictions subject to the statute which are states or political subdivisions that have tests or other devices that are prerequisites to voting and have historically had low voter registration or turnout. Section 5 provides that no change in voting procedures can take effect in covered jurisdictions (meeting the Section 4(b) criteria) prior to approval by federal authorities.

The Supreme Court held that the determination of which governmental entities are subject to the Act will take effect only if Congress updates the system for determining which entities are covered jurisdictions. The Act is constitutional and, by its terms, will remain in effect until 2031. The Court holds that the coverage formula in Section 4(b) is unconstitutional. Section 5 remains constitutional, but without knowing which jurisdictions are subject to it, there is no way for it to be applied. Consequently, there is a regulation but no identification of whom it applies to or how it can be enforced.

The *Shelby County* case is interesting for another reason. It is a 5 to 4 decision in which Justice Clarence Thomas was one of the five Justices who voted to allow for voting rights to be diminished. In vol. 4, I discuss several issues related to the current situation (in 2023) in which the Supreme Court has become so conservative that it is overruling decisions that have established civil rights, including the right to have an abortion. Well-recognized rights, including constitutional rights, are being eliminated.

The reason being given for overruling the precedents that established these rights involves the application of an inappropriate test for declaring that certain precedents were incorrectly decided. While I disagree with the "incorrectly decided" test, I do accept that a case is incorrectly decided if there is a bribe or a similar impropriety. Corruption leads to an incorrect decision. This occurs when a Justice refuses to recuse himself when ethical rules and procedures are ignored.[197]

In section 6.3, I discussed gerrymandering and the recent decision of *Moore v. Harper* that reinstated judicial review of partisan gerrymandering in establishing election districts.[198] Therefore, it is obvious that voting rights are diminished by gerrymandering. Gerrymandering occurs when legislative districts are not designed to provide for equal voting rights. The district lines are drawn to perpetuate a political party's control of the legislature. Neighborhoods that have minority voters are underrepresented because their voting districts are designed to perpetuate the control of the legislature.

There is a potential judicial remedy that may be available to challenge the effects of gerrymandering on the right of African Americans to have an equal opportunity to vote. This decision could affect the drafting of maps for congressional districts in Alabama, Louisiana, Georgia, Texas, and South Carolina, and potentially several other states. By a 5-to-4 vote in *Allen v. Milligan*, the Supreme Court decided that Alabama's congressional districts map will have to be redrawn because of the racial discrimination evident in the map that was used for the 2022 elections.[199]

In this case, the judge in the district court held that "Alabama concentrated Black voters in one district, while separating them out among the state to make it much more difficult to elect more than one candidate of their choice."[200] Even though more than 25% of the residents in Alabama are African Americans, there is only one district out of seven congressional districts in which they are a majority of the voters. In the new map, there will be at least two districts in which they will be able to elect candidates of their choosing.

In addition to gerrymandering, many states are adopting measures to make voting more difficult. Instead of encouraging voting, restrictions are being imposed. The number of polling places is being reduced, mail-in ballots are being restricted or prohibited, and other forms of voter suppression are prevalent. Stricter voter identification requirements are being implemented. Voting rolls are being purged. Early voting opportunities, and Sunday voting before or after church, are being challenged. Polling locations in minority neighborhoods are being reduced. These practices disproportionately affect minority neighborhoods.

There is one more decision to discuss that supports the observation that African American voters are being denied equal voting opportunity. A recent decision also illustrates the interplay of state courts and federal courts with constitutional and statutory issues on voting rights. As already discussed, voting rights in America are a combination of federal, state and local law, with state and federal courts grappling with providing equal voting rights for all citizens.

The case is *Brnovich v. Democratic National Committee*.[201] It concerns section 2 of the Voting Rights Act (VRA) and the rules about voting in Arizona, one of the 2020 battleground states. Arizona does not have the same history of racial discrimination as Alabama demonstrates. In Arizona, in general, it is much easier to vote than it is in Alabama. Voters may vote in person at a traditional precinct or at a "voting center" in their county of residence. They may also cast an early ballot by mail, and they may also vote in person at an early voting location in each county.

Arizona amended its regulations concerning precinct-based election-day voting and early mail-in voting. You must now vote in the assigned precinct. A vote in the wrong precinct in the county will not be counted. If you vote early by mail, it is now a crime to collect such votes if you are not a postal worker, election official, or a caregiver, family member or household member. These two changes were challenged in court on the grounds that they restrict the voting rights of the State's American Indian, Hispanic and African Americans in violation of section 2 of the VRA.

The District Court rejected the claims of the plaintiffs on the basis that the changes were not enacted with a discriminatory effect. The American Indians live on reservations without postal addresses on their houses. They have community leaders who gather the early mail-in ballots. Therefore, the effect on them is obvious, but the District Court held that it was not a "meaningful inequality".[202] A panel of the Ninth Circuit affirmed the District Court, but the en banc court reversed the District Court. It held that the new restrictions imposed a disparate burden on minority voters. The Supreme Court reversed the Court of Appeals and held that the VRA was not violated.

In light of the great variation in results in these different levels of the federal judicial system, this raises the question of whether Hart's premise of a consensus of opinion about what the law is can be supported by the reality of judicial decision-making. This case also illustrates the difficulty of establishing discriminatory intent. Section 2 of the VRA was amended in 1982. The amendment changed "discriminatory intent" to the phrase "in a manner which results in a denial or abridgment of the right ... to vote on account of race or color." To meet this standard, the plaintiff must establish that the voting opportunity is not "equally open."[203]

The size of the burden of the change in the voting rules will be relevant. The extent of the departure from what used to be standard procedure will be considered. The size of the disparity of the impact will be weighed. The court will look at the state's entire voting system. In considering the totality of the circumstances, the Supreme Court held that there was no violation of Section 2 of the VRA. The Supreme Court divided entirely on partisan lines, with the majority consisting of Justices Alito (who wrote the majority opinion), in which Roberts, Thomas, Gorsuch, Kavanaugh and Barrett joined. Justice Kagan filed a dissenting opinion, in which Breyer and Sotomayor joined.

Here is the bottom line. Even if the plaintiffs are able to establish a disparate burden, the State's "compelling interest in preserving the integrity of its election procedures" would be adequate to avoid a violation of the VRA. The Court of Appeals had found the State's defense unconvincing because there was no evidence of voting fraud in Arizona. Hence, there was no reason to make voting more restrictive. The Supreme Court held that a State may take action to prevent election fraud without waiting for it to occur within the State. This approach indicates that the ongoing efforts to reduce voting opportunities will not be able to be successfully challenged in the courts, even though the effect on minority voters is obvious and is the reason why the voting restrictions are being imposed.

7.6 Juries

Jury decisions are not reviewable if there is no error at the trial. They are final and binding, but they are not authoritative, and they do not create precedents. The jury is instructed about the applicable law by the trial judge in his charge to the jury. If the charge is incorrect regarding the judge's description of the applicable law, the case may be reviewable by an appellate court.

During the 19th and 20th centuries, there were close to 5,000 reported lynchings in the U.S. While most lynchings involved hangings, there were other methods for murdering persons viewed as undesirable. It is estimated that approximately 73% of the victims of lynching were African Americans. Many more lynchings have been unreported.

An overwhelming majority of the perpetrators of lynching were neither charged nor convicted. Because only white citizens could sit on the juries that heard the criminal cases when there was a lynching, it was difficult to convict the perpetrators. During 50 to 75 years in the U.S., in a large area of the nation, the juries nullified the laws that made lynching a criminal act.[204]

7.7 Law enforcement

Law enforcement is another area in which racial discrimination has been evident. The broad issues that are involved include biased police policies when minority individuals are disproportionately targeted. This sometimes results in disproportionate use of force. African Americans are more likely to experience incidents of excessive force. Racial discrimination can lead to over-policing in some communities and under-policing in others.

Some of the current issues involve racial profiling, stop and frisk procedures, unfair traffic stops, choke holds and other issues that are too numerous to discuss at length. The flashpoint regarding racial relations in the 21st Century has been in the area of law enforcement— the interaction between police officers and African American individuals. This issue is very important, but it is outside the scope of this book. The one contribution that I can make to the discussion is the case that I filed in an effort to establish a new legal rule reflecting the right of dignity.

7.8 The right of dignity

Many years ago, I tried to convince the courts to recognize the right of dignity. In 1968, I was retained by the NAACP and the ACLU to represent four African American teenagers who had been arrested for disorderly conduct in Bristol Township, Bucks County, Pennsylvania. I filed a complaint in federal court for the violation of the civil rights of the young men. The civil right that was involved was characterized as the right of dignity, a new civil right that I wanted the court to create. If this effort had been successful and we'd won the case, the decision would have been a just and wise decision (and an incorrect one, because no such cause of action existed in the pre-existing law.

Here are the facts in the case. The four young men were standing on the street corner and two Bristol Township police officers drove by in a marked police car. One of the officers yelled at the youngsters: "Hey there, Chinese Niggers." The boys responded in kind, but without any racial overtone. They were arrested for disorderly conduct. Our approach was that when the government puts men in uniform, gives them badges and revolvers and grants to them the authority to make arrests, the police officers have a responsibility to treat the citizens with dignity and respect.

We expected to lose at the District Court level. Our goal was to appeal the case to the Court of Appeals and to attempt to convince the Court of Appeals (and, maybe even the Supreme Court to establish the right of dignity as a precedent. We lost in the District Court.[205]

After we lost in the District Court, we filed our appeal to the Third Circuit Court of Appeals. We were offered a cash settlement before the case was heard by the Court of Appeals. While the NAACP and the ACLU wanted to continue the litigation in order to see if we could convince the Court of Appeals to establish a right of dignity, the four young men decided that they wanted to accept the cash settlement (each of them wanted to purchase a car. While I was acting on behalf of the NAACP and the ACLU and these organizations were paying the costs of the case, I concluded that my clients were really the four individuals and that my obligation to them required that I honor their request and that I accept the settlement and end the litigation.

Here is the important aspect of the District Court opinion. The District Court declared that the four young men would be entitled to prevail in their claim of the violation of their civil rights if the State of Pennsylvania had established a right of dignity as a right of their citizens. The right of dignity would, in that event, require that public officials, or other persons with authority from the government, when acting pursuant to such authority, treat all citizens with dignity and respect. The right of dignity would provide that all persons must be treated with dignity and respect and be protected from discriminatory treatment because of their race, religion, etc. by public officials or other persons in authority while acting pursuant to such authority.

For the right of dignity to be recognized in Pennsylvania, the Pennsylvania General Assembly must establish such right. If there was a right of dignity, it would be the guidepost for how police officers and other governmental officials would be obligated to act when exercising the authority of their office.

While we were unsuccessful in our case, the right of dignity has been recognized in the EU Charter of Fundamental Rights, the Universal Declaration of Human Rights of the United Nations, and in some national and state constitutions. The bottom line is that there is much room for improvement in how public officials interact with citizens. The reality on the streets does not match the goals of equal treatment by law enforcement officials. In short, the real rules (in the situation just discussed, the real rules of law enforcement), which is our next subject, are different than the paper rules.

8.
Real Rules

8.1 Real rules

Hart's primary rules are legal norms that are part of the law. When these primary rules are applied to make the correct decision, the correct decision is presumptively justified. The decision may also be a just and/or wise decision. If a new legal norm must be created to make the just and/or wise decision, the decision may be justifiable. The just and/or wise decision is consistent with the tertiary rules (which I describe in *The Judge and the Incorrect Decision*) or with a modified version of the secondary rules. Unlike the obligation to make the correct decision, the "obligation" to make the just or the wise decision is not obvious because it is based upon a customary rule that does not have the force of law.[206] This customary rule is part of the legal culture.

In addition to these two types of alternate source decisions (the just or the wise decision), there are decisions that cite other sources for making judicial decisions that clearly are not regarded as being obligatory. These could be decisions applying rules found in cases from other jurisdictions, rules endorsed by text writers or in law review articles, rules codified in restatements that have not been adopted as statutes, and other similar situations where new potential rules are considered. I discuss some of these sources in the next chapter.

Finally, there also are real rules that may be cited in order to make judicial decisions, though the real rules may not be regarded as obligatory. If they are also customary norms with the force of law, they could be part of the law and their application would result in a correct decision. If the real rule in question is not a customary rule with the force of law, it is the paper rule that will dictate whether the decision is correct, rather than application of the real rule. The concept of the real rules is a legal theory developed by several of the American Legal Realists, though they have endorsed several different versions of real rules.[207]

The distinction between "paper rules" and "real rules" is a central theme in all of Karl Llewellyn's writings. Paper rules are the prescriptive rules, which the judge may or may not apply. To be distinguished from paper rules are real rules. But real rules are not paper rules that the judge has accepted and cited. Real rules are presented, in Llewellyn's version of this theory, as descriptive terms. They are not really rules at all in the sense that the word "rules" is used in the term "paper rules." Real rules refer to the descriptive sense of rules, not the prescriptive sense.[208] Real rules, according to Llewellyn, express the behavior of the courts. They are empirical rules describing what the courts do (or should do if you accept, which I do not, that legal rules are predictions of what the courts will do).

The real rules that I am describing are similar to the settled and established practices that Chief Justice Roberts refers to in *Moore v. Harper*.[209] In the majority opinion, which I discussed in section 6.3, he referred to settled and established practices as being relevant to the interpretation of constitutional provisions. These practices could be considered to be real rules that are also customary rules with the force of law (since they are recognized as being authoritative in this recent SCOTUS precedent).

Just as the rule of recognition is a social fact, real rules are also social facts. The rule of recognition is not a rule in the same way in which the primary rules are rules. Many real rules are customary rules and, as such, they may conflict with paper rules. Real rules may also promote changes in the paper rules. Real rules may be utilized by lawyers in advising their clients. An advocate may request that a paper rule be modified to make the law consistent with the real rules.

In summary, real rules are presented in factual terms that describe the activities of courts or other law-applying agencies. The implication from this proposition is that there can be a study of the paper rules, the traditional prescriptive rules, which is an analytical study. There could also be a study of the real rules, the descriptions of official behavior, which would be an empirical study. The question of whether judges are obligated to, and do apply, the paper rules is not a necessary part of the study of the real rules. The real rules are descriptions of the behavior of judges and other officials. The paper rules, even if they are disregarded or disobeyed, remain in the legal system as valid rules.[210]

Llewellyn may even be suggesting that many of the paper rules are also an element in real rules. In fact, he acknowledges that lawyers advising clients refer to the paper rules. Advocates cite the paper rules. Judges justify their decisions by reference to the paper rules. Real rules, even if we all agree that paper rules are the law, still are a real phenomenon and we should account for them in our understanding of the law and the legal system. The practice of law includes consideration of the real rules as well as the study of the paper rules.

Jerome Frank, another prominent American Legal Realist, also endorses real rules as a concept to be used in explaining that "the rules that lawyers would like to (but do not) have are rules which would aid them in precisely predicting specific decisions in contested cases and in bringing about such specific decisions."[211] Llewellyn and Frank contend that paper rules could not be used for predicting what judges would do, so they were led to look for another type of rules that could be used to predict judicial decisions. The role of the lawyer, then, in performing the function of advising clients is described by Frank as follows: "A lawyer is a predictor, really, a prophet. He says to a client, because this and this is true, and since this and this might be true, then your alternatives are such and such, and here's what's most likely to happen."[212]

John Gardner offers an analogy involving sculpture:

> Sculpture is the genre to which sculptures belong, but it is also (differently) what sculptors do. Law, likewise, is the genre to which legal systems and legal norms belong, but it is also, differently, what lawyers and legal officials do.[213]

Laws, therefore, may be viewed as artifacts, which is the network of overlapping and hierarchical norms that form the basis for lawyers advising clients and judges deciding cases. Law is also the practice of performing these tasks, which, in fact, explains why we commonly refer to lawyers as practicing law.

The activities of police officers, when they apply the paper rules, do not create, or change, the paper rules. Their daily activities, with their customary methods of law-applying or of exercising discretion not to apply the law, reflect unwritten practices that I am calling the real rules. Real rules, then, are rules that describe what legal actors do in performing their duties to enforce the law. These activities may or may not be consistent with the paper rules (which are the primary rules). Let me offer some examples of situations in which looking at real rules might be useful.

8.2 Paper rules that are not enforced

My first type of real rule is the rule that reflects or explains the situation when a paper rule is not enforced. If the rule of recognition is based upon a social fact, as Hart describes it, how do we account for the social fact of non-enforcement of legal norms? It is not unusual that there are legal norms that are not enforced. The established practice of non-enforcement is a different situation from violations of the laws that do not result in criminal liability because the perpetrator is not identified or arrested. The President's Crime Commission estimates that 91% of all Americans have violated laws that could subject them to terms in prison.[214]

The rule of recognition is not a prescriptive rule. It is also not viewed as an explanatory statement about general compliance with the law (the compliance being a demonstration of acceptance). It is, then, merely the acknowledgement of a social fact. It may, therefore, be characterized as a descriptive statement or an explanatory statement about general agreement on what is the law.

The statement of the rule of recognition includes the supposition that the law exists because the legal subjects accept it as law. It would exist even if there were disobedience, so long as it is still accepted as law. But putting aside for the moment the disobedience, are all laws accepted as the law or are there some laws which exist on the books which are not regarded as law? Are there paper rules that, speaking solely now from a factual point of view, are in such disregard that the social fact (and this could be the real rule) is that they do not function as law and are not accepted as law?

The pedigree theory of the legal positivists is the contention that a norm is a legal norm only if it is accorded such status by the rule of recognition. The rule of recognition is not itself validated by itself but is a social rule, an observable accepted practice. Real rules, then, which are also social rules, could be like the rule of recognition. In the same way that the rule of recognition is part of the legal system, real rules could also be assumed to be part of the legal system.

8.3 My personal example of a real rule

My own personal experiences lead me to incorporate the concept of real rules into my description of how legal systems operate. Let me return to my childhood years (when I was approximately eight years old) for my first example of the real rules.

When I lived with my family in South Philadelphia, everyone who lived in that area, including my father, placed bets daily on what was called "playing the numbers." The number writers (called "bookies") were well-known, they walked around openly in the neighborhood and bets were placed with them in a public way. I even witnessed the policemen patrolling the neighborhood placing their bets with Stumpy, the neighborhood bookie (he was called "Stumpy" because he had one leg amputated and walked with crutches).

I was fascinated with this social practice because I did not understand how it worked. Bets were placed by giving Stumpy one to five dollars and a number between 000 and 999. My father frequently used "513". We lived at 513 Carpenter Street. The winning number was then based on the results of the early races at a designated racetrack. If a better had the winning bet, Stumpy made a payment to him, and there was a small neighborhood celebration.

The oddity in this procedure, in my young mind, was that Stumpy never seemed to write the numbers down. I never understood how disputes were resolved as to what number was bet. I asked my father many times how he could be sure that he would be paid if he had bet the winning number or how he could be certain that Stumpy would remember the number accurately. He just laughed and said that there would never be a problem, and there never was. There was complete trust in Stumpy. My father insisted that Stumpy was the most honest person in the neighborhood.

The only problem was that every so often Stumpy was arrested. But he never stayed in jail very long and never even went to trial. My father would drive to the police station and bring him back to our street. If this was a crime, and number-writing certainly was a crime, there was a general common understanding that it was "no big deal". No one, including the local police, considered it to be a real crime. Hence, the real rule was that the paper rule was non-enforceable. There was also the common understanding that there was no obligation to obey the paper rule. No one believed that they were participating in a crime. Moreover, non-obedience carried with it no sense of immorality. This common belief and practice, like the rule of recognition, was a social fact.

Another example of a real rule took place during my teenage years, when I was old enough to drive, and I frequently received parking tickets for parking where one was not supposed to park. I, like everyone else in the neighborhood, did not pay the parking tickets and there was never any enforcement of them. In fact, for almost my entire life, until approximately 2014, the Traffic Court in Philadelphia was notoriously ineffective (actually, it was so corrupt that it had to be replaced by a new system because parking and other traffic tickets were "fixed" on a regular basis. Once again, very few persons viewed not paying parking tickets as a crime, though the corrupt judges in the traffic court were clearly committing a crime. This common practice was also a social fact.

8.4 Obsolete statutes

In every legal system, there are obsolete statutes.[215] During my first 20 years practicing law, adultery was a crime.[216] Before Pennsylvania recognized no-fault divorce, you had to offer a reason for being entitled to a divorce (something your spouse had done that the divorce code designated as grounds for a divorce. In a non-contested divorce action, adultery was a popular accusation. Even though it was declared as having occurred in many divorces, it never led to police enforcement. In fact, I do not think there was ever an arrest for adultery in Philadelphia and the surrounding suburbs during the years I practiced law even though it clearly was a crime until 1973 and was a common event with sworn testimony as to its frequent occurrence.

Taking this one step further, I once explained this situation to a friend who was a professor who taught political science. He did not seem to believe that what I was describing as the real rule for obtaining a divorce was true. The real rule was that, if the divorce was uncontested, it was almost always granted based upon fictional grounds for the divorce. Everyone knew that, in most cases, they were fictional. There was sworn testimony that was then presented to the administrative official, called the master (when serving in divorce cases). The master always recommended that the court issue the divorce order, and the court almost always did. The fictional narrative presented to the master as sworn testimony was a script in a repetitive play.

So, the professor and I took a survey of the lawyers in Bucks County, Pennsylvania. We sent out questionnaires to all the lawyers. In more than 95% of the uncontested divorce cases, the divorce was granted. The applicants for divorce lied in over 60% of the uncontested divorce cases according to the responses. Obviously, the lawyers and judges knew that lying was institutionalized and part of the system for obtaining divorces. Lying was a known common and ongoing practice. My professor friend and I published an article about this practice.[217]

Recognition of the real rule leads to the conclusion that the law in the books may be sometimes regarded as not applicable. In some places, for example, there are laws in the statute books governing horse-drawn vehicles on urban streets. In other jurisdictions, there is a traffic code for vehicles that is also applied to horse-drawn carriages. If someone wants to navigate a wagon with a horse on an urban street, they are likely to not even know what the applicable rules are. As they proceed slowly, blocking traffic and causing traffic jams, it is possible that the traffic police officer does not know the applicable rules. There are general traffic rules that could be applied to some situations, but there also are special problems presented by horse-drawn wagons for which the present traffic code designed for motorized vehicles does not work well.

The old, antiquated rules from 100 years ago sometimes do not make sense, and no one remembers what they are anyway. If you look through the books of statutes in your jurisdiction, you will find many curious examples of obsolete statutes.

8.5 Litigation costs

In many legal systems, high litigation costs can have the effect of rendering the legal rules in statutes or common-law precedents unenforceable or enforceable only by those who can afford to pursue litigation. Very few civil cases go to trial. Quite often, the costs associated with litigation preclude letting a jury or a judge in a non-jury case conduct a trial and make the decision. If all the civil cases were tried, the courts could not handle the flow of lawsuits in the United States. The real rule is that litigation costs are so high that litigation is unavailable to many people in many situations. Self-driving cars will make the traffic code obsolete.

8.6 Plea bargaining in criminal cases

In criminal cases today, the number of cases which go to trial is minute. Almost all cases are settled by plea bargaining, so that enforcement of criminal offenses is a negotiating process. If the defendant elects to go to trial, the potential sentence is pushed to an extreme level to force the defendant to agree to plead guilty to a much lower-level crime for a much-reduced penalty. The real rule is that, while someone charged with a crime has the right to insist upon a trial, the system works in such a way that there are very few actual trials and most criminal cases are resolved by a negotiating process.

8.7 Constructed rules

Constructed rules are rules that exist within the legal system which have not yet been pronounced. There are, at a minimum, three types of constructed rules: (1) rules that have not been pronounced but can be derived from deep analysis of the precedents; (2) rules that have not been pronounced but which can be constructed by study of the practices of legal officials when no reasons are given for their legal actions; and (3) idiosyncratic rules that are descriptive of the practices of a specific official, such as a particular judge.

For the first type, take a series of precedents about a specific subject and construct a rule that describes the decisions, though the rule has not been pronounced in any of the decisions. In section 7.8 of *The Judge and the Umpire*, I provided an example of this type of constructed rule. I looked at the cases concerning adequacy of consideration in employment agreements (such as in the *O'Brien* case discussed in chapter two of that volume). In this hypothetical example, the constructed legal rule was that consideration of less than 5% of the prior year's compensation was inadequate consideration for the non-compete agreement. More than 10% was adequate consideration. This was not a rule that had been pronounced in any case.

A text writer is not authorized by the customary rules of the legal system to make an authoritative constructed statement of the legal rule. His statement of what is the law is a descriptive statement of the legal norms that control the decisions. If you are an official with authority, such as a judge, and you place the statement of the constructed rule in an opinion resolving a particular case, it will be an authoritative statement of what the applicable legal norms are thereafter in your jurisdiction. It will be authoritative, even though it is not the ratio decidendi of any single precedent of the pre-existing law before the decision was made and the legal rule has never previously been pronounced by an authoritative source in your jurisdiction.

In short, then, this pronouncement of what the legal norms are as to adequacy of consideration for existing employees for signing non-compete agreements will be a descriptive statement if made by the text writer. It will be both a descriptive statement (a real rule) and a prescriptive statement if made by the judge in deciding a case (a paper rule in a published decision). The statement contains the real rule of the summary of the precedents even though that rule has never been expressed in a precedent before this decision is made. By the way, based upon this real rule, the payment made in the *O'Brien* case was inadequate consideration which would have rendered the non-compete contract unenforceable.

My awareness of the second type of constructed rule is based upon my representation of young men who refused to report for duty when they were drafted during the Vietnam War. Two federal judges heard their cases on alternate Fridays. If you went before Judge X, your sentence was generally five years of probation. If you went before Judge Y, your sentence was generally five years of imprisonment. There were two real rules, dependent upon which judge heard the case.

My third type of constructed rule relates to the rules applicable in the courtroom when trying a case. This is also based upon my experience as a trial lawyer. There are the codified rules of civil procedure. There are also local rules of the courts in that jurisdiction. Then, some judges have printed rules about how things are done in their courtroom (standing orders for trial procedures in that judge's courtroom). There will also be unwritten rules. For a trial lawyer, it is important that you know or find out when preparing for trial what all these rules are. The outcome of the trial may be dependent upon knowing all these procedural rules. When you try the case, these are the real rules that are applicable to how the trial is conducted, and, sometimes, they may affect the outcome of the trial.[218]

8.8 Ascertainment and application of non-laws

Much of the discussion so far has been about laws that are either not enforced, or present-day inadequacies in the way the legal system functions. The real rule may relate to the reality of how trials are conducted or avoided. Let me offer the converse example to law non-enforcement, which is the situation in which a non-law is enforced.

If you are building a real estate project in Pennsylvania, you need to obtain an NPDES Permit (National Pollutant Discharge Elimination System Permit). This is a permit that is issued by the Department of Environmental Protection of the Commonwealth of Pennsylvania (DEP), which has deputized the local County Conservation District (CCD) to administer the program.

The CCD, in turn, in administering the program, has created a protocol, sometimes in a written document and sometimes unwritten, referring to best management practices (BMPs). The BMPs are not legally enacted rules or regulations, but the CCD treats them as though they are. If you choose not to comply with the CCD's imposed requirements, you will experience lengthy delay, inconvenience and substantial cost associated with challenging this protocol. This is enforcement of a non-law, where there is no paper rule (no enacted legal rule). The BMPs are the real rules that are generally followed and are systematically applied even though they were not formally posited as authoritative rules.

While the BMPs are not technically authoritative rules, they are written rules. You can find the BMPs in the Pennsylvania Stormwater Best Management Practices Manual 363-0300-002.[219] Regarding applicability, the Manual states that: "This guidance applies to all persons conducting or planning to conduct activities that require a written post-construction stormwater management plan". The Manual, however, also states that "the guidelines herein are not an adjudication or a regulation". Moreover, "The Department [DEP] reserves the discretion to vary from this guidance as circumstances warrant". In short, the BMPs are not law, and are not legally required. DEP and its agent, the CCD, retain discretion to apply or not apply the guidance of the BMPs. The BMPs may look like law if the regulatory agencies decide to apply them, even though they are not regulations.

Another example of a non-law is the stop sign in a shopping mall or office park. Usually, the parking lots and traffic aisles are private property controlled and maintained by the owners of the facility. These are not public streets. These stop signs are not traffic controls like those on public streets under the supervision of the local police. The owners of the malls and office parks have no legal authority to issue traffic tickets for not stopping at their stop signs. In other words, these are not governmentally erected controls or public traffic controls though the signs appear to look exactly like official governmental traffic controls.

While you are not compelled by the law to stop at this type of stop sign, drivers in this private facility expect you to stop. If you fail to stop at the stop sign and thereby cause an accident, you are negligent and legally liable for the accident. Stopping at this stop sign is not a privately enacted customary rule with the force of law because you cannot be issued a traffic citation for not honoring the stop sign. It is not, in that sense, a legally enacted traffic control. It functions like a legally enacted traffic control for the purpose of ascribing liability if not stopping causes an accident. Failure to stop, however, does not mean that you have acted illegally. You may have civil liability, but you have not violated a traffic law.

8.9 Applying a customary rule without the force of law

Let me present another situation which is like the non-legal stop sign, in the sense that the rule that is applied is not erected by a legal authority. This case involves a customary rule that does not qualify as a legally binding customary rule. In a specific type of case, the real rule functions in a way that provides for significant legal consequences. The case that presents this unusual situation is *Alimota Farmers Elevator and Warehouse Co. v. United States.*[220]

The *Alimota* case involves the condemnation (a taking of property by eminent domain) of a grain elevator on land leased to the plaintiff tenant (who is called the "condemnee"). The leasehold interest according to the lease agreement would terminate at the end of seven years. The condemnee testified that he expected to renew the lease and he based this expectation on the general practice of the landlord (the railroad which owned the land) in renewing leases in the past.

When the leased premises were taken by the exercise of the power of eminent domain, just compensation from the perspective of the condemnee tenant required that the condemnor (the condemnor was the United States government) compensate him for a longer period than the seven years left in the term of the lease. He had a legal right of only seven years to remain in possession of the leased premises. He wanted to also be compensated for the additional period for which he had a reasonable expectation that his tenancy would continue. The U.S. Supreme Court agreed with the condemnee and decided that the condemnee was entitled to compensation for the entire period that he expected to be a tenant on the property that was taken.

The Supreme Court declared the following:

> At the time of the taking in this case, there was an expectancy that the improvements would be used beyond the lease term. But the government has sought to pay compensation on the theory that at that time there was no possibility that the lease would be renewed, and the improvements be valued as though there were no possibility of continued use. That is not how the market would have valued such improvements; it is not what a private buyer would have paid.[221]

In other words, it was legally possible that the lease would not be renewed. In the real world of leases by this railroad, it was reasonable to assume that the lease would be renewed. Thousands of dollars had been invested in building the structure that was condemned, even though spending that amount of capital could not be justified by the short-term lease (short-term considering the capital investment).

The tenant condemnee was given more by the Supreme Court than the law provided for prior to the decision in this case. The tenant did not have a contractual legal right to have his lease renewed before or after the decision in this case. He also had no right prior to the decision in this case to compensation for denial of the opportunity to continue to be a tenant at the condemned premises beyond the termination of his leasehold period.

I view this decision as a just and wise decision. This decision may also be considered an incorrect decision because the customary rule of renewing leases does not have the force of law. In other words, the condemnee did not have the legal right to require that the landlord renew its lease. It could be argued that it would be a correct decision only if the customary rule had the force of law, which it did not have.

Offsetting the argument that the decision is incorrect because there is no legal right to have the lease renewed is the question of what is the condemnee's right to compensation. There is a constitutional right to receive just compensation for the taking. If the condemnee is not compensated for the real value of its leasehold interest, including the customary rule that this landlord, the railroad, would renew its lease, it would not receive just compensation. The railroad renews its leases because the tenants next to the railroad tracks are customers of the railroad. The railroad has a vested interest in seeing its tenants remain on its property. The Supreme Court, in effect, applied the real rule to decide the case. My conclusion, as I explain below, is that this is a correct, just, and wise decision.

The Supreme Court may be criticized, of course, for having disregarded the legal rules (the paper rules) which were in existence prior to the decision in the *Alimota* case. The Supreme Court, however, might also be criticized if it denied the condemnee (the tenant) damages for the structure it had erected on the leased premises based upon the condemnee's reasonable expectation that its lease would be renewed. Alimota has a constitutional right to just compensation for the taking. The Supreme Court could be criticized for reaching an unjust result if it had denied the condemnee's claim.

I would cite this case if I were asked to justify the just decision. I believe that judges should dispense justice as well as apply pre-existing legal rules. They may not be able to do both in all situations. They may be criticized for deciding either the correct decision or the just decision. They obviously cannot be bound to do both if the just result conflicts with the correct result. The judge cannot be equally obligated to do mutually inconsistent acts if doing one or the other necessarily means that the result is subject to criticism for being either incorrect or unjust. The judge is both bound in some difficult to measure fashion to apply the pre-existing legal rules and to also disregard them or to alter them in the appropriate cases.

I see no conflict between justice and correctness in the *Alimota* case because I maintain that the condemnee has a legal right to just compensation. Just compensation would require that he be compensated for his reasonable expectation that his lease would be renewed and that, based upon this expectation, he erected the structure on the leased premises. So, this decision is not only just but it could also be regarded as a correct decision.

Moreover, it is a correct decision because (and therefore I am including it in this discussion) the Supreme Court recognizes the real rule of how the marketplace would view the situation in making decisions. The real rule is that it is the reasonable expectation of the condemnee based upon the custom of renewal of the leases, a custom recognized in the marketplace, even though there is no legal right requiring renewal of the lease. The renewal of the leases is not based upon a legally-binding requirement—the tenant has no legal right to compel the landlord to renew the lease.

The Supreme Court is honoring the real rule in the *Alimota* case. The real rule, the rule in the marketplace, is the reasonable expectation that the lease will be renewed. This reasonable expectation induced the condemnee to construct the structure. He did so even though he only had a twelve-year lease, which only had seven years remaining in the term of the lease when the property was condemned. The likelihood of renewal of the lease provides the basis for the valuation of the property. Notwithstanding the paper rule that no court would require that the landlord renew the lease, SCOTUS looked behind the curtain and applied the real rule.

8.10 Summary of the real rules

Real rules are descriptive rules of how the legal system functions in the real world. Prescriptive rules, Hart's primary rules, exist in the real world as enactments of law-creating bodies. In addition to these enactments, there also exist practices of the law—the way the law operates by the actions of the law-subjects and the governmental officials involved in law enforcement and law-application. The description of these practices can be formulated into real rules which, in turn, may be like the paper rules or may depart, in small or in larger ways, from the paper rules. In the *Alimota* case, the Supreme Court recognized the real rules of the marketplace, which it adopted and adapted to create a legal rule.

General acceptance of the law, according to Hart, is required in order to have a legal system. This general acceptance is a social fact. There must be a level of compliance with the law in order to conclude that there is "the rule of law". The rule of law requires that there be some congruence between the paper rules and the law in action in the conduct of the persons who are obligated to obey the rules.

For congruence between the paper rules and the rule of adjudication, there must be, in general, correct decisions. This is an indicator that the legal system is functioning in accordance with the rule of law. The correct decision, in turn, requires not only accurate law-ascertainment but also law-application. To some minimal extent, the rule of recognition must reflect the law in action. The real rules, in short, cannot deviate too much from the paper rules. If they do, there is no rule of law and no legal system that functions like a legal system.

Ultimately, there must be general obedience to most norms, general agreement on what the law is, and correct decisions in order to demonstrate that there is a functioning legal system. There may be some disobedience, as is illustrated in the real rules. In a limited number of cases, there may be agreement on what the law is, but the court decides to disregard the pre-existing law and to create a new legal rule in order to reach a more desirable decision. In other words, the court may decide to make the just decision and/or the wise decision rather than the correct decision. In short, the legal system can accommodate a limited number of cases in which the rule of change predominates over the rule of recognition and a correct decision is not made. Similarly, there can be a limited number of factual situations where the real rules are not the same as the paper rules.

For Hart's legal theory to work, the rule of recognition must be expanded to cover the situations where the rule of adjudication allows for alternate sources to be utilized in making judicial decisions. The rule of recognition and Hart's legal theory must be reconstructed to accommodate those factual situations where the real rules are part of the legal culture, while retaining the paper rules and the administration of the law in accordance with the paper rules to the extent necessary to retain the rule of law.

8.11 Studying the real rules

My suggestion is that students of the law and the legal system should not ignore the real rules because they are also part of the legal system, and they present a picture of the real-world operation of the legal system. Study of the law is not just study of the paper rules. The point is not that the paper rules should be ignored. The contention is that the paper rules do not in themselves tell the whole story. The real rules are not outliers or oddities. They are descriptive of the actual functioning of the law in action.

Sometimes, as the *Alimota* case demonstrates, the real rule is applied to decide the case. In general, principles cannot be applied to decide cases. They are too broad, and principles may conflict with each other and with the legal rules. The principle in *Alimota*, however, is a constitutional principle. It is an enacted principle because it is in the written Constitution that was adopted when the Constitution was adopted or amended. Principles other than the constitutional principles are not enacted. The constitutional principle that was recognized in the *Alimota* case establishes the right to just compensation when someone's property is taken, and just compensation includes consideration of the likelihood of the lease being extended beyond its legal limits.

The real rule, when that happens, when Alimota's property was taken, is the alternate source that was utilized to create a legal rule that was applied to make the decision. And, to make the decision that would be consistent with Alimota's constitutional right to just compensation. To make, in other words, a just decision. Judges are not like umpires; they not only have an obligation to make the correct decision, but they may also strive to make the just decision. They may look to an alternate source to make the just decision and/or the wise decision. Let's now look at some other alternate sources.

9.
Alternate Sources

E ven though judges may look to alternate sources in making judicial decisions, this does not mean that the exercising of discretion by judges is unlimited. There are constraints upon judges based upon the law and upon self-executing customary rules. Customary rules, in fact, control many of the activities of law-applying officials. The type of customary rules that I call real rules, which are not generally considered to be part of the law, should also be studied since the real rules affect the behavior of citizens and the legal advice given by lawyers to their clients.

For the purpose of evaluating and criticizing judicial decisions, I have offered the just decision and the wise decision as standards that may be employed. The correct decision is always presumptively justified. There are situations, however, in which the correct decision may not be the most desirable decision and the just decision and/or the wise decision may lead to a better result. When the critic of a judicial decision maintains that the just decision or the wise decision will result in a better decision than the correct decision, creative positivism views this as support for an alternate source for the decision other than the application of a rule of the pre-existing law that could have been applied to make the correct decision.

Some of the situations that I mention may be incorporated into Hart's rule of adjudication and rule of change. Alternatively, they could be tertiary rules that supplement Hart's primary and secondary rules. All these concepts form part of creative positivism. I describe the foundation for creative positivism, its tertiary rules and the principles of creative positivism in *The Judge and the Incorrect Decision*. I want to consider here the additional sources for judicial decisions that may be the result of looking to sources other than the legal norms of the pre-existing law.

The judge (and the critic of judicial decisions) should start with the correct decision because the correct decision is presumptively justified in all cases. Law is by its nature obligatory (mandatory or normative) and judges and other officials take an oath to perform their roles as legal officials in accordance with the law.[222] Citizens are also obliged to obey the law in their own conduct. One of Hart's contributions to understanding the law is his concept of the internal aspect of the law, and the internal aspect, as Hart recognizes, is different for officials in comparison to citizens.[223]

For duty-imposing rules, the internal aspect of the law illustrates that citizens acknowledge that they are obliged to obey the law. It is accepted by the citizenry that, in general, one acts morally when the law is being obeyed. Sanctions may be imposed if citizens fail to obey the law, and the public agrees that the application of sanctions is an appropriate response to disobedience. There is, as a social fact, what John Austin calls "habitual obedience to the law".

In addition to duty-imposing norms, there are power-conferring norms. These do not carry with them an obligation by the law-subjects to obey the law, but the power-conferring norms provide citizens with the means by which various legal actions can be performed and goals achieved. They can, for example, marry, sign contracts, and write wills.

In some situations, when you exercise your right granted to you by the power-conferring rule, you also are assuming duties. For example, when you marry pursuant to the power-conferring rule that authorizes citizens to marry (if they meet the standards for doing so), you accept the obligations associated with being a member of a married couple. Also, in a slightly different manner, as a married person you qualify for being subject to duties that apply only to married persons. For example, spousal abuse is a crime only if you are married. Therefore, it is an obligation imposed upon you only after you get married.

For officials, the power-conferring rules authorize their taking official action. The power-conferring rules that enable and support official action take on a different posture for various types of officials at various levels of the government. If you go to the clerk who issues marriage licenses, and you meet the criteria that are relevant for obtaining a marriage license, the clerk has no discretion. She is obligated to issue the license, even if she disagrees with the relevant legal norms. She must give the license to same-sex couples if the law permits them to marry. It makes no difference whether she thinks the law is just or wise.[224]

For a judge, the obligation to obey the law, or, more accurately, to apply the law in making decisions, is very different from the role of the marriage-license clerk because a judge has the legal authority to make the law. The judge is subject to power-conferring secondary rules about how she makes the law. She takes an oath to apply the law, but also has the authority to decide what the law is; and she may also change the pre-existing law.[225]

This sounds quite circular when you describe it in this way, but judges, acting as judges are supposed to act, and being authorized to so act, have the authority to determine what the law is and to change the law in the process of doing so. There are norms governing how judges create new laws. When I discuss the abortion cases in *The Judge and the Incorrect Decision*, I outline some of the norms that should be honored in deciding whether to overrule or not overrule *Roe v. Wade*.

9.1 Looking to sources other than the legal norms

The law consists of the constitution, legislation, precedents, and customary norms with the force of law. All statutes (those that are not repealed) and all precedents (those that are published and have not been reversed or overruled) are law. There are customary norms that may be law (and customary norms that would not be regarded as law).

The correct decision is a law-applied decision which is made by finding a rule of the pre-existing law that may be applied to the instant factual situation (law-ascertainment) and applying that law to decide the case (law-application). In addition, in order to be a correct decision, the ratio decidendi of the decision will not materially modify the pre-existing law. Correct decisions, in general, are authorized, authoritative and binding. There are some correct decisions that are not precedents because they are not published and, therefore, they are not authoritative.

There are also decisions that are not precedents because the decision states that the legal rule being applied is restricted to that case and is not intended to apply to any other factual situation. The "rule" being applied is an individual norm rather than a general norm (rules, in general, have to apply to more than one instance). Hart's rule of recognition, then, has to apply not only to the general norms (the legal rules) but also to what Hans Kelsen described as individual norms. The legal system includes the law as applied and the law as it operates in our world of law application (the real rules). Some of the real rules are also part of the law, such as the customary rules with the force of law.

Hart never accepted the concept of the real rules and never agreed that judges can and do create new law in the areas in which the pre-existing law was certain (this is the primary subject in vol. 2). Hart did acknowledge that there are rules that confer authority on individuals and institutions to create legal norms. Creative positivism refers to this type of rule as the rule of identification, which is part of the rule of recognition. These rules are within the realm of secondary rules rather than primary rules. These rules are not mandatory, and they authorize individuals and institutions to introduce new legal rules or modify existing rules. They are, then, part of the rule of change. If judges are involved, they are also part of the rule of adjudication.

An originalist will start with asking what the author of the text of the legal rule intended regarding how the legal rule should be applied. For example, you might ask what the Founding Fathers intended when they placed the cruel and unusual punishments clause in the Eighth Amendment. Would executing a defendant who committed a horrible murder when he was 17 years old be a cruel and unusual punishment and thereby be prohibited from being the penalty for committing the crime? Would it make a difference if he told his friends before he did so, that he wanted to kill somebody? Suppose he went to the house of a 46-year-old neighbor, placed duct tape around the woman, put a hood over her head, and threw her off the bridge while she was still conscious and alive, and she drowned? Add that he bragged about killing her to his friends and told them that he would get away with it since he was a minor, even though the penalty for murder in the State of Missouri where the act was committed could be execution if the jury decided that the crime was heinous enough to warrant execution and the judge agreed?[226]

The originalist would ask if the drafters of the Eighth Amendment would consider execution to be a cruel and unusual punishment. The Constitution would mean today what the drafters of the document intended it to mean when it was ratified. Its meaning would not change unless it was amended.

A textualist will look to the text to determine the plain meaning of a legal rule. He would ask what do the terms in the legal rule (in this case, the cruel and unusual punishments clause) mean. He would consider the context in which the terms were used, probing for their meaning in order to apply the legal rule.

The non-textualist will start with the text and consider the intention of the legislators or the purpose of the legal rule in applying the legal rule. For the non-textualist, the intent or purpose are part of the process of statutory interpretation. Judges may consider statements by legislators in order to interpret statutes. They may go beyond the text.

In the factual situation of the murder case that I described above, which are the facts of *Roper v. Simmons*, the majority opinion held that the execution of the defendant who was a juvenile when the crime was committed would violate the cruel and unusual punishments clause. In the 5-to-4 decision, the majority opinion considered multiple factors in deciding the case. The holding in the case is that it is unconstitutional to impose capital punishment for a crime that was committed when the juvenile was less than 18 years old.[227]

SCOTUS considered the following factors in arriving at the conclusion that the cruel and unusual punishments clause prevented Missouri from executing Simmons: a national consensus had developed against the execution of juvenile offenders; evolving standards of decency prohibited the execution; and most foreign countries would prohibit execution.

Here is the conclusion in the majority opinion:

> The prohibition against 'cruel and unusual punishments,' like other expansive language in the Constitution, must be interpreted according to its text, by considering history, tradition, and precedent, and with due regard for its purpose and function in the constitutional design.[228]

Hart accepts that judges may rely upon a variety of sources in making legal rules. Judges may, also, by extrapolation from Hart's legal theory, look to non-mandatory sources in making judicial decisions. Judges may consider, for example, foreign law or legal text writers as a source for creating new legal rules. Hart, consequently, distinguishes mandatory legal sources from non-mandatory sources.

Therefore, Hart, by inference from his legal theory, refers to sources that are available to judges and are non-mandatory. Judges may refer to them in order to explain their decisions or justify their decisions. They are empowered to make the just decision or the wise decision, and they should be viewed as part of the rule of change.

For this use of alternate sources (using them to create new legal rules when making judicial decisions, Hart should be read as distinguishing the new legal norms from legal norms provided by the rule of recognition. The alternate sources are a source of new legal rules that are created by judges when they exercise judicial discretion. Judges may refer to them, but they are no obligated to apply them.[229]

9.2 Looking to alternate sources

Creative positivism contends that the legal system includes alternate sources which may affect the making of judicial decisions. The alternate sources used to create new legal rules may be considered to be persuasive sources for making judicial decisions even though they are not part of the law. While the potential legal rules that are the result of using persuasive sources to create new legal rules do not qualify as law, they also do not qualify as non-law. Even though applying a new legal rule derived from a persuasive source does not lead to a correct decision, it does lead to a binding, authoritative decision if it is published. The judge is authorized to reach such a decision.

Judges can and do create new law when the pre-existing law is clear, but the judge concludes that applying it will not result in a desirable decision. In those cases, the judge evaluates the potential correct decision and the rule that will reach that result and he looks to an alternate source to make his decision. For example, in deciding *Roper v. Simmons*, SCOTUS did not apply the pre-existing law (the leading precedent, *Stanford v. Kennedy*, was overruled and a new legal rule was created.

Creative positivism offers as two alternate sources the just decision and the wise decision. Creative positivism does not claim that judges actually try to reach the just decision and/or the wise decision. Creative positivism proposes that the critic of the judicial decision could use these two evaluative standards. The judge may cite the alternate sources that lead to the just decision or the wise decision. Neither Hart nor creative positivism would include alternate sources within the law.

Sometimes, correct decisions are also consistent with alternate sources, such as those that provide for the just and/or the wise decision. The just decision and the wise decision may also be a correct decision. Sometimes, decisions are made that are not correct. The decision that is not correct may refer to alternate sources.

9.3 Cases without a majority opinion, concurring opinions, and dissenting opinions

A decision will not create a new legal rule when a panel of judges hears the case and there is no majority opinion written to decide the case. Most appellate decisions are made by a panel of judges. No new legal rule will be created when no combination of a majority of the judges who heard the case agree upon the result for the same reason. Similarly, proposed legal rules presented in concurring and dissenting opinions are not considered to be legal rules of the pre-existing law for the next case. They have no precedential value. In that respect, even though the opinions may be published, they are like the non-published decisions.

While it is true that appellate courts are more likely than trial courts to change the legal rules, it is also true that, in general, appellate courts will not consider issues that have not been raised in the lower courts. There are exceptions, of course, and *Erie Railroad Co. v. Tompkins* is an example.[230]

Contrary to the view expressed by some legal philosophers, lawyers not only argue about what the correct decision would be, but they may also argue that an alternate source decision should be made (though they will not generally use this terminology). To establish that point, I present in Appendix A of *The Judge and the Incorrect Decision* the oral argument in the *Knick* case.[231]

When a later court refers to an opinion that is not a majority opinion, this does not lead to a correct decision. Those legal rules that are not cited in majority opinions in appellate courts are not authoritative legal rules. They are only potential legal rules that may be alternate sources.

9.4 The incorrect decision by mistake

The incorrect decision by mistake also creates law, though you could view this as accidental law since it represents a legal rule created by making a mistake. Just as an invalid statute is not invalid until a court declares it to be invalid, a legal rule created by mistake will be a legal rule if the case creating that legal rule is not reversed.

My example of the incorrect decision by mistake is in *Cincinnati Insurance Co. v. Flanders Motor Service Co. (Cincinnati 1)*.[232] This case, however, is not an instance of a legal rule being created in a decision that is an incorrect decision. The reason why it is not a good example for this purpose is because the decision is not a precedent in either the federal legal system or in the State of Indiana legal system.

The point that I am making here is that even incorrect decisions can be authoritative. A better example of this point is the *Erie* case when the U.S. Supreme Court decided that *Swift v. Tyson* would be overruled in regard to its interpretation of the Judiciary Act.[233] The Supreme Court overruled *Swift v. Tyson* and changed the legal rule regarding which legal system's laws should be used to decide diversity-of-citizenship cases in federal courts. Prior to the *Erie* decision, the legal rule of the *Swift* case was the law of the land. *Swift v. Tyson* was not overruled because it was an incorrect decision. It was overruled because the Supreme Court wanted to make a wise decision.

9.5 Cases decided pursuant to the Erie Doctrine

Since the *Erie* case was decided, it is a very common occurrence for a federal court sitting in a diversity-of-citizenship case to apply the law of the relevant state. This is not the law of the federal legal system but is the law of a specific state. The decision of the federal court though authorized and binding is not authoritative regarding the pre-existing law of the legal system whose law is being applied.

Since the federal decision in a diversity-of-citizenship case is not an authoritative decision in the legal system of the state whose law is being applied, it would not be a correct decision if the state court elects to cite the legal rule in the federal decision. This would be a reference to an alternate source. The federal court decision is not a binding precedent in the state-court setting, just as a decision by an inferior state court would not be binding on a superior state court.

By the way, this citing of the inferior court decision can be regarded as another type of alternate source decision. In other words, the decision may be viewed favorably by the higher court, but it is not authoritative in the higher court. It would be like citing with approval a legal rule in a dissenting or a concurring opinion. These generally accepted rules for which decisions constitute authoritative precedents are themselves customary rules. Many of the rules related to how the legal system functions are customary rules.

9.6 The conflict-of-law case

Another type of case which would qualify as an alternate source would be the conflict-of-law case in which the laws of another jurisdiction are applied by a court. The conflict-of-law rules give the legal system authority to make decisions using the laws of another jurisdiction. The decision which is made will not be authoritative in either the state whose court is making the decision (it does not change the law in that jurisdiction) or in the state whose laws are being applied.

This is different from the situation where one court cites the decisions of another court, not because they are applying another state's laws, but because the court citing the case finds the decision being cited to be persuasive. For example, the Supreme Court in the *Conway* case cited the decisions of four sister states.[234] Citing persuasive cases from another jurisdiction that are not authoritative in the legal system citing them is another type of alternate source decision.

9.7 Rules derived from statutory interpretation in another jurisdiction

Another example of an alternate source decision would be the interpretation of a statute that is like a statute applicable in a similar situation in another state. In the U.S., we have model statutes that may be adopted in individual states. I have previously mentioned the Uniform Commercial Code, of which Karl Llewellyn, a leading American Legal Realist, was a principal author. This is one of those model statutes. The interpretation of the model statute in a specific state will be binding on the courts within that state. If another state has adopted the same statute with exactly the same statutory language, the interpretation of the statute in one state will not be binding upon courts in another state, though the interpretation of the statute may be cited as an alternate source.

9.8 Customary norms in another state

Similarly, customary norms in one state may be regarded as binding while the very same customary norm in a neighboring state may not be viewed as a customary norm with the force of law. The same could be said about constitutional interpretations when two states have the exact same, or very similar, language in their constitutions. Obviously, the interpretation of the U.S. Constitution by the U.S. Supreme Court will be binding in the entire nation. An interpretation of a statute or constitutional provision in one circuit in the federal system will not be binding on another circuit though it will be binding on the district courts in the circuit in which the interpretation in question was made. Citing of a customary norm in a sister state may be viewed as looking to an alternate source.

9.9 Rules of non-governmental agencies

While I would not necessarily regard it as an example of citing an alternate source to make a judicial decision, I previously mentioned homeowners' associations (HOAs) as "law-making" agencies. HOAs adopt rules and regulations that govern the affairs within a specific community. In other words, the HOA is an entity that creates norms. If these norms are violated, the HOA may seek court enforcement of its rules and regulations. The judicial decision will be binding upon the members of the HOA, which is not a public agency but has authority to adopt rules pursuant to a state statute. The law accommodates these rules and regulations by the courts enforcing them.[235]

9.10 Rules of quasi-judicial agencies

In Appendix A of *The Judge and the Philosopher*, I discussed how zoning law works. The decisions granting variances by zoning hearing boards are another example of decisions being made by an agency with limited jurisdiction (usually within a single municipality) that will be binding on the parties. These decisions are authorized decisions, but they are only to a small degree viewed as authoritative. In other words, these decisions are not law-creating, though they are, but only in a limited sense, law-applying. As Hans Kelsen explains, these decisions create individual norms that apply to a single property. Hart does not offer a concept in his legal theory that is comparable to Kelsen's individual norms. Since the individual norms are not authoritative, citing the decision creating the individual norm could be viewed as referring to an alternate source.

9.11 Text writers

Other alternate source decisions could be references to descriptions of the law by legal experts, such as the text writers. These descriptions of the law by prestigious text writers could represent astute reasoning. It is not unusual for courts to cite their works when they are believed to be accurate presentations of the law. These texts are not authoritative, however, even if the text writer was the original author of the statute being interpreted. Citing the text writer's version of the legal rules or her interpretation of the legal rules is another example of the citing of a permissive source.

9.12 Foreign law

In *Roper v. Simmons*, SCOTUS refers to the laws in several foreign jurisdictions. Those laws are not authoritative in the U.S. Therefore, reference to them should be regarded as looking to alternate sources.[236]

9.13 Islamic law

Finally, let me return to one outlier case that discusses the question of whether Islamic law may be an acceptable alternate source for judicial decision-making. Oklahoma adopted an amendment to its constitution prohibiting judges in Oklahoma from considering the legal precepts of other nations or cultures in making their decisions and, more specifically, international law or Islamic law.

A Muslim community leader in Oklahoma City filed an action challenging the constitutionality of the constitutional amendment. This case illustrates a question about the rule of recognition, which is whether a constitutional amendment can be valid or invalid. If it can be invalid, this affects our description of the rule of recognition. The constitutional amendment in this case precludes a potential alternate source from being cited as a source for creating legal rules in making judicial decisions.

The supporters of the constitutional amendment argued that it was intended to prevent courts from applying all religious laws and the reference to Islamic law was just an example of a set of religious laws. The state senator who sponsored the constitutional amendment claimed that the purpose of the constitutional amendment was to ensure that judges in Oklahoma apply only Oklahoma or U.S. law. He declared that Islamic law conflicted with the Oklahoma Constitution.

The District Court in 2010 ruled that the constitutional amendment could not take effect. The 10th Circuit Court of Appeals affirmed the decision of the District Court.[237] The Court of Appeals could find no case in Oklahoma in which an Oklahoma court applied Islamic law or the legal precepts of other countries. Oklahoma courts could, however, based upon this decision, consider Islamic law to be an alternate source for making judicial decisions. This does not mean that Islamic law can override either the Oklahoma Constitution or the U.S. Constitution. All that the court has decided is that judges may look to Islamic law as an alternate source.

An alternate source is not an authoritative source. Citing an alternate source will not lead to a correct decision. Creative positivism contends that judges are obligated to make correct decisions, and they are authorized to (have the authority to) create new legal rules by looking to the alternate sources that would provide for a just decision or a wise decision. The customary rules that govern judicial decision-making, the legal culture, allows judges to look to alternate sources. There is, however, no obligation comparable to the obligation to make the correct decision when looking to alternate sources.

IO.
Criticizing a Judicial Decision

10.1 Revisiting the obligation to make the correct decision

This section sets forth the philosophical basis for legal positivism. Some of the American Legal Realists in the first half of the 20th century proposed the theory that there is no such thing as the correct decision because law is too indeterminate to allow for finding and applying the legal rules. Ever since Hart's *The Concept of Law* was published in 1961, many legal philosophers believe that judges are obligated to make the correct decision. Creative positivism, the legal theory that I am proposing, includes the concept that the correct decision is presumptively justified. You may extend that view to acknowledging that there is an obligation imposed upon the judge to make the correct decision. But this then requires that you explain what it means to have such an obligation.

The law is comprehensive and complete, and I contend that there are no gaps in the law. It is not logical to argue that a decision for either of two contesting parties can both be the correct decision. For example, you cannot claim that a decision in *Conway v. Cutler Group* for either Conway or for Cutler Group can each be a correct decision.[238] This is the case in which the Conway family was not the purchaser from the Cutler Group, the builder of the house. In Pennsylvania, if the house is defective, the purchaser from the builder has a cause of action against the builder for the breach of the judicially created implied warranty of habitability.

The decision in most cases will be the correct decisions. In some cases, the decision that is made is not a correct decision. The bottom line is that a decision for Conway would not be the correct decision because there is no legal rule in the pre-existing law that may be applied for Conway to prevail. The only way that Conway can receive a decision in his favor is if a new legal rule is created and applied. A decision in favor of Cutler Group is the correct decision.

Since, prior to the *Conway* case, there was no case in Pennsylvania in which the purchaser of a home could prevail against a builder in a contract suit when the builder was not the seller of the home (there are inapplicable exceptions to this proposition), I conclude that Conway could not make out a contractual cause of action against the Cutler Group. Since Conway has no cause of action, a decision in favor of Conway would not be the correct decision and a decision in favor of the Cutler Group would be the correct decision.

I define the correct decision as a decision that is made by applying a legal rule of the pre-existing law. In addition, the legal rule that is applied is not materially modified by the decision. After the decision is made, if it is published, regardless of whether or not it qualifies as a correct decision, the decision is a precedent. As a precedent, the ratio decidendi of the decision becomes a legal rule that is now the standard for whether the next decision will be correct or incorrect. Every decision is either correct or incorrect (it is an either-or concept).

Consequently, when the Court of Common Pleas decided in favor of the Cutler Group, this was a correct decision. Then, the Superior Court reversed that result and decided for Conway. The Superior Court did not make the correct decision.

Here is the important point. The Superior Court did not reverse the trial court because the judges in the Superior Court thought that the pre-existing law did provide a cause of action. They did not find an existing legal rule in the pre-existing law that the trial court missed or conclude that the trial court had made a mistake regarding what the pre-existing law was. Instead, they decided that the implied warranty of habitability created in the applicable precedent (the *Elderkin* case) should be extended to include a cause of action for the second purchaser against the original builder.[239]

The Cutler Group took an appeal to the Supreme Court. They, once again, made the same argument in the Supreme Court that they had made in the trial court and in the Superior Court. They argued that the implied warranty of habitability from the builder to the first purchaser should not be extended, or, if it were to be extended, it should be by the legislature and not by the courts. The Supreme Court, like the Superior Court, did not conclude that the inferior court had applied the wrong rule of the pre-existing law. Instead, the Supreme Court opted for applying the pre-existing law and making the correct decision.

The reason given by the Supreme Court for deciding in favor of the builder is that the issue in the case involves creating a new legal rule and that the new legal rule would involve a policy decision that should be made by the legislature. Courts do not have the resources to study policy issues; they are limited by the trickle of cases in a specific confined area of the law being presented in an unorganized and haphazard manner. Courts may change the law only if, and only when, cases are presented to the court that allow for the change to be made.

Courts are, and should be, deferential to the legislature. The legislature has more resources than the courts have for analysis of legal rules and their consequences. Legislatures can hold hearings and spend more time than courts on complex issues. Moreover, legislators are generally elected, while judges are often not elected, so that, in a democracy, the legislature reflects the will of the people.

The fundamental role of courts is to resolve disputes, though they also have a role in regulating the behavior of those subjected to the law or those utilizing the law to accomplish social results. Bear in mind that the individual judge and even panels of judges are not systemically coordinating the flow of cases.

For lower-court judges, following the legal rules established in the precedents of the superior courts is based upon one or some of the following reasons: the easiest way to do their jobs (the most efficient course of action); the way to avoid having their decisions reversed (though that did not work for the trial court in *Conway* when the Superior Court reversed the trial court); implementing the obligation to apply the law in deciding cases; applying legal rules pronounced by higher courts is a policy-oriented strategy; and acting in a way that is compatible with the judge's view of the role of judges in the legal system.

Appellate judges have more discretion than trial-court judges. Therefore, appellate judges have more opportunity to create legal rules. But no judge has the authority to create legal rules in the same manner as a legislature. Courts are more limited in their authority to create law than legislatures are and even more limited in their opportunity to do so.

All three courts in the *Conway* case, and their multiple judges, agreed that Conway did not have a cause of action if the pre-existing law was applied and that a decision for the builder would be the correct decision. The issue for all three courts and their multiple judges was whether the legal rule should be extended to make a just decision (and, maybe, a wise decision), even though such a decision would not be a correct decision. My theory of creative positivism accepts that judges usually make the correct decision. It also presupposes that, in a particular case, the judge has the authority (the judicial power) to avoid the correct decision and make the more desirable decision. The judge does so by creating a new legal rule to apply in deciding the case.

None of the judges involved in the various phases of the *Conway* case acted illegally. All the judges performed their duties in accordance with their sworn responsibility to act in a professional manner in accordance with their oath of office. None of these judges made a mistake about law-ascertainment. In accordance with the rule of recognition, there was a general consensus among all of these judges about what the law is before they decided the case.

The *Conway* case presents a prime example of how to use the three elements (correctness, justice and wisdom) as useful criteria for analyzing decisions after they are made. When the trial court and the Supreme Court decided in favor of the Cutler Group, their decision was the correct decision. The decision that the Superior Court made for Conway was not the correct decision, though it was a just decision. After all, the Cutler Group built the house with the defects in the house when Conway purchased it. The decisions of the trial court and the Supreme Court were unjust decisions.

In section 3.2 of *The Judge and the Umpire*, I introduce the apple sorter. He has four bins for four different grades of apples. He sorts the apples in accordance with the criteria he has been given, apple by apple. He puts each apple into one of the four bins based upon his understanding of the criteria and he applies those criteria to each apple. He is not making moral decisions as to each apple. He makes a moral decision to apply the criteria to perform his assigned task. Regarding this task, the apple sorter is like the umpire, merely applying the rules he has been given.

Underpinning the decision to apply the criteria for sorting the apples is the more basic decision that the apple sorter has made. He has made the moral decision to do his job and not to challenge the criteria. He does not make a moral decision as he examines each individual apple. He came to work with the basic understanding (the underlying moral decision) that he was going to do his job the way his job is supposed to be done. That is the moral decision. The sorting of the individual apples are not individual moral decisions; they are just judgment calls on applying the criteria given to the apple sorter apple by apple.

I introduced judging apples to provide an example of a rational judging process that is non-evaluative. Grading apples based upon size, color, lack of blemishes and shape requires making judgments according to established criteria but does not involve evaluation of the criteria. If the apple sorter decides to question the criteria or the results of applying the criteria (were the criteria to be modified), the process becomes evaluative. But the mere sorting without questioning the criteria requires judgment, not evaluation. I view the apple sorting as an analytical process, just as applying legal rules to make judicial decisions is an analytical process.

The trial judge applying the rules of the pre-existing law does not have to make a moral decision each time he makes a ruling in the case (like a ruling on the admissibility of evidence) or decides a case. He makes a moral decision to perform his duties in accordance with the customary rules of being a judge. Making the correct decision is what is expected of him. He is authorized to make correct decisions. He need not pause to decide whether he should make correct decisions. It is his practice to make correct decisions, just like the apple sorter's practice in judging apples.

In this very limited sense, the judge making correct decisions without evaluating the decision he is making is like the umpire calling balls and strikes. He need not consider the moral outcome in the case to make the correct decision. The judge is always presumptively justified in making the correct decision. The difference between the judge and the umpire, however, is that the judge may change the legal rules and the umpire has no authority to change the rules of baseball. The rules of baseball may be modified, but not by the individual umpire or panel of umpires.

Let me try to explain this point about the correct decision by considering another situation. You open your business of selling bagels. The decision to open this business is an economic decision. You decide upon your pricing based upon economic considerations. Too high a price will result in your competitors with lower prices getting the customers. Too low a price means that you will not make a profit. You may also make some moral decisions, such as not to sell cigarettes and not to engage in price gouging if the opportunity to do so presents itself. There may be a moral element to some of these decisions, but many are primarily business decisions.

When a customer buys a dozen bagels, you charge him five dollars, which is the price you have established. If he looks like he can pay much more than your price, you make the moral decision not to take advantage of him. If he looks like he cannot afford to pay your price, you make the moral decision not to discount your price. If he gives you a ten-dollar bill, you give him five dollars back. This is not a moral decision. It is a mathematical decision. The decision not to cheat your customers is a moral decision. The decision to give five dollars back when you receive a ten-dollar bill is the correct decision. It probably never occurred to you to cheat the customer. You just made a correct decision without engaging in an evaluative process. Often, trial judges similarly just make correct decisions without evaluating whether their decision is the best decision.

If the judge does evaluate his decision, he may decide in the rare case to not apply the law that is available to him in accordance with the rule of recognition. He may not be content with the decision that he would make if he applied the legal rule in the pre-existing law. He may decide to make a better decision than the correct decision. This is when he looks to an alternate source for creating a new legal rule in order to make a more desirable decision.

Creative positivism offers the evaluative criteria of the just decision and the wise decision. The judge may create a new legal rule (which may or may not be based upon an alternate source) in order to make the just or the wise decision. Hart accepts that this might occur if the law is uncertain. Creative positivism contends that it may also occur when the law is determinate, and there are examples of such decisions in *The Judge and the Umpire*.

10.2 Making the judicial decision

The judge differs from the umpire and the apple sorter because the judge is not only presumptively justified in making the correct decision, but she is also authorized to avoid making the correct decision by creating a new legal rule. The judge may select the criteria for making the decision. The judge may create a new legal rule, which she applies to make the decision. Neither the apple sorter nor the umpire has authority to change the rules.

Consequently, the obligation of the judge to apply the rules does not preclude the judge from applying new rules, rules of her creation. She is not obligated to make a new legal rule. She is authorized, however, to do so. I maintain that making the new legal rule is justified if two conditions are met: (1) applying the new rule will result in a just and/or wise decision; and (2) the just and/or wise decision is a better decision than the correct decision. Deciding upon whether there would be a better decision is an evaluative process.

The judge is authorized to engage in this evaluative process. When the judge decides that the just decision and/or the wise decision is the preferable decision, she will not apply the legal rule that would otherwise have been applicable. The judge is not only applying the law, but she is also deciding what the law is that she will apply. When the judge does so, the judge is not breaking the law. The judge is not violating her obligation to obey the law because she has authority to create a new legal rule.

Justice Scalia, in his dissenting opinion in *Roper v. Simmons*, maintains that the role of the Supreme Court is to say what the law is and not what it should be. And the law is, according to his originalist interpretation of the Constitution, what the drafters of the cruel and unusual punishments clause intended it to be. The fallacy in this approach, however, is that the decision to apply this originalist theory is itself a decision about what the law should be rather than a decision about what the law is. The law is not necessarily limited to what the law was intended to be almost 250 years ago.

In the concurring opinion by Justice Stevens in the *Roper v. Simmons* case, he responds to Justice Scalia by pointing out that the interpretation of the Eighth Amendment is not frozen with the meaning it had when it was originally drafted. In the best tradition of the development of the common law, our understanding of the Constitution and its interpretation changes from time to time.[240]

Making the correct decision, as I have explained, does not necessarily involve evaluation. Law-ascertainment and law-application are parts of a rational reasoning process, which may not include evaluation of the legal rule being applied. The correct decision is not, in theory, based on who is making the decision. In theory, each judge who makes the correct decision should reach the same conclusion. Every case provides the opportunity to make the correct decision. Every decision is either correct or incorrect. There is, in theory, and in my experience in practice, general agreement on what the correct decision will be.

10.3 Evaluation in the judicial process

Evaluation enters the judicial process when you decide whether the correct decision is a good decision or a bad decision. Deciding if the legal rule that one would apply to make the correct decision is a good or bad legal rule is also an evaluative process. Deciding not to make the correct decision but to make the just or the wise decision is an evaluative process. Making the correct decision allows for greater certainty and predictability in what the judicial decision would be.

Certainty and predictability are very important values for a workable and efficient system for regulating human behavior.

Stability and change are coupled features of legal systems. Without change, laws over time will become obsolete and as social mores change, the laws will appear to be old-fashioned and out-of-date. Change, however, cannot appear to be too extreme or so pervasive that the law loses its stability, certainty, and predictability. It follows that stability and change need each other and neither can exist without the other. In this sense, they are coupled, always appearing together in the legal system.

In the same way, the correct decision is coupled with the two alternate source decisions, the just decision and the wise decision. The correct decision is needed for continuity and consistency in decision-making. The law must be determinate to be predictable and dependable. But correct decisions that lead to unjust results will be unacceptable and will appear to be influenced by prejudice and bias. Unjust decisions will be contrary to expectations of the parties in the case who anticipated that the result would be fair. So, the correct decision and the just decision are coupled, with the former providing for stability and predictable results and the latter providing for the appearance of being non-partisan and fair. And the same is true of the correct decision and the wise decision.[241]

The three elements of the judicial decision are interconnected and overlapping while remaining distinct and independent. Making the judicial decision is always ultimately evaluative because the judge must decide whether to make the correct decision or an alternate source decision. In most cases, making the correct decision is the obvious choice, the most convenient way to proceed and is unchallengeable in the sense that the correct decision is always presumptively justifiable.

My starting point in consideration of justice is that the court is a court of justice as well as a court of law. I take this to mean that the court must dispense justice as well as apply the law.[242] In applying the law, the court has the authority to change the law to make a just decision. Making the judicial decision becomes a critical evaluative process when the official evaluates the outcome for the participants and for the general society. If the official evaluates the outcome, and he has the authority to do so, he may want to change the criteria for making his judgment calls. Evaluation of the outcome could involve considering the effect on the individuals affected by the process (the just decision) and the consequences for the society going forward (the wise decision).[243]

10.4 The just decision v. the wise decision

Sometimes, when the just decision is made, the consequences are less significant because the judge makes it clear that he considers the instant case to be an unusual or extraordinary case. He creates a narrow rule to apply in the instant case that will not affect many future cases.[244] Justice Black, in his dissenting opinion in the *Darrow* case had no objection to the rule that the majority wanted to create, but he urged that the rule not be applied to Darrow. If that suggestion had been accepted, the decision would have been a just decision.[245] As Llewellyn notes, it is the judge's duty to decide the case based upon a rule of law, but not necessarily a rule of law that can be applied to all seemingly like cases.[246]

It is also possible that the consequences of the wise decision may be so favorable that the effect upon the parties becomes very much secondary or even non-existent as a factor in evaluating the decision. I would characterize the *Darrow* case as an example of the wise decision overwhelming the just decision and the correct decision. The focus of the Supreme Court was on establishing a workable legal rule for the future that would control trustees, be easily administered, and protect creditors and the bankrupt entity. The goal was to establish a clear rule that would eliminate uncertainty and be dogmatic regarding what activities would be permissible in the future regulation of trustees.

Darrow, who did nothing wrong from a moral or ethical point of view, but who did make a mistake, was the victim of the wise decision.

I am using the term "policy" to include policies, principles, standards, and values. Policy is part of the element of the wise decision. The wise decision could also be the result of applying the law. In other words, the wise decision could also be the correct decision.

Every law, each legal norm, has a purpose, sometimes explicit and other times implicit. For example, the legal norm could be "in order to improve worker safety, every worker in the factory must wear a hard hat". Here, the purpose is clear. Some laws could have multiple purposes. There should be no conflict between the purpose(s) and the legal norm, unless there is a gross example of sloppy drafting of the language of the legal norm.

The purpose of a legal norm, however, has only a small degree of influence on the interpretation of the legal norm, even though some would argue that it could be part of applying the legal norm to make the correct decision. The purpose of the rule is often unclear. It may conflict with other values of the legal system. The rule can be over-inclusive or under-inclusive in relation to the rule's supposed purpose. The rule may result in consequences that are contrary to the rule's purpose, or the rule may result in unintended consequences or unthought of consequences.[247]

If you are looking for the purpose of a statute to aid in interpreting the statute, you are asking "what are the consequences that the legislature was seeking to accomplish?". Then, in applying the language of the statute to the factual situation in the case, you can ask whether the consequences are those that were sought by the legislature. Therefore, looking to the purpose of a statute is really an inquiry into the proposed consequences of the statute. Looking at the proposed consequences is part of evaluating the consequences.

When you are evaluating the consequences, you are considering whether you agree that they are beneficial or not. When you are applying the legal rule, you are accepting the intended consequences and determining if the literal language of the statute, when applied to the factual situation, leads to those consequences. The court does not have the authority to rewrite the statute. The court does have the authority to interpret the statute in a way that activates the intended consequences. This is an attempt, regardless of the desirability or undesirability of the consequences, to achieve the result desired by the legislature.

When the critic considers the desirability or undesirability of the consequences, the critic is evaluating the legal rule to be applied. When making the wise decision, the emphasis is on the consequences of the rule being applied or created, not only on the parties in the case, but also on the resolution of future disputes. This evaluation should be based upon sound legal policies embedded in the law, time-honored and generally acknowledged.

The legal system reflects many policies. These policies may conflict with each other. The laws themselves, however, never conflict in the sense that disputes must be resolved, correct decisions are presumptively justified, and correct decisions are made by applying the pre-existing law. If there is a potential conflict in the legal norms, it is resolved by applying the legal norm that is most applicable in order to make the correct decision.

The law cannot require that a citizen both act in a specific manner and penalize the individual for so acting. The law cannot specify the conduct of the person to do or not to do something at the same time. It cannot require contradictory acts. The legal rules must be non-contradictory.

There is always a potential legal norm to apply to resolve every dispute because the law is coherent, comprehensive, complete, and consistent so that, in making the judicial decision, the decision necessarily eliminates any potential conflict among the legal rules. There is never a tie; every case will result in a decision.

Policies will be a factor in the legal system in many ways, though policies may conflict with each other. The element of the wise decision presupposes that there is a decision that will provide for the best consequences. The best decision may be an alternate source decision (the just decision and/or the wise decision). To make the wise decision, policies must be evaluated. For the wise decision to be compared to the correct decision, the legal norm that would result in the correct decision has to be evaluated. The correct decision is the decision that would be made by applying pre-existing law with no requirement of evaluation of the legal norm to be applied to do so.

There are policies embedded in the law (in the legal norms) and there are also policies inherent in the legal system. These are all public policies. These policies, from these multiple sources, could conflict. The wise decision must resolve that conflict by selecting from among the policies. The policies that the judge considers should not be the result of bias or prejudice. The policies should be those that are universal and reflect the views of the citizenry.

The decision to avoid making the policy decision (as in the *Conway* case) is itself the implementation of a policy: to wit, the policy to leave policy decisions to the legislature. In the *Elderkin* case, the decision was made to adopt a policy to protect home purchasers who had less bargaining power and knowledge than home builders. This was accomplished by creating the implied warranty of habitability.[248] Thus, the Pennsylvania Supreme Court in the *Elderkin* case created a legal norm, which the Supreme Court declined to modify but which it left intact in the *Conway* case.

John Ladd, a professor of philosophy at Brown University, contends that judges must make rational decisions:

> By a 'rational decision' I mean a decision by which the agent can give good reasons. A nonrational decision would be one for which the agent has no reason, whereas an irrational decision would be one for which he has only

bad reasons, that is, one which, though ostensibly rational, violates the norms of rationality and thus conflicts with rationality.[249]

To be rational is to give reasons, but the reasons may be the wrong reasons. So, the kind of decisions we are considering are not just rational, reasoned decisions, but are rational, well-reasoned decisions. In other words, the reason being given must be an acceptable reason in accordance with the legal culture and the customary norms applicable to judges when they are making decisions.[250] The customary norms create the judicial culture that then sets the guideposts for judicial behavior.

It is the authority of the judge to make the just decision that is missing in Hart's legal philosophy. If the rule of recognition is based on a social fact, and the rule of recognition is not superior to the rule of change and the rule of adjudication, it follows that the rule of change and the rule of adjudication are also based on social facts. They are not subordinate to the rule of recognition. All three of the secondary rules are interconnected and they may conflict in certain cases, which means that there will be cases where the judge does not apply the rule that is derived from the rule of recognition. Hart does not directly address this point and offers no guidance on resolving this potential conflict among the secondary rules.

The real rule is that judges do not just make correct decisions. They do not decide cases in a mechanical method but employ an analytical method. This analytical method does not involve evaluation from the perspective of making the correct decision. It does involve evaluation when an alternate source decision is made.

For the just decision, the focus is on the effect upon the parties in the case.[251] In some cases, there are other interests involved in the case besides those of the parties. From the perspective of the decision being a precedent, the effect of the decision upon individuals who are not before the judge and their interests may become a factor. Creative positivism refers to this aspect of judicial decision-making as the consideration of the wise decision.

A good illustration of the contrast between the interests of the parties and other interests occurs in the case involving the publication of a book entitled *Too Much and Never Enough, How My Family Created the World's Most Dangerous Man*. The book is by Mary L. Trump, the niece of former President Donald J. Trump.

President Trump's brother, Robert S. Trump, sued Mary L. Trump, the author of the book and Simon & Schuster, Inc., the publisher of the book to enjoin its distribution. The Supreme Court of Duchess County, which is a trial court, issued an injunction prohibiting distribution of the book on June 30, 2020. The Supreme Court of the State of New York, Appellate Division, affirmed the injunction against Mary L. Trump but reversed the injunction against Simon & Schuster on July 1, 2020.[252]

The case for an injunction against Mary L. Trump is based upon a contractual dispute. She signed a non-disclosure agreement (also called a confidentiality agreement) as part of the settlement of the estate of her grandfather. There will ultimately be a hearing about whether publishing this book can be enjoined based upon it being a possible breach of contract. This will be the subject of a later trial.

Simon & Schuster was found by the trial court to be the agent of Mary L. Trump. As her agent, they were also enjoined because the prohibition applied to her agents. The appellate court found that this ruling was incorrect because they held that there may be no agency relationship. The reason that I am referring to this case is not because of the contractual issue regarding Mary Trump and her publisher.

The case also raises interesting freedom of speech issues. Whether, based upon the First Amendment freedom of speech clause, Mary L. Trump may disregard the non-disclosure agreement is an issue that will be resolved in further proceedings. The confidentiality agreement may be enforceable against her.

While Mary L. Trump's grandfather was a prominent real estate developer, and there may be some public interest involved, the fact that her uncle was the President when the case was tried creates heightened public interest. This is especially true when he is a candidate for re-election in 2020. The court in the opinion of President Justice Alan D. Scheinkman points out that there is a legitimate interest in preserving family secrets for a family involved in real estate development. It is another matter, however, for the family of the President.

Regarding the publisher, the important point is that Simon & Schuster is not a party to the settlement agreement of the Trump family. The First Amendment rights of the publisher may not be restricted by the settlement agreement.

To a certain extent, then, the rights of the public are involved in the *Trump v. Trump* case. Therefore, this case may have some general public importance in addition to its relevance as a precedent. While the weighing of the interests of the litigants in a lawsuit is the paramount concern of the just decision, when we wander into the interests of the society, we approach the realm of the wise decision.

In summary, judges are presumptively justified in making correct decisions. In addition to the authority to make correct decisions, judges are also authorized to make decisions that will not qualify as correct decisions because the decisions create new legal rules. Making new legal rules is consistent with the legal culture and is controlled by, constrained by, and authorized by customary rules. These customary rules are social facts, just as the rule of recognition is a social fact.

The judge made a wise decision in the *Trump v. Trump* case in allowing the publisher to distribute the book. The general interest of the public in the book was acknowledged by the judge as a relevant factor in refusing to prohibit the publisher from distributing the book. Even though the public is not a party in the case, the interests of the public are a factor in the decision. The judicial culture allows for the judge to consider those interests in making his decision.

APPENDICES

APPENDIX A: Volume 1 and Volume 2 and a Preview of Volume 4, *The Judge and the Incorrect Decision*

Volume 1

In the first book of my quartet, *The Judge and the Umpire*, I establish that judges are not like umpires for a variety of reasons. The most important of these is that judges have the authority to (are empowered to, have the capacity to, and actually do) change the legal rules that they will apply in making judicial decisions. Judges may create new legal rules. I introduce H.L.A. Hart's legal philosophy as the springboard for creative positivism. The starting point for any legal philosophy is to describe the law and its role in the legal system. Hart provides the foundation for finding the law and applying it to make judicial decisions.

Hart describes the law as consisting of two types of legal rules. Primary rules are the basic legal rules that apply to the behavior of the citizens. There are two types of primary rules: duty-imposing rules that require conduct to conform to prescribed behavioral patterns (the duties) with sanctions for non-compliance and power-conferring rules that authorize citizens to achieve desired results by fulfilling specified criteria. The power-conferring rules allow citizens to enter into contracts, own property and get married.

The second type of rules are the secondary rules. There are three of them. The rule of recognition is the rule that allows for the primary rules to be found (law-ascertainment) and to be applied (law-application). The rule of change provides for changing the primary rules. The rule of adjudication allows for courts to resolve disputes. Some theorists assumed that the primary rules were duty-imposing, and the secondary rules were power-conferring, but I contend that Hart should be interpreted to allow for the two types of primary rules and the three types of secondary rules.

Some theorists have assumed that the rule of recognition is the paramount rule, but Hart's legal theory does not require this. The way in which the legal system works is that judges may create new legal rules in accordance with the rule of adjudication and the rule of change, and, once the new legal rule is created, it becomes part of the law pursuant to the rule of recognition.

Creative positivism presents the three elements—correctness, justice and wisdom—as the conceptual construct for studying, analyzing and criticizing judicial decisions. The correct decision is a decision that is made by applying a legal rule of the pre-existing law without making a material change in the legal rule that has been applied. I refer to the pre-existing law as the law that was in existence when the judicial decision was made. Any decision that is not a correct decision will be an incorrect decision. Each judicial decision can also be considered to be just or unjust and wise or unwise.

To prove that judges may create new legal rules, I discuss six cases. The six cases include trial court decisions and appellate court decisions. While appellate courts are more likely than trial courts to create new legal rules, trial courts may also do so. In fact, appellate courts will not, in general, consider issues that have not been raised in the trial courts, though there are exceptions.[253]

When judges change the legal rules, they are not simply applying the legal rules of the pre-existing law (the law in existence before the case was decided). They may not, therefore, make the correct decision. As I mentioned, I define the correct decision as a decision in which a rule of the pre-existing law has been applied and the rule that is applied is not materially modified by the decision. When modifying the rules of the pre-existing law, the judge must look to an alternate source other than the pre-existing law. The judge does so in order to create the new legal rule to apply to decide the case.

Instead of applying the rule of the pre-existing law in order to make the correct decision, the judge may strive to make the just decision or the wise decision, which may provide a more desirable decision than that of the correct decision. In most instances, the judge will decide the case by applying a legal rule of the pre-existing law, and, in those cases, the just decision and/or the wise decision may also be the correct decision.

Some legal theorists contend that judges, and lawyers arguing cases before judges, are concerned only with the correct decision. I maintain in *The Judge and the Umpire* that the six cases which I discuss demonstrate that courts sometimes consider alternate sources in order to make the just decision and/or the wise decision.[254] The role of umpires is to make correct decisions. Judges, in contrast to umpires, consider the effect of their decisions upon the parties in the case and the consequences to the society of their decisions. These decisions may be precedents that create legal rules that will affect future decision-making.

Volume 2

In *The Judge and the Philosopher*, the second book in this series, I expand upon the discussion of Hart's version of legal positivism. I agree with the legal positivists about the pedigree theory which is the contention that we look to the source of the law to determine what the law is. I also agree with most of the legal positivist discussion of the separation theory, which is that judges and lawyers should distinguish legal rules from other types of rules such as moral rules.

I divert from legal positivism in my consideration of the discretionary theory. Hart contends that discretion may be exercised by judges only in deciding the hard cases, which he describes as the cases in which the law has gaps, open texture or penumbral factual situations. The hard cases are the cases in which the pre-existing law is not clear. The six cases I discuss in Volume 1 offer examples of judges creating new law in the easy cases – the cases that do not meet the criteria of Hart's hard cases. The easy cases are cases in which the pre-existing law is determinate. In both the hard cases and the easy cases, the judges may make the correct decision. Judges may also make the just decision or the wise decision, which may or may not be the correct decision.

In *The Judge and the Philosopher*, I provide examples of legal reasoning, such as applying a legal rule by reference to an analogy.[255] Legal reasoning is employed in making the correct decision. This is an analytical process rather than an evaluative process. Applying the rules created in precedents, and making new legal rules, are activities that are subject to customary rules that are part of the legal culture.[256]

Hart provides the concept of the rule of recognition as the source for law-ascertainment and law-application in making the judicial decision. The rule of recognition is a social fact. It is necessary in order to have a legal system that there be a general consensus among the officials in the society regarding what is law. Law consists of the legal rules that may be found in the constitution, statutes, precedents, and customary rules with the force of law.[257]

Customary legal norms are not enacted but exist as part of, and because of, the legal culture. There are two types of self-executing customary legal norms. Some customary legal norms have the force of law, and some do not. The customary legal norms that have the force of law are waiting to be recognized as law. The customary legal norms that have the force of law may be applied to make the correct decision.

It is fundamental to Hart's concept of the law, or at least to my understanding of his concept of the law, that the legal system provides a clear answer as to whether the judge has made a correct decision.[258] It is absolutely crucial in analyzing a case to begin with whether the court has made the correct decision.

Consider *Mosser v. Darrow*, one of the six cases discussed in *The Judge and the Umpire*, for an example of why you start your analysis with some understanding of what the correct decision would be.[259] This case involves a trustee who hired two employees to manage the bankrupt estate and the two employees defrauded the estate. The trustee was then surcharged for the loss suffered by the estate, even though he received no personal benefit from the fraudulent acts of the two employees.

In the *Darrow* case, there was no rule of the pre-existing law that allowed for the trustee to be surcharged. The U.S. Supreme Court created a new legal rule to provide that result. It should be of interest for the critic of the judicial decision to understand whether it is pre-existing law that is being applied or new law that is being created that does not qualify as pre-existing law, even though the judge may claim to have discovered the legal norm rather than created it.

It is also important to consider how that new legal rule will affect the parties, such as making Darrow personally responsible to make a payment to the trusts when he has not received any benefit from the wrongdoing of the employees. Also, there was no rule of pre-existing law that would make him liable. The Justices of the Supreme Court hearing the *Darrow* case had to consider how the new legal rule will affect future trustees who will be liable for the wrongful acts of their employees. This would include whether anyone would agree to be a trustee if he could be subject to a surcharge such as the one imposed on Darrow.

Surely, there are highly important practical consequences of the *Darrow* decision that cannot be ignored. Meanwhile, criticism of the decision must also include whether the decision is based upon pre-existing law and is, therefore, a correct decision. For the law to be effective, the law must be certain and there must be general agreement on what the rules of law are and what a correct decision would be. Finally, the critic should not ignore the retroactive impact of the decision upon Darrow.

Hart recognizes that some theorists believe that morals are part of the pre-existing law. They maintain that a moral judgment is relevant in determining the law or in making a new law. When Ronald Dworkin, Hart's successor as the Professor of Jurisprudence at Oxford University, argues that moral norms are inevitably intertwined with the legal norms, he obscures the determination of the correct decision. Hart should be read as acknowledging that there is a correct decision as part of his theory. Moral judgments are not part of the application of the law, but they are relevant to whether the correct decision is the best decision and to making the just decision and the wise decision.[260]

Since Hart recognizes that his theory is based upon the acceptance of the law as a social fact, it is an important part of his legal theory to include customary legal norms with the force of law within his description of the law. They are, and Hart might agree with this, social facts that are part of the pre-existing law. My point is not that Hart ignores customary legal norms but that he sometimes fails to acknowledge that they are an important part of his legal theory.

Hart starts his legal theory by explaining his "practice theory" of social rules. Hart's practice theory recognizes social patterns that present two features—patterns of conduct that are regularly followed by most members of the group and the "acceptance" of the normative characteristic of these social patterns that allow them to be called social norms. These social norms have both an external point of view and an internal point of view. The external point of view is that of an observer of the social patterns. The internal point of view is that of a participant, who exhibits both his acceptance of the social norms to guide his own conduct and his use of the social norms as a standard by which to criticize the conduct of others.[261]

Dworkin contends that good moral grounds are justification for doing what the legal system requires and this is the basis for converting the social conventions into legal rules. Hart maintains that Dworkin's explanation is not satisfactory. The social practices in question, he points out, may be morally neutral. The key issue from the point of view of making and criticizing judicial decisions is whether the customary rule has the force of law or is a customary rule that lacks the force of law. If it has the force of law, then applying the customary rule will result in a correct decision.

Hart's legal theory is designed to reflect multiple legal systems in many different countries and cultures. In order to do this, Hart is forced to downplay the complexity of the law in modern mature common-law nations.

Volume 4

The fourth volume in this series is entitled *The Judge and the Incorrect Decision*. This title is the result of the Supreme Court deciding on June 24, 2022, to overrule two well-established precedents—*Roe v. Wade* and *Planned Parenthood v. Casey*. In doing so, the Supreme Court declares that these two precedents were incorrect decisions, though they did not use this term. A decision is a correct decision if it is made by applying a rule of the pre-existing law and the decision does not materially modify the legal rule. If the decision is not a correct decision, it is an incorrect decision.

In *Dobbs v. Jackson Women's Health Organization*, the Supreme Court declared that the two precedents were wrongly decided. The reason given for their being wrongly decided is that they are declared to be inconsistent with the text of the Constitution and American history and traditions. As I will explain in *The Judge and the Incorrect Decision*, there is a profound and fundamental difference between a decision being incorrect and a decision being wrongly decided. The former is the result of an analytical process, while the latter must involve an evaluative process.

As the reader of the first three volumes in this series knows, any decision that is not a correct decision is an incorrect decision. It is an either/or choice. No decision is both correct and incorrect. Every decision is either correct or incorrect. The courts have authority to make incorrect decisions as well as correct decisions and incorrect decisions are authorized and binding. Being designated as an incorrect decision does not imply or suggest that the decision is not a good decision. It may, in fact, be the best decision that could have been made in that situation.

Every correct decision is presumptively justified. If the correct decision is not the best decision, the judge may create a new legal rule to be utilized to make the decision, and the decision will be an incorrect decision. The judge may decide to make a just decision or a wise decision. The just decision and/or the wise decision will be justified, according to my theory of creative positivism, even if it will not qualify as a correct decision, so long as the just decision and/or the wise decision will result in a better decision than the correct decision.

An incorrect decision can be reversed on appeal. At some point the decision, whether correct or incorrect, becomes a final decision. If it is published, it becomes a precedent. A precedent should not be overruled because it was an incorrect decision when it was made. The judicial culture treats reversal on appeal as a different process from overruling an established precedent.

The judicial culture also includes a customary norm that provides the authority for judges to create new legal rules, such as the legal rule created to make the alternate source decision. The legal rule created to make an incorrect decision may be grounded in legal principles, policies, standards and values. As I explain in more detail in *The Judge and the Incorrect Decision*, there are several problems associated with a precedent being overruled because the decision was incorrect when it was made.

First, the incorrect decision, as I am defining it, is an authorized and binding decision. It is also authoritative. Second, as I already mentioned, there is a difference between reversing a decision and overruling a precedent. The Supreme Court's decision in *Dobbs v. Jackson Women's Health Organization*, which is the decision overruling *Roe and Casey*, ignores this distinction. Third, the Court in *Dobbs* uses an inappropriate test for overruling the two precedents. The Court, in the majority opinion in *Dobbs*, refers to the text of the Constitution, and American history and tradition. This test, if applied to multiple well-established precedents, would result in a massive rewriting of American legal history.

The decisions that would be in jeopardy if the Court's test were applied to the overruling of precedents would include, for example, the following important and significant well-established precedents. *Gideon v. Wainwright* is a 1963 decision. It overruled *Betts v. Brady*, a 1942 decision. In the *Betts* case, the Supreme Court decided that the text of the Constitution was not intended to apply to states regarding the right to counsel. The Sixth Amendment recognizes the right to counsel in federal courts. In state courts, according to *Betts*, the appointment of counsel is not a fundamental right. The Framers of the Fourteenth Amendment did not, according to *Betts*, intend to include within that Amendment the application of the Sixth Amendment right to counsel to apply in state courts. Florida law, which was applicable in the *Gideon* case, provides for appointment of counsel only for poor defendants.

In *Gideon*, the Supreme Court looks to the due process clause of the Fourteenth Amendment and applies the Sixth Amendment right to counsel to state courts. It overrules *Betts* in doing so. The Supreme Court in *Gideon* admits that the Framers of the Constitution intended the Sixth Amendment right to counsel to apply only to the federal courts. There is no reference in the majority opinion in *Gideon* to the intent of the Framers of the Fourteenth Amendment. There is also nothing in the text of the Fourteenth Amendment in the due process clause that would qualify as a legal rule that may be cited to support the decision in *Gideon*.

Moreover, U.S. history and tradition do not provide support for the constitutional right to counsel in state courts. Instead of text, history and tradition supporting the *Gideon* decision, the majority opinion refers to "reason and reflection". The concurring opinion by Justice Harlan refers to the evolution of the law since the decision in *Betts*. Therefore, he agrees with the majority that it is not history and tradition that supports overruling *Betts*. Based upon the reasoning in the *Dobbs* case, *Gideon* is an incorrect decision and *Betts* should be reinstated because *Betts* is consistent with the text, history and tradition and *Gideon* is not.[262]

The second decision that illustrates that the Supreme Court in overruling *Roe and Casey* is utilizing the wrong test for doing so is *Miranda v. Arizona*.[263] *Miranda* is similar to *Gideon* in that it also involves a constitutional right that is applicable in the federal courts but not in the state courts. The issue in *Miranda* concerns custodial interrogation and the admissibility of confessions or other information obtained in questioning of criminal defendants. Historically, confessions made when the defendant is in custody without warnings being given to the defendant regarding the introduction at trial of their statements into evidence were not admissible in federal court. But they were admissible in state courts if voluntarily given.

The Fifth Amendment to the Constitution provides the right to remain silent, commonly called the privilege against self-incrimination. The question in *Miranda*, as in *Gideon*, is whether this right is included within the due process clause of the Fourteenth Amendment and is thereby made applicable to the state courts. The Framers of the Fourteenth Amendment did not include the issue of custodial interrogation specifically in the language of the Amendment. Therefore, it could be argued that it is not in the text of the Constitution, as far as admissibility of confessions without specific warnings in state courts is concerned.

In addition, providing the warnings against the use of confessions is not part of the history and tradition of the methodology of state police organizations. Some states could have statutes controlling the questioning of persons who were arrested, but *Miranda* concerns the practices in multiple states that did not have such statutes. The majority opinion reviews the history of interrogations involved in police practices in the various states. The majority opinion encourages Congress and the States to adopt rules to protect the rights of individuals "while promoting efficient enforcement of our criminal laws".[264]

Until such time as Congress and the States adopt the necessary rules, the Supreme Court lays out in canonical fashion the rules that must be followed. These rules, item by item, constitute what has come to be referred to as "the *Miranda* warnings". The Court's instructions to the local police agencies are very clear and direct:

> The warnings required and the waiver necessary in accordance with our opinion today are, in the absence of a fully effective equivalent, prerequisites to the admissibility of any statement made by a defendant.[265]

The Court then compares its instructions with the practices of the Federal Bureau of Investigation and the opinion contains the questions asked by the Court of the FBI and the answers provided.[266]

The Court also recites the English and the Scottish instructions. The Court acknowledges again that the Congress and the States have the opportunity to adopt their own sets of rules, so long as the protection to the defendants is as efficacious as the rules promulgated by the Court in *Miranda*. The Court considers the facts in the four cases it is deciding and finds in three of the four cases that the police interrogation was improper.

The majority opinion mentions "the nature of the problem" and "its recurrent significance". Consequently, it is fair to conclude that the history and tradition of the state police practices do not include acknowledging that the rights of the defendants are adequately protected if the *Miranda* warnings, in their exact canonical terminology, are not recited. History and tradition are disregarded because new rules have to be enacted. The rules that are adopted must be in the exact language prescribed by the Court, or its equivalent if the rules are created by the Congress or the various States.

Justice Clark files a dissenting opinion in *Miranda* because he cannot "join in the Court's criticism of the present practices of police and investigatory agencies as to custodial interrogation".[267] Once again, those present practices are the history and tradition of the then current state of law enforcement. It is those practices (that history and tradition) that the Court wants to change. Justice Clark quotes from the majority opinion that "we might not find the defendants' statements [here] to have been involuntary in traditional terms".[268]

Justice White also writes a dissenting opinion. He points out that the history of the privilege and the language of the Fifth Amendment do not relate to custodial interrogation.[269] Rather, they are concerned with the right to counsel at trial and to the compelling of testimony in a trial. Therefore, both the text and the history do not support the imposition of the *Miranda* warnings. In addition, the Court, according to Justice White, has failed to look at the consequences of its decision. Though he does not use these words, according to Justice Clark, this is not a wise decision.

There are many other cases that illustrate that the test of text, history and tradition does not reflect judicial practices. My point is not that *Gideon* and *Miranda* are bad decisions. They are both efforts to resolve what the Supreme Court viewed as defects in current practices. Their focus is on solving problems. If you consider only text, history and tradition, and you ignore justice and the consequences of the legal rule being created and the effect of the decision upon the society, you may not make a good decision. The Supreme Court should overrule a precedent only if it has a good reason to do so.

The due process clause of the Fourteenth Amendment is a broad concept (maybe even a principle) and its text, history and tradition is not entirely clear. The current Supreme Court does not apply the same approach to the equal protection clause as it is adopting in *Dobbs* regarding the due process clause. The Supreme Court, in order to be consistent, will have to reexamine many of its decisions relating to how the equal protection clause will be interpreted in cases involving issues concerning racial discrimination. For example, affirmation actions taken to enhance racial equality should be viewed as consistent with the text, history and tradition of the equal protection clause and the purpose and intent of the drafters of the Fourteenth Amendment.

In other words, the text, history and tradition of the equal protection clause is much more determinate than that of the due process clause. One of the unintended consequences of the Supreme Court's concept of constitutional interpretation will result not only in inconsistency with well-established due process precedents but also with a different approach to equal protection issues.

Read *The Judge and the Incorrect Decision* for a full explanation of why the *Dobbs* decision is incompatible with previous judicial practices (the legal culture) and prudent judicial decision-making. This book will be published sometime in 2023 or 2024.

APPENDIX B: References and notes for the indictment in section 3.11

Note: Numbers in parentheses are to the 130 statements in the indictment.

Alternate electors:
See section 2.4.

Defendant used dishonesty, fraud, and deceit to organize the alternate electors, get them to sign false certificates, and to submit them to Congress. (47-52)

Trump and Eastman told many potential alternate electors that the certificates signed by the alternate electors would be used only if the voter fraud lawsuits were successful.

Arizona (14-19):
See section 2.5.

The campaign manager told Co-conspirator 1 that the claim that there was fraud in the election was false.

Trump called the Arizona House Speaker on December 4 to request that the legislature decertify the State's legitimate electors. He replied that there was no fraud. Co-conspirator 2 said that he did not know enough about the facts on the ground but that he should decertify "and let the courts sort it out". He refused and asked for evidence of fraud.

On January 6, Trump claimed that 36,000 non-citizens had voted in Arizona.

Regarding the certificate of the Arizona alternate electors, see Bender, William and Tamari, Jonathan, "Was Doug Mastriano Trump's Pa. 'point person' in fake elector plot? Or barely involved? Campaign remains silent…" *The Philadelphia Inquirer*, July 22, 2022.

Co-conspirators:
For Jeffrey Clark, see Endnote 68.
For Kenneth Chesebro, see sections 2.1 and 3.7.

Costa, Robert, Legage, Robert, Triay, Andres, and Kates, Graham, "Who Are The Co-Conspirators in Trump's Jan. 6 Incitements," *CBS News, August 3, 2023*

Bailey, Holly, et al., "Here are the Trump co-conspirators described in the DOJ incitement," *Washington Post*, August 1, 2023

See also Roebuck, Jeremy and Seidman, Andrew, "Trump indictment: A Philly strategist played a 'major operational role' in Trump's fake elector scheme," *The Philadelphia Inquirer*, August 2, 2023. This article identifies Mike Roman, a former GOP ward leader in Philadelphia as the possible Co-conspirator 6. The article states the following:

> Roman took on more responsibility in the aftermath of the November election. Giuliani, serving as a lawyer for Trump at the time, tapped him as 'the lead' for organizing the slates of fake Trump electors from key battleground states, according to emails obtained by Congress.

It is known that he has talked to federal prosecutors. Roman is mentioned in *Endnote 33*.

Crimes charged in the indictment:

Count 1—Conspiracy to defraud the United States, 18 U.S.C. Section 371

Count 2—Conspiracy to obstruct an official proceeding, 18 U.S.C. Section 1512(k)

Count 3—Obstruction of and attempt to obstruct an official proceeding, 18 U.S.C. Section 1512©(2).2

Count 4—Conspiracy against rights, 18 U.S.C. Section 241

Bunch, Will, "It's justice that Trump, who wanted to toss Black votes, gets charged un a KKK Act," *The Philadelphia Inquirer*, August 4, 2023

Tucker, Eric, "Donald Trump indicted for efforts to overturn 2020 election and block transfer of power," *Associated Press*, August 1, 2023

Fraudulent claims made to the alternate electors:
Hasen, Rick, "'Fake' elector plot raised concerns over legal peril, indictment shows," *Election Law Blog*, August 7, 2023, about the article with the same title that appeared in *Washington Post*, on August 7, 2023.

Georgia (20-33):
See Endnote 46.
Giuliani appeared at a subcommittee meeting in Georgia. He claimed that dead people had voted there. He showed a misleading video. He showed the video at a hearing and accused election workers of fraud.

In a now-famous phone call with Georgia election officials, Trump asked that they find 11,780 additional votes in a phone call that the Georgia Secretary of State recorded.

Trump made statements the next day about the phone call that were false.

He repeated the claims of voting fraud in Georgia on January 6.

Georgia lawsuit:
See Endnote 46.
Walfe, Jan and McWhirter, Cameron, "Donald Trump Faces Looming Threat of Racketeering Charges in Georgia case," *Wall Street Journal*, August 7, 2023.

Michigan (34-42):
Trump claimed that election workers in Detroit had delivered phony ballots that were counted.

Trump repeated these claims in meetings with Michigan Republican legislators. They denied that there was fraud.

Giuliani requested that hearings be held and that the electors be decertified.

Pence Card:

I describe the Eastman memos and the interactions with Pence in *section 2.2* and *Chapter Three.* See in addition to 2.2, *sections 2.3, 3.3 and 3.4.*

The Eastman memos are also described in the indictment.
Blanchet, Ben, "'Not a Smart Move': Ex-Prosecutor Spots Trump Attorney's 'Admission" in Jan. 6 Case," *HuffPost*, August 4, 2023 about John Lauro, Trump's attorney, stating in an interview on television that Trump wanted Pence to delay the proceedings to count the votes for 10 days, which admission is admissible in evidence and the delay would be a criminal offense.

Pennsylvania (42-52):

See section 2.6.

Trump claimed fraud in Philadelphia in the vote count.

On November 15, Giuliani held a meeting in Gettysburg with state legislators and made false claims of voter fraud.

In Pennsylvania, notwithstanding the claims of voter fraud in Philadelphia, the Republican officials responded that there was no fraud. They placed a disclaimer in the certificate that the alternate electors signed indicating that it would take effect only if there was a successful lawsuit establishing fraud. Here is the disclaimer that was included in the Pennsylvania alternate elector certificate:

> We, the undersigned, on the understanding that if, as a result of a trial, non-appealable Court Order, or other proceeding prescribed by law, we are ultimately recognized as being the duly elected and qualified Electors
> …

See Bender, William and Tamari, Jonathan, "Was Doug Mastriano Trump's Pa. 'point person' in fake elector plot? Or barely involved? Campaign remains silent," *The Philadelphia Inquirer*, July 22, 2022. This article also states that other Pennsylvanians besides Bunny Welsh (who I said in the text and endnotes refused to sign the certificate) also refused to sign the certificate.

Bender, William and McGoldrick, Gillian, "'POTUS just called me': Pa. GOP emails shed new light on 2020 election upheaval," *The Philadelphia Inquirer*, June 16, 2023. The subtitle is as follows: "The emails show how conspiracy theories permeated the Legislature. One lawmaker said a fellow Republican was spreading 'crazy' and 'hurting our party' by trying to invalidate millions of votes."

Roebuck, Jeremy and Seidman, Andrew, "Trump indictment: Charges feature former president's effort to subvert Pennsylvania election results," *The Philadelphia Inquirer*, August 1, 2023

Sentence:
Orden, Erica, "641 years behind bars? No, but Trump's risk of prison is real," *Politico*, August 2, 2023. If Trump is convicted, the maximum sentence is high. But there is no mandatory minimum sentence for any of the crimes for which he has been charged. In my opinion, there is very little chance that Trump will get a prison sentence. At most, there may be fines and house confinement for several years.

Supreme Court:
Bolton, Alexander, "Legal experts predict Supreme Court won't spare Trump from trial and verdict," *The Hill*, August 7, 2023

Chen, Fran, "Trump wants Supreme Court to 'intercede' in legal fights," *CNN Politics*, August 4, 2023

Vlachou, Martha, "Trump Calls on The Supreme Court He Stacked to Intervene in His Criminal Cases," *Yahoo News*, August 4, 2023

Trial judge:

Rabinowitz, Hannah, and Cohen, Marshall, "The judge who will preside over Trump's criminal 2020 election case is no stranger to January 6 litigation," *CNN Politics*, August 4, 2023.

The trial judge assigned to the indictment case is Tanya Chutkan. She has heard dozens of January 6 defendant cases.

Trump's role in the January 6 riot:

Trump told his advisors that the crowd on January 6 would be angry. (88).

Trump issued a false public statement that he and Pence are in total agreement that the Vice President has the power to act. (89).

To keep pressure on Pence, Trump had Giuliani and Eastman speak to the mob on January 6.

Wisconsin (47-52):

See section 3.7.

Even though the Wisconsin Supreme Court decided that there was no fraud in their election, Trump continued to claim that there was.

Notes

Chapter One: Electing the US President

[1] The written Constitution is a document. In addition to the words in the document, there are other concepts that are generally considered to be so engrained in the legal system that they are also part of the Constitution, though they are not written in the document that we refer to as the Constitution. For example, we will discuss in several sections in this book *Roper v. Simmons*, 543 U.S. 551 (2005). Justice Kennedy mentions these additional factors in the majority opinion of the U.S. Supreme Court: "The prohibition against 'cruel and unusual punishments' [in the Eighth Amendment to the Constitution] like other expansive language in the Constitution, must be interpreted according to its text, by considering history, tradition, and precedent, and with due regard for its purpose and function in the constitutional design." *Id.* at 560-61. Justice Kennedy's method of constitutional interpretation helps us to understand the following constitutional concepts that are not explicitly mentioned in the written Constitution: federalism, separation of powers, checks and balances, the peaceful transfer of power, specific guarantees for the accused in criminal cases, and broad provisions that give rise to additional individual freedoms and constitutional rights.

[2] Article II, Section 1 of the U.S. Constitution.

[3] Article I, Section 3 of the Constitution: "The Vice President of the United States shall be President of the Senate but shall have no vote unless they be equally divided."

[4] Article 1, Section 1 of the U.S. Constitution. See also Conrad, Emily, *The Faithless? The Untold Story of the Electoral College.*

The reasoning for this system for electing the president and the vice president is explained and defended in the Federalist Papers. Federalist No. 68 is by Alexander Hamilton and is titled "The Mode of Electing the President":

"The method of electing the president has not received as much criticism as many of the other constitutional provisions. In order to ensure that the voice of the people is heard, the election of the president is not assigned to any preestablished body. Instead, the president will be chosen by people who are assembled for this specific purpose and at the time of making the decision. This group is more likely to make the right choice because it will be a small number of people selected for this purpose who will have the necessary information and discernment.

"It is preferable to have the selection not made by one person but by a small group of people. Since the electors will be chosen in each state and will vote in the state in which they are chosen, 'this detached and divided situation will expose them much less to heats and ferments, which might be communicated from them to the people, than if they were all to be convened at one time, in one place.'"

The goal was to make it more difficult for foreign influence to affect the selection: "They have not made the appointment of the President to depend on any preexisting bodies of men, who might be tampered with beforehand to prostitute their votes; but they have referred it in the first instance to an immediate act of the people of America, to be exerted in the choice of persons for the temporary and sole purpose of making the appointment. And they have excluded from eligibility for this trust, all those who from situation might be suspected of too great devotion to the President in office. No senator, representative, or other person holding a place of trust or profit under the United States, can be of the numbers of the electors."

Since the electors will be meeting in separate locations, it will be more difficult for corruption to occur. Another important factor is that the president should be independent when he seeks reelection, and it should be the people who decide if he should continue in office. This procedure will avoid his reliance upon certain people because reelection will depend upon a special body of representatives, selected in each state for the single purpose of making this decision. A majority of the votes will be required to be elected. If there is no majority, the House may choose from among the five persons who received the most votes. The Senate selects the Vice President in the same manner as the House selects the President.

[6] Amendment XII of the U.S. Constitution: "The Electors shall meet in their respective states and vote by ballot for President and Vice President…" There will be separate ballots for President and Vice President.

[7] Section 1 of Amendment XV of the U.S. Constitution: "The right of citizens of the United States to vote shall not be denied or abridged by the United States or by any State on account of race, color, or previous condition of servitude."

[8] Amendment XIX of the U.S. Constitution: "The right of citizens of the United States to vote shall not be denied or abridged by the United States or by any State on account of sex."

[9] Section 1 of Amendment XXIV of the U.S. Constitution: "The right of citizens of the United States to vote in any primary or other election for President or Vice President, for electors for President or Vice President, or for Senator or Representative in Congress, shall not be denied or abridged by the United States or any State by reason of failure to pay poll tax or other tax."

[10] Section 1 of Amendment XXVI: "The right of citizens of the United States, who are eighteen years of age or older, to vote shall not be denied or abridged by the United States or by any State on account of age."

[11] The Electoral Count Act of 1877 is codified in *3 USCA* Chapter 1.

[12] This issue is resolved in *Bush v. Gore*, 531 U.S. 98 (2000), discussed in section 1.4. For the state's determination to be

binding on Congress, it must be made pursuant to a state statute that was adopted prior to Election Day. The Supreme Court ruled in *Bush v. Gore* that Florida had not established a recount procedure within the safe harbor deadline so that the recount ordered by the Florida courts did not satisfy the requirement in the Act. The decision ended the election contest when the Democratic candidate, Albert Gore, conceded that he had lost the election.

[13] In the contest resolved in *Bush v. Gore*, Florida submitted a "Certificate of Final Determination of Contests Concerning the Appointment of Presidential electors." This is a Florida procedure. We need not discuss that aspect of the case.

[14] For example, according to "Electoral Count Act" in *Wikipedia*, the standard is whether the certificate has been "regularly given" by the elector. Examples could be that the governor of the state did not certify the votes properly pursuant to the ascertainment process, or the votes themselves did not qualify as having been "regularly given". For the latter, there could be bribery or corruption, mistake or fraud, or the elector did not satisfy constitutional or statutory requirements (for example, the elector held federal office as a senator).
https://en.wikipedia.org/wiki/Electoral_Count_Act#

[15] *"Bush v. Gore," Wikipedia*:
https://en.wikipedia.org/wiki/Bush_v._Gore

[16] *Bush v. Gore*, 531 U.S. 98 (2000)

[17] *Bush v. Gore*, 531 U.S. 98 (2000). Another case in which the U.S. Supreme Court reversed a state's top-ranking election official's ruling that the state's mail-in ballots had been legally counted occurred regarding a 2021 election. It illustrates again the conflict between federal and state law. The acting Secretary of State in Pennsylvania interpreting state law ruled that county election officials should count mail-in votes that arrive in exterior envelopes with inaccurate or nonexistent handwritten dates.

The Third Circuit Court of Appeals held that mail-in ballots without a required date on the return envelope had to be counted in a 2021 Pennsylvania election involving judicial candidates. According to the Court of Appeals, the requirement of the date is immaterial so long as the vote was cast in a timely manner.

The Supreme Court reversed the decision of the Court of Appeals in a 7-2 decision. The Supreme Court did not decide whether the votes should or should not have been counted. The result is that the decision of the Court of Appeals is not a precedent and state law, consequently, remains the same as it was before this case was decided. See Weber, Lindsay, "U.S. Supreme Court rules against use of undated mail-in ballots prompted by Lehigh County candidate," *Daily Local*, October 12, 2022.

The sub-heading of the article is as follows: "It threw out a lower-court's ruling allowing undated mail-in ballots to be counted in the judge's race David Ritter lost." It did not change the outcome of the election. *See also* "U.S. Supreme Court vacates key ruling that allowed undated Pa. mail-in ballots to be counted," *Pittsburgh Post-Gazette*, October 11, 2022. As this article points out, "the high court decision did not affect a separate previous ruling by the Commonwealth Court [an intermediate appellate court in Pennsylvania] in favor of counting ballots without properly dated exterior ballots." The state law is clear, while the federal law remains unsettled. State law allows local boards to decide the issue. Local rules control many aspects of the election process. See section 3.7.

The case is *Ritter, David v. Micliori,* No. 22-30. decided on October 11, 2022. See "SCOTUS Vacates Ruling Requiring Counties of PA Undated Mail-in Ballots," *Democracy Docket*, October 11, 2022:
https://www.democracydocket.com/news-alerts/scotus-vacates-ruling-requiring-counting-of-pa-undated-mail-in-ballots/

Here are the instructions to the local boards of election described in this article: "On Tuesday, Oct. 11, the Pennsylvania acting secretary of state released a statement that counties are 'expected to include undated ballots in their official returns for the

Nov. 8 [2022] election.' The secretary notes that the 'order from the U.S. Supreme Court does not affect the prior decision of [the] Commonwealth Court in any way. It provides no justification for counties to exclude ballots based on a minor omission, and we expect that counties will continue to comply with their obligation to count all legal votes.'" See section 3.7.

[18] See section 6.2.

[19] *"Bush v. Gore,"* *Wikipedia*: "A number of legal scholars have agreed with the dissenters' argument that Bush failed to carry the 'heavy burden' of demonstrating a 'likelihood of irreparable harm.'" https://en.wikipedia.org/wiki/Bush_v._Gore

Chapter Two: The 2020 Presidential Election

[20] I will discuss the importance of customary rules to the election process in the sections which follow. An example of customary rules without the force of law in another subject matter comes from Issacson, Walter, *The Code Breakers,* which is about the rules regarding the use of CRISPR. The rules were created at a conference of academic scientific scholars and leaders.

[21] This comes from Woodward, Bob and Costa, Robert, *Peril:* "They [Secretary of the Department of Defense Esper and Chairman of the Joint Chiefs of Staff Milley] had a constitutional obligation to ensure the president was fully informed on his options. But once Trump decided and issued an order, they were required to execute it. The only exception was an illegal, immoral or unethical order. That would be the point at which someone might consider resigning Milley reasoned. But Milley could not recall a time in history when a cabinet official, one as essential as the secretary of defense, had angrily slapped a paper down on the Resolute Desk." *See also* Schmidt, Michael S., "In a call with Pelosi after the Capitol riot, Milley agreed that Trump was 'crazy,' book says," *New York Times,* September 28, 2021:
https://www.nytimes.com/2021/09/28/us/politics/in-a-call-with-

pelosi-after-the-capitol-riot-milley-agreed-that-trump-was-crazy.html

[22] Feuer, Alan, Haberman, Maggy and Brandvater, Luke, *N.Y. Times* article on February 2, 2022, entitled "Memos Show Roots of Trump's Focus on Jan. 6 and Alternate Electors." https://www.nytimes.com/2022/02/02/us/politics/trump-jan-6-memos.html

[23] Another article discussing these early memos was published on February 2, 2022, by American Oversight entitled "Legislative Leaders in Arizona, Wisconsin were sent memos regarding the ability of state lawmakers to alter selection of electors following 2020 election." Both memos declared that "state lawmakers cannot alter electors' selections or actions taken after an election." An attorney from the Wisconsin Legislative Reference Bureau wrote: "You have asked whether the legislature after a presidential election may affect the selection or actions of the state's presidential electors." The attorney explained that the legislature cannot retroactively change the selection or actions of presidential electors:

"On Dec. 14, 2020, the day of the Electoral College's official vote, Republicans in Wisconsin, Arizona and five other states that Trump had lost met to submit to Congress phony certificates declaring themselves the true electors, either outright or contingent upon court decisions finding the elections to have been compromised by fraud (an outcome for which there was and is no evidence)."

The two memos submitted to the legislators in Wisconsin and Arizona resulted in advice being given that there was no way that alternate electors could change the election results: https://www.americanoversight.org/legislative-leaders-in-arizona-wisconsin-were-sent-memos-regarding-the-ability-of-state-lawmakers-to-alter-selection-of-electors-following-2020-election

[24] See "Eastman Memos," *Wikipedia*. Eastman impressed former President Trump by his views on immigration law. John R. Bolton, the former national security advisor, said that Mr. Trump was

listening to an outsider "without the institutional learning that has gone on for a couple of hundred years that undergirds the advice that is normally given to presidents that keep them in safe channels." Eastman's view on immigration is that Trump "could use his executive authority to impose limits on birthright citizenship—the fundamental concept that anyone born in the United States is automatically a citizen—by saying it should not be applied to people born in the United States to noncitizens." Eastman also suggested that Kamala Harris could not legally become president because her parents had not been born in the United States. https://en.wikipedia.org/wiki/Eastman_memos

[25] Schmidt, Michael S. and Hagerman, Maggie, "The Lawyer Behind the Memo on How Trump Could Stay in Office," *The New York Times,* published on October 2, 2021, and updated on November 8, 2021. https://www.nytimes.com/2021/10/02/us/politics/john-eastman-trump-memo.html

[26] I first read about these memos in Chapter Thirty-Eight in Woodward, Bob and Costa, Robert, *Peril.*

[27] See section 6.2 where non-justiciability is discussed.

[28] See "Eastman Memos" in *Wikipedia.* https://en.wikipedia.org/wiki/Eastman_memos. *See also* Feuer, Alan, Haberman, Maggie, and Brandvater, Luke, "Memos Show Roots of Trump's Focus on Jan. 6 and Alternate Electors," *New York Times,* February 2, 2022. https://www.nytimes.com/2022/02/02/us/politics/trump-jan-6-memos.html. *See also* Jacobs, Ben, "Trump found the holes in our election laws. Congress is trying to patch them," *Vox,* September 13, 2022: "The other effort to exploit the ECA [Electoral Count Act] was the one to persuade Pence to throw out electoral votes. It was a last-ditch effort to unilaterally reject certified electoral votes for Biden from certain states. If pro-Trump electoral voters could not be manufactured, this could at least invalidate enough Biden votes to throw the race into a joint session of Congress." The roots for this strategy recall the 1876 election: "The fake elector effort was

an attempt to trigger an 1876-type crisis by forcing Congress to decide between two competing sets of returns from competitive states. However, the process was so bungled and so lacking in any validity or political support from key players that it did not come to fruition." *Ibid.* https://www.vox.com/policy-and-politics/2022/9/13/23344990/electoral-count-reform-act

[29] See Chapter Thirty-Eight in Woodward, Bob and Costa, Robert, *Peril.*

[30] Woodward, Bob and Costa, Robert, *Peril*, Chapter 44.

[31] *Gohmert v. Pence*, 510 F. Supp. 3d 435 (E.D. Tex. 2021).

[32] Hellerman, Rosalind S., "How the Trump elector slates took shape," *Washington Post*, reprinted in *The Philadelphia Inquirer,* January 21, 2022. https://www.washingtonpost.com/politics/2022/06/20/trump-documents-fake-elector-plan/.

John Eastman not only wrote the memos, but he also was an active participant in trying to convince the state legislators to implement his program:

"Eastman spent the final weeks of the Trump administration stoking false claims of election fraud in order to put pressure on GOP-led state legislatures to appoint alternate slates of presidential electors. In Eastman's view, those alternate slates would form the basis of a dispute that only Pence could resolve. But no state legislatures agreed to appoint those alternate electors." Cheney, Kyle, "He [Eastman] devised a fringe legal theory to try to keep Trump in power. Now he's on the verge of being disbarred," *Politico*, June 11, 2023. *See also* fn. 83.

[33] Haberman, Maggie and Broadwater, Luke, "'Kind of Wild/Creative': Emails Shed Light on Trump Fake Electors Plan," *The New York Times,* July 26, 2022. Here are some other statements from this article:

"In emails reviewed by The New York Times and authenticated by people who had worked for the Trump campaign at the time [when they were planning to arrange for Trump to be the winner of the election rather than Biden], one lawyer involved in the detailed discussions repeatedly used the word 'fake' to refer to the so-called electors, who were intended to provide Vice President Mike Pence and Mr. Trump's allies in Congress a rationale for derailing the congressional process of certifying the outcome. And the lawyers working on the proposal made clear they knew that the pro-Trump electors they were putting forward might not hold up to legal scrutiny.

"We would just be sending in 'fake' electoral votes to Pence so that 'someone' in Congress can make an objection when they start counting votes, and start arguing that the 'fake' votes could be counted, . . .

"Mr. Epshteyan [the coordinator for people inside and outside the Trump campaign and the White House], the emails show, was a regular point of contact for John Eastman,...

"Mr. Epshteyan and Mr. Roman [director of Election Day operations for Mr. Trump's campaign], the emails show, coordinated with others who played roles in advising Mr. Trump.

"The House committee investigating the Jan. 6 attack on the Capitol has produced evidence that Mr. Trump was aware of the electors' plan.

"His idea [the idea of Kenneth Chesebro, an ally of John Eastman] is basically that all of us (GA, WI, AZ, PA, etc.) have our electors send in their votes (even though the votes aren't legal under federal law—because they're not signed by the Governor); so that members of Congress can fight about whether they should be counted on January 6th..."
https://www.nytimes.com/2022/07/26/us/politics/trump-fake-electors-emails.html

Vice President Mike Pence asserts that the Trump team and Trump himself knew that Eastman's strategy was flawed and that what they were doing was illegal. "Mr. Eastman [at the January 4 meeting] repeatedly qualified his argument, saying it was only a legal theory. I [Pence] asked, 'Do you think I have the authority to reject or return votes?' He [Eastman] stammered, 'Well, it's never been tested in the courts, so I think it is an open question.' . . .I [Pence] later learned that Mr. Eastman had conceded to my general counsel that rejecting electoral votes was a bad idea and any attempt to do so would be quickly overturned by a unanimous Supreme Court. That guy didn't even believe what he was telling the president." Pence, Mike, "My Last Days With Donald Trump," *Wall Street Journal*, November 13, 2022. https://www.wsj.com/articles/donald-trump-mike-pence-jan-6-president-rally-capitol-riot-protest-vote-count-so-help-me-god-stolen-election-11668018494

[34] See Farmouth, Amiri, "Jan. 6 committee subpoenas fake Trump electors in 7 states, including Pennsylvania," *The Philadelphia Inquirer,* January 22, 2022: "The House Committee investigating the U.S. Capitol insurrection subpoenaed more than a dozen individuals Friday who it said falsely tried to declare Donald Trump the winner of the 2020 election in seven swing states.

"We believe that the individuals we have subpoenaed today have information about how those so-called alternate electors met and who were behind that scheme." https://www.inquirer.com/politics/nation/jan-6-committee-fake-trump-electors-20220128.html

See also Barrett, Devlin and Wingett Sanchez, Yvonne, "Arizona fake-electors subpoenas show breadth of DOJ Jan. 6 probe," *The Washington Post,* July 25, 2022. https://www.washingtonpost.com/national-security/2022/07/25/fann-townsend-subpoenas-arizona-trump/

After the election, Trump called Republican National Committee chairwoman Ronna McDaniel and asked her for help from the RNC in identifying potential Trump alternate electors in various states. Ali, Shirin, "What Exactly Was the Fake Electors Scheme," *Slate*, July 22, 2023.

[35] An aide for Republican Senator Ron Johnson attempted to hand to Vice President Pence a few minutes before the Congress met on

January 6 for the electoral college vote count the certificates of the alternate electors. Ali, Shirin, "What Exactly Was the Fake Electors Scheme," *Slate*, July 22, 2023.

[36] This group of alternate electors is one of the groups discussed in Section 2.4.

[37] *Gohmert v. Pence*, 510 F. Supp. 3d 435 (E.D. Tex. 2021).

[38] This is where the risk to the entire electoral system is at its highest. I will address this issue in Section 3.6.

[39] The Electoral Count Act of 1887, 3 U.S.C. Section 5, 15. This statute should be amended to incorporate the provisions that are necessary to ensure that there is a peaceful transition of power after the presidential election and that the electors in the states vote in accordance with the popular vote in their state. A more dramatic reform would be to make the vote for president a national vote and the winner of the national popular vote would be the president. It is the ambiguities in this statute that John Eastman relied upon to support his theories about why Biden should not be the president. See section 1.3.

[40] See the discussion of the faithless electors in section 3.4.

[41] *Gohmert v. Pence*, 510 F. Supp. 3d 435 (E.D. Tex. 2021.)

[42] The plaintiffs appealed to the Fifth Circuit Court of Appeals, which affirmed the decision of the District Court. The Court of Appeals order is an unpublished order, so the decision is not a precedent. The opinion is only one paragraph. The District Court is affirmed for the reasons stated by the District Court. The Court of Appeals expresses no view on the underlying merits of the case, and it gives no reasons for its decision. I discuss non-publication of judicial decisions in section 5.6.

[43] Additional information comes from Bunch, Will, "What fake 2020 Electoral College certificates tell us about America's fragile democracy," *Philadelphia Inquirer*, January 13, 2022: https://www.inquirercom/search/?query=will%20bunch

[44] *Ibid.* While the meeting was not publicized, it would be unfair to characterize it as a secret meeting. The Pennsylvania Republican

Party issued a press release about it. It was not known until much later, however, that the meeting was part of an organized campaign to overturn the election results. We also now know that Trump himself, after the election, called Bryan Cutler, the Republican leader of the Pennsylvania House, to solicit his help in support of the alternate elector strategy. Ali, Shirin, "What Exactly Was the Fake Electors Scheme," *Slate*, July 22, 2023.

[45] Carolyn "Bunny" Welsh, Delaware County, former Chester County sheriff was listed as one of the Republican Party's electors. See Albigles, Marie, "Meet Pennsylvania's Electoral College voters: Everything they can do—and can't do," *WHYY*, November 12, 2020: https://whyy.org/articles/meet-pennsylvanias-electoral-college-voters-everything-they-can-and-cant-do/

[46] *Ibid.* It is unlikely that there will be a prosecution of the Pennsylvania alternate electors. In contrast to this, there is likely to be an indictment of the Georgia alternate electors. Georgia Secretary of State Brad Raffensberger recorded a now-famous telephone call from Trump in which Trump asked him to "find 11,780 votes," the number that he thought he needed to win the election. There were two rounds of recounts in Georgia. Biden was the clear winner in every recount (there may also have been a third partial recount). The first recount reduced Biden's margin of victory from 14,186 votes to 12,284 votes. The second recount had Biden winning by 11,799 votes. See Cummings, William, Garrison, Joey and Sergent, Jim, "By the numbers: President Trump's failed efforts to overturn the election," *USA Today*, January 6, 2021. The Fulton County District Attorney Fani Willis has been conducting a criminal investigation for many months and it is expected that she will indict multiple parties for the efforts to overturn the election results in Georgia. The Arizona Attorney General Kris Mayes has also conducted a criminal investigation. See Ali, Shirin, "What Exactly Was the Fake Electors Scheme," *Slate*, July 22, 2023.

[47] The Pennsylvania statute is codified in 25 P.S. Electors & Electoral Districts, Section 2191, Election of presidential electors.

This statute was adopted in 1937 and applied to the 1940 election and subsequent presidential elections. It states that the number of electors in Pennsylvania will be the same as the number of members of the House of Representatives and two for the two U.S. Senators. For the 2020 election, Pennsylvania had 20 votes. The statute also provides that the electors will meet at 12:00 P.M. in Harrisburg on the day fixed by Congress. In other words, they will meet in accordance with the Electoral Count Act. The third section of the statute provides for the appointment of a replacement elector if the named elector cannot meet on the day the Electoral College meets. The fourth section provides for the electors to be paid $3.00 for the day they serve. They are also entitled to payment for mileage at the rate of three cents per mile from their home to Harrisburg. The statute presupposes that the electors are those persons whom the party which won the election picked to be the members of the Electoral College.

[48] "Pennsylvania state code doesn't say anything about so-called 'faithless electors,' or electors who cast a vote for a candidate other than the one who won the state popular vote." *Ibid.* See: https://whyy.org/articles/meet-pennsylvanias-electoral-college-voters-everything-they-can-and-cant-do/

[49] *Ibid.*

[50] I have the official agenda of the meeting and I have discussed it with Marian. I watched it on C-Span, and it is available there: https://www.c-span.org/video/?36137-1/pennsylvania-electoral-college-proceedings

[51] The twenty Electors are as follows (with the description of them in the Journal of the Proceedings of the 59th Pennsylvania Electoral College):

Nina Ahmad, Philadelphia, Former Philadelphia deputy mayor, defeated 2020 Democratic candidate for auditor general

Val Arkoosh, Montgomery County, Montgomery County Board of Commissioners chair

Cindy Bass, Philadelphia, Philadelphia City Council member

Rick Bloomingdale, Dauphin County, Pennsylvania AFL-CIO president

Ryan Boyer, Delaware County, Laborers District Council of the Metropolitan Area of Philadelphia, and Vicinity business manager

Daisy Cruz, Philadelphia, 32 BJ SEIU Mid-Atlantic District leader

Kathy Dahlkenper, Erie County, Erie County executive

Janet Diaz, Lancaster County, Lancaster City Council member; defeated 2020 Democratic candidate for state senate

Paige Gebhardt, Lackawanna County, Scranton mayor

Charles Hadley, Philadelphia, Former Democratic candidate for state House

Jordan Harris, Philadelphia, State representative

Malcolm Kenyatta, Philadelphia, State representative

Gerald Lawrence, Delaware County, Delaware County Board of Elections chair

Clifford Levine, Allegheny County, Attorney

Virginia McGregor, Lackawanna County, Democratic National Committee deputy national finance chair

Nancy Mills, Allegheny County, Pennsylvania Democratic Party chairwoman

Marian Moskowitz, Chester County, Chester County commissioner

Josh Shapiro, Montgomery County, Pennsylvania attorney general

Sharif Street, Philadelphia, State senator

Connie Williams, Delaware County, Former state senator.

Chapter Three: The Aftermath of the 2020 Election

[52] As I discussed in section 3.4 and will discuss in section 3.11, the certificates of the voting of the alternate electors were designed to appear just like the official certificates of the electors for Biden. In New Mexico and Pennsylvania, the certificates had an additional

paragraph that stated that the alternate electors would vote for Trump if he prevailed in the lawsuit in that state challenging the election of Biden. There were many lawsuits in all of the states except New Mexico, so one had to be filed there so that it would be possible to have a successful challenge to the election. None of the challenges in the seven battleground states were successful except for a small victory in Pennsylvania which did not affect the outcome of the election.

[53] See Cummings, William, Garrleon, Joey, and Sergent, Jim, "By the numbers: President Donald Trump's failed efforts to overturn the election," *USA Today*, January 6, 2021.

[54] *Gohmert v. Pence,* 510 F. Supp. 3d 435 (E.D. Tex. 2021). See sections 2.3 and 2.5. I return to this case in section 5.5. *See also* Nouvelade-Getty, Ellen, "Give Mike Pence 'Exclusive Authority' on Which Electoral College Votes to Count: Lawsuit," *Newsweek*, December 28, 2020. https://www.newsweek.com/give-mike-pence-exclusive-authority-which-electoral-college-votes-count-lawsuit-1557596

[55] The U.S. Supreme Court declined most of the writs of certiorari filed by Trump-endorsed lawsuits after the 2020 election. SCOTUS did consider two cases. *Texas v. Pennsylvania*, 592 U.S. _____ (2020) was filed by the Texas Attorney General under SCOTUS' original jurisdiction (when one state is suing another state). The defendants included, besides Pennsylvania, the States of Georgia, Michigan and Wisconsin. The contention was that these States had violated the Independent State Legislature theory by changing election procedures through non-legislative means.

The plaintiffs wanted to withhold temporarily counting the certified votes from these four states on December 14, 2020, when the Electoral College would meet. Over 100 Republican Representatives and 18 Republican state attorneys general filed motions in support of the Texas claims. SCOTUS issued orders on December 11, 2020, declining to hear the case. Texas lacked standing to challenge the results of the election held by another state. Alternatively, this could be viewed as lack of a cause of action because SCOTUS declared that Texas did not demonstrate "a judicially cognizable interest in the manner in which another state conducts its elections."

Justice Alito, joined by Justice Thomas, filed an opinion disagreeing with the ruling. As I will discuss in *The Judge and the Incorrect Decision*, this is obviously a case in which Justice Thomas should have recused himself.

The second case also involves Pennsylvania. Representative Mike Kelly and two other House candidates who attempted to decertify the results of the election in Pennsylvania. In *Kelly v. Pennsylvania*, 592 U.S. _____ (2020), in a one-sentence order, without comment or dissent, the request was denied.

The *Kelly* case is just one of a torrent of litigation over the conduct of the election in Pennsylvania. See Lai, Jonathan, "U.S. Supreme Court dismisses the last challenge over Pennsylvania's 2020 election," *Philadelphia Inquirer*, April 19, 2021.
[56] Republican Party of Pennsylvania v. Veronica Degraffenreid, Acting Secretary of Pennsylvania, and Jake Corman v. Pennsylvania Democratic Party, 592 U.S. ____ (2021). The petitions for writ of certiorari are denied. There is no opinion in regard to the denial except for the dissenting opinions. One is by Justice Thomas. Justice Alito also filed a dissenting opinion with whom Justice Gorsuch joined. See also Stern, Mark Joseph, "Clarence Thomas Promotes Trump's Voter Fraud Lies in Alarming Dissent," *Philadelphia Inquirer*, February 23, 2021, reprinted from *Slate*, February 22, 2021. https://slate.com/news-and-politics/2021/02/clarence-thomas-voter-fraud-trump-pennsylvania.html

For a review of several of the Trump lawsuits, see Blank, Jr., Mark, "The Litigious President" *New Matter*, 1st quarter, 2023.
[57] Nouvelade/Getty, Ellen, "Give Mike Pence 'Exclusive Authority' on Which Electoral College Votes to Count: Lawsuit," *Newsweek*, December 28, 2020. https://www.newsweek.com/give-mike-

pence-exclusive-authority-which-electoral-college-votes-count-lawsuit-1557596

[58] Whitney, Jake, "How Trump's Judges Stuck a Pin in the 'Stop the Steal' Balloon," *Daily Beast,* March 14, 2021. https://www.thedailybeast.com/how-trumps-judges-stuck-a-pin-in-the-stop-the-steal-balloon

[59] Chung, Andrew and Hurley, Lawrence, "U.S. Supreme Court Formally Pulls the Plug on Election-Related Cases," *Reuters Wire Service Content,* February 22, 2021, printed in *U.S. Legal News,* February 23, 2021. https://www.reuters.com/article/us-usa-court-election/u-s-supreme-court-formally-pulls-the-plug-on-election-related-cases-idUSKBN2AM1S1

[60] Chapter 46 in Woodward, Bob and Costa, Robert, *Peril.*

[61] Nedio, Harper, "Judge questions Eastman's work for Trump amid House committee allegation," *The Hill*, March 6, 2022. The House Committee filed a 221-page brief that contained the following statement: "The committee said that it had evidence that Trump sought to obstruct an official proceeding—in this case the certification of the election results—by trying to strong-arm Pence to delay the proceedings so that there would be additional time to 'manipulate' the results." https://thehill.com/regulation/court-battles/597398-judge-questions-eastmans-work-for-trump-amid-house-committees/ *See also* Amimi, Farmush, Tucker, Eric and Jalonick, Mary Clare, "Jan. 6 panel sees evidence of Trump's 'criminal conspiracy,'" *Yahoo News,* March 3, 2022. https://www.yahoo.com/entertainment/jan-6-panel-claims-trump-031356056.html

As more emails became available, it has become clear that Trump was advised that he did not have proof of voter fraud and that his purpose in filing the lawsuits was to delay the counting of the electoral college votes. It has also become clear that John Eastman knew that his proposals for not counting the votes would not be sustained in any challenge to the votes in a judicial proceeding.

See the following articles:

Swan, Jonathan and Beau, Zachary, "Exclusive: Emails reveal warning to Trump team about fraud claims," *Axios*, October 22, 2022.

Cohen, Zachary and Snead, Tierney, "Trump knew voter fraud claims were wrong, federal judge says as he orders John Eastman's emails turned over," *CNN*, October 19, 2022

Cheney, Kyle and Gerstein, Josh, "Judge: Trump signed court document that knowingly included false voter fraud stats," *Politico*, October 19, 2022.

[62] Cohen, Marshall and Polantz, Katalyn, "Judge challenges John Eastman's privilege claims in hearing over January 6 documents," *CNN Politics*, March 8, 2022. Judge Carter questioned where the line is between legal advice and political strategizing. It was not clear what litigation Eastman was offering advice about when he sent the email messages. Eastman declared that the strategy would work because they were no longer playing by Queensbury Rules. https://www.cnn.com/2022/03/08/politics/eastman-documents-hearing/index.html

[63] *Eastman v. Thompson*, 594 F.Supp.3d 1156 (C.D.Cal. 2022).

[64] I discuss the prediction theory of law in EndNote 77 in Chapter Three of *The Judge and the Philosopher*.

[65] The crime is described in 18 U.S.C. Section 1512(c)(2). The Committee also claims that Trump and Eastman violated 18 U.S.C. Section 371 because they conspired to defraud the United States by disrupting the electoral count.

[66] See Jurecic, Quinta, "John Eastman and the Limits of Bar Discipline," *Lawfare* (February 2, 2023).

[67] Stone, Peter, "US investigators zone in on Trump election-plot lawyer John Eastman," *The Guardian* (July 4, 2023): https://www.theguardian.com/us-news/2023/jul/04/us-investigators-trump-election-plot-lawyer-john-eastman#

The subtitle of this article is "Experts say Eastman faces possible disbarment in California under increasing scrutiny in federal and state inquiries."

This meeting is discussed in Section 2.2.

As the article indicates, it is difficult to anticipate what charges will be filed by the Department of Justice: "It remains to be seen whether the fake electors' scheme will serve as the basis of a standalone indictment or whether it will be merged into a broader case involving the multiple ways Trump and his allies attempted to reverse the outcome of the 2020 election. . .

"A standalone case may have less jury appeal than a case in which it is one of many sets of tactics used to overturn the election, . . . but [he] noted that 'a broader case will almost inevitably be longer, more complex, include numerous defendants, and be more difficult to try." *Ibid*.

Trump has already been indicted by the Department of Justice for retaining hundreds of classified national security documents after he left office. This case is pending as of writing this book.
[68] "For example, amid pressure from bar authorities in Colorado, Trump attorney Jenna Ellis admitted in March [2023] that she had repeatedly misrepresented evidence about the integrity of the 2020 election. Rudy Giuliani's law license was suspended in December after D.C. bar disciplinary proceedings resulted in a finding that he violated professional ethics and rules. Giuliani's law license has also been suspended in New York. And former Justice Department attorney Jeffrey Clark is awaiting similar proceedings in Washington, which were cleared to proceed last week after an eight-month delay." Cheney, Kyle, "He devised a fringe legal theory to try to keep Trump in power. Now he's on the verge of being disbarred," *Politico*, June 11, 2023
[69] *Ibid*.
[70] See Stone, Peter, "US investigators zone in on Trump election-plot lawyer John Eastman," *The Guardian* (July 4, 2023):

https://www.theguardian.com/us-news/2023/jul/04/us-investigators-trump-election-plot-lawyer-john-eastman#

[71] "Willis has said she will announce charging decisions in August [2023], and experts say the Georgia inquiry looks poised to include criminal charges against Trump and some elite lawyers." *Ibid.*

[72] I discuss constitutional norms in section 1.1. I contend that constitutional principles, as distinct from other legal principles, may be viewed as part of the law because they have been enacted when they were included in the Constitution.

[73] Hernandez, Elizabeth, "John Eastman used CU email account to advise Pennsylvania legislator on challenging that state's 2020 election results," *The Denver Post*, May 10, 2022: https://www.denverpost.com/2022/05/10/john-eastman-cu-boulder-emails/

[74] *Ibid.*

[75] *Ibid.*

[76] Roebuck, Jenny, "Emails reveal plan to undo Pa. vote," *The Philadelphia Inquirer*, May 13, 2022. *See also* Amiri, Farmush, "How fake electors tried to flip election," *The Philadelphia Inquirer,* February 22, 2022.

[77] Amiri, Farmush, "Jan. 6 committee subpoenas fake Trump electors in 7 states, including Pennsylvania," *The Philadelphia Inquirer,* January 22, 2022:

"The House committee investigating the U.S. Capitol insurrection subpoenaed more than a dozen individuals Friday who it says falsely tried to declare Donald Trump the winner of the 2020 election in seven swing states.

"We believe that the individuals we have subpoenaed today have information about how those so-called alternate electors met and who were behind that scheme."
https://www.inquirer.com/politics/nation/jan-6-committee-fake-trump-electors-20220128.html

The Department of Justice has appointed a special prosecutor to investigate whether crimes have been committed as part of former

President Trump's efforts to overturn the election results. In addition, there are ongoing investigations in several of the seven battleground states. The investigation in Georgia appears likely to lead to indictments.

Regarding the alternate electors, in addition to their potential indictment in Georgia, the alternate electors have been indicted in Michigan. See Cohen, Zachary, Cohen, Marshall, Rabinowitz, Hannah, and Schneider, Jessica, "Michigan AG charges participants in 2020 fake elector plot," *CNN politics,* July 19, 2023:

"The group of electors from Michigan include current and former state GOP officials, the Republican National Committee member, a sitting mayor, a school board member and Trump supporters who were the plaintiffs in a frivolous lawsuit that tried to overturn the 2020 results.

"The 16 fake GOP electors from Michigan met in Lansing on December 14, 2020, and signed certificates falsely proclaiming that Trump won the state and they were the rightful electors." https://www.cnn.com/2023/07/21/politics/michigan-fake-electors-charging-documents/index.html

[78] See Conrad Emily, *The Faithless? The Untold Story of the Electoral College.*

[79] *Ibid.* Conrad discusses the study conducted every four years by a professor from North Ohio University. He suggests that there could be as many as 37 Republican electors who would not vote for Trump or who were considering whether to vote for Trump in the 2016 election. Trump in 2016 received 306 Electoral College votes. There were faithless electors in 2016 but not enough to overturn the result. Jim McErlane, one of the Trump electors in the 2016 election (in Pennsylvania) told me that he received 7,000 pieces of mail, 87,000 emails, and ten people came to his house and knocked on his front door, all of which urged him not to vote for Trump. There have been 180 faithless elector votes for either president or vice president out of over 23,000 electoral college votes cast. Berman, Mitchell N., "How Practices Make Principles,

and How Principles Make Rules," Page 54 (January 2022):
https://scholarship.law.upenn.edu/faculty_scholarship/2765/

[80] *Ray v. Blair*, 343 U.S. 214 (1952).

[81] *Chiafalo v. Washington*, 591 U.S. ____ (2020).

[82] *Colorado Department of State v. Bacca*, 591 U.S. _____ (2020).

[83] Snead, Tierney, "Lawsuit against GOP operatives accused in rare presidential electors scheme filed in Wisconsin," *CNN politics*, May 17, 2022. The suit is filed in the Dane County Circuit Court. https://www.cnn.com/2022/05/17/politics/fake-presidential-electors-wisconsin-suit/index.html. *See also* Epstein, Reid J., "Wisconsin Democrats Sue G.O.P. Fake Electors Over 2020 Election," *The New York Times*, May 17, 2022: https://www.nytimes.com/2022/05/17/us/politics/wisconsin-fake-electors.html

[84] *Ibid.*

[85] *Ibid.*

[86] Bauer, Scott, "Wisconsin judge allows for lawsuit against fake Trump electors to proceed," *AP News*, May 15, 2023.

[87] Levine, Sam, "The Trump loyalist who could be a major threat to US democracy," *The Guardian*, May 20, 2022. Mastriano has retained Jenna Ellis, one of Trump's lawyers, to work on his campaign. She is mentioned in section 3.3 and in e.n. 72. https://www.theguardian.com/us-news/2022/may/20/doug-mastriano-pennsylvania-republican-governor-trump

[88] *Ibid. See also* Haberman, Maggie and Broadwater, Luke, "'Kind of Wild/Creative': Emails Shed Light on Trump Fake Electors Plan," *The New York Times,* July 26, 2022. In regard to Mr. Mastriano, this article states the following: "As they organized the fake elector scheme, lawyers appointed a 'point person' in seven states to help organize those electors who were willing to sign their names to false documents. In Pennsylvania, that point person was Douglas V. Mastriano, a proponent of Mr. Trump's lies of a stolen election who is now the Republican nominee for governor."

https://www.nytimes.com/2022/07/26/us/politics/trump-fake-electors-emails.html

See also Orso, Anna, Terruso, Julia, and Bunch, Jesse, "What the House Jan. 6 report says about Doug Mastriano, Scott Perry, and other key Pa. Republicans," *The Philadelphia Inquirer* (December 23, 2022). This is not an unrealistic threat that Mastriano has made. Fulton County in Pennsylvania allowed a third-party company, Wake TSI, to access the county's 2020 voting machines. The county had first given the firm access to its Dominion voting machines in the weeks after the 2020 election. Mastriano had requested that the county allow an audit of its machines. The Pennsylvania Department of State, which is the state agency that supervises the county election boards, asked the court to block the county from giving the firm access to its voting machines. Third party access of voting machines is considered to be a significant breach of security and the state said that the machines could no longer be trusted for further use. The court ordered the county to keep the machines secure.

Fulton County disobeyed the court order, which led the Pennsylvania Supreme Court to impose sanctions on the county. Justice Dougherty of the Supreme Court made the following statement: "In fact, let it be known far and wide that this Court can—and will—exert the full might of its constitutional authority against those who seek to delegitimize this Commonwealth's elections, or its judiciary." See Lai, Jonathan, "Pa. court: County erred in access to voting machines," *The Philadelphia Inquirer,* April 20, 2023.

[89] *Ibid.*

[90] The information about the local election regulations comes from the following article: Huangru, Kate, "Unequal election policies disenfranchised Pennsylvania voters in 2022," *Spotlight PA, The Philadelphia Inquirer,* February 21, 2023.

[91] Note to the reader: In order to avoid multiple endnotes interrupting the flow of the discussion about the indictment, I will

provide in Appendix B the sources for the statements made in this section 3.11.

Chapter Four: Customary Legal Norms

[92] Dicey, A.V., Introduction to the Study of the Law of the Constitution, Introduction, Page clv.

[93] See Waldron, Jeremy, "Are Constitutional Norms Legal Norms," 75 Fordham Law Review 1697, 1702-09 (2006).

[94] Postscript, Page 258.

[95] *Ibid.* Hart would qualify as an exclusive positivist in his original version of the rule of recognition. He is an inclusive positivist in his modified version. The pedigree theory is discussed in chapter six of *The Judge and the Philosopher.*

[96] Bederman, David J., *Custom as a Source of Law*, chapter 4, f.n. 13. *See also* Llewellyn, Karl, *The Cheyenne Way*, Page 25.

[97] Bederman, David J., *Custom as a Source of Law* at chapter 3.

[98] *Id.* at chapter 3, f.n. 34.

[99] *Id.* at chapter 6, f.n. 55.

[100] *Id.* at chapter 7. I discuss Karl Llewellyn's legal philosophy in chapter three of *The Judge and the Philosopher.*

[101] *Id.* at chapter 6. See *County of Hawaii v. Sotomura*, 55 Haw. 176, 517 P.2d 57, 62 (Hawaii 1973). *See also* Tom, Michael D., "Hawaiian Beach Access: A Customary Right," 26 Hastings Law Journal 823 (1975).

[102] *Lucas v. South Carolina Coastal Council,* 505 U.S. 1003, 112 S. Ct. 2886 (1992).

[103] *Stevens v. City of Cannon Beach*, 114 Or. App. 457, 835 P.2d 940 (Or. 1992), *affirmed*, 312 Or. 131, 854 P.2d 449 (Or. 1993), *cert. denied*, 510 U.S. 1207 (1994).

[104] See Havey, Melody F., "*Stevens v. City of Cannon Beach*: Does Oregon's Doctrine of Custom Find a Way around *Lucas?*" 1 *Ocean & Coastal Law Journal* 109, 122 (1994).

[105] *Swift v. Tyson*, 41 U.S. 1 (1842). See section 6.2 of *The Judge and the Umpire.*

[106] *Black & White Taxicab & Transfer Co. v. Brown & Yellow Taxicab & Transfer Co.*, 276 U.S. 518 (1928). See section 6.3 of *The Judge and the Umpire.*

[107] *Erie Railroad Co. v. Tompkins*, 304 U.S. 64 (1938). See section 6.4 of *The Judge and the Umpire.*

[108] Consider, for example, *Roper v. Simmons*, 543 U.S. 551 (2005), which is a case involving interpretation of the Eighth Amendment provision of "cruel and unusual punishment" being prohibited. The defendant was 17-years old when he killed a woman. The question in the case is whether execution of the defendant would violate the cruel and unusual punishment clause. Unlike the test in *Dobbs v. Jackson Women's Health Organization*, 597 U.S. _____ (2022), which I will discuss in *The Judge and the Incorrect Decision*, in which the Supreme Court looks at just text, history and tradition. Instead, the Supreme Court in *Simmons* considers international human rights laws and the laws in other countries. The Court could have considered the customary norms to aid in the interpretation of the constitutional norms. Unlike in *Dobbs*, the Supreme Court in *Simmons* does not consider just text, history and tradition in its interpretation of the constitutional norms.

[109] Raz, Joseph, *The Concept of a Legal System*, Page 164. In criminal law, this is called the rule of lenity, which means that there is no crime if the act is not prohibited in the criminal code. See Lachman, Steven F., "Applying The Rule of Lenity And The Void For Vagueness Doctrine: The Ambiguous Approach of Pennsylvania Courts," *XCIII Pennsylvania Bar Association Quarterly* 115 (July 2022).

[110] Hans Kelsen, in *The Pure Theory of Law*, has the same difficulty Hart has in trying to fit custom into a legal positivist narrative, though Kelsen has a more complete description of the relationship of custom to legal norms. Custom may create a legal norm because it is posited by human behavior. Kelsen, Hans, *The Pure Theory of*

Law, Page 9. The application of customary norms by courts is considered to be legitimate because it may be presupposed that custom is binding in the same sense that a written constitution has the character of an obligation. *Id.* at 223. But customary law may only be applied by the law-applying agency if such application is authorized. "This means a basic norm must be presupposed, which institutes not only the fact of the creation of a constitution, but also the fact of a qualified custom as law-created fact." *Id.* at 226.

Then, Kelsen qualifies that observation with this statement: "The question of whether a law-creating custom is present may be decided only by the law-applying organ." *Id.* at 227. Therefore, Kelsen appears to agree with Hart that custom may be legally-binding only if a court recognizes the custom as binding in a judicial decision. So, is Kelsen saying that a customary norm is part of the law? Here is Kelsen's reasoning on that fundamental point: "...[T]he 'source' of law in the specific sense of the term (that is, the origin of law, that from which the law arises, that which creates law) can be 'law' only because it is a peculiarity of the law to regulate its own creation." *Id.* at 255.

[111] Just to establish that this hypothetical example is not entirely hypothetical, consider this example from Japan: "Japan's crackdown on errant diners in the wake of 'sushi terrorism' has intensified after two men were arrested for using their chopsticks to remove a condiment from a communal container at a restaurant in Osaka... Oka, 34, and Shimazu, 33, are accused of obstruction of business after they used their chopsticks to eat pickled ginger from a container intended for all customers at a restaurant.... Diners are supposed to use separate chopsticks to add toppings to their dish." In this case, "obstruction of business" is equivalent to "disorderly conduct" and the failure to use separate chopsticks and not your own personal chopsticks is the violation of a customary rule with the force of law. See McCurry, Justin, "Diners in Japan arrested for dipping own chopsticks in communal bowl of ginger," *AP News*: https://apnews.com/article/japan-food-prank-arrest

[112] Postscript, Page 256. Mitchell Berman distinguishes social norms from legal norms. Berman, Mitchell, N., "Dworkin versus Hart Revisited: The Challenge of Non-Lexical Determination," Pages 10-11. His theory is similar to the distinction between customary rules with the force of law and those without the force of law. Hart might also agree with this distinction. It is the legal culture (described by Stanley Fish) or the judicial culture (described by Joseph Raz) that authorizes judges to make new legal rules. They do so by looking to alternate sources that may be employed to make judicial decisions. These alternate sources for making judicial decisions are not sources of the law (not statutes, published precedents, or customary rules with the force of law). It is not the rule of recognition that authorizes the creation of the new legal rules but the rule of change. It is the rule of recognition that validates the creation of the new legal rules as being part of the law for the next decision. See this link for Mitchell Berman's article: https://scholarship.law.upenn.edu/faculty_scholarship/2763/
[113] Article I, Section 4, Clause 1.

Chapter Five: Expanding the Rule of Recognition

[114] The exception to this statement is when the law in one jurisdiction requires the courts in that jurisdiction to apply the law of another jurisdiction rather than its own law.
[115] *In re: Appeal of Brandywine, Jennersville, and Phoenixville Hospitals, et al.,* Chester County Nos. 17-11220, 17-11222, 17-11223, 17-11226, 17-11227, 18-11854, 18-11855, 18-11857, 18-11858, 18-11859 Judge Sommer ruled that the three Chester County hospitals were more aligned with for-profit companies than non-profit companies and should be paying real estate taxes. The three hospitals do not provide enough free services to qualify as non-profit entities. The doctors in the hospitals have for-profit practices. They receive lucrative compensation based upon their

performance. In order to qualify for tax-exempt status, the corporation must operate completely free from for-profit motivation. In fiscal 2021 (ending June 30, 2021), of the six Tower Health hospitals, only Reading Hospital (in Berks County) made a profit. Tower Health has announced that it will be closing Jennersville Hospital in Chester County and Chestnut Hill Hospital in Philadelphia. See Maye, Fran, "Tower Health loses bid to have 3 Chester County hospitals deemed tax exempt," *Daily Local*, February 11, 2022.
https://www.dailylocal.com/2021/10/19/tower-health-3-chester-county-hospitals-tax-exemption-denied/

On February 10, 2023, the decision of the Court of Common Pleas of Chester County that Tower Health was not tax exempt was affirmed by the Commonwealth Court. See Brubaker, Harold, "School districts score major win over Tower Health in property-tax cases," *The Philadelphia Inquirer*, February 11, 2023.

[116] *Pottstown School District v. Montgomery County Board of Assessment Appeals*, 2017-27756 (O.C. Montco 2021). Judge Saltz mentions in his opinion that the previous owner of the Pottstown Hospital, Community Health Systems, was a for-profit corporation and paid real estate taxes. He finds that Tower Health does not operate in a manner similar to that of for-profit companies and that it should not have to pay real estate taxes. He rejects the claim of the Pottstown School District that the hospital operates like a for-profit company. This decision was made just days before the Chester County decision. Tower Health was disappointed that they were less successful in their Chester County case than they were in the Montgomery County case. I should mention that there is one factual difference between the two cases. Before Tower Health purchased the hospital in Montgomery County, it sought and obtained a tax-exempt status ruling from the Montgomery County Board of Assessment. This did not happen in Chester County. I do not consider this to be a relevant difference in the two cases.

On February 10, 2023, the decision of the Montgomery County Court of Common Pleas that Tower Health was tax exempt was reversed. See Brandt, Evan, "Court ruling puts Pottstown Hospital back on the tax rolls," *Daily Local*, February 14, 2023.

[117] The location of the county may affect how the law is interpreted. This is especially true in regard to jury verdicts when juries apply the law.

[118] In August 2021, the Pennsylvania Department of Health issued an order requiring everyone to wear a mask inside schools. Some parents, schools and Republican politicians filed a lawsuit in the Pennsylvania courts challenging the validity of the order. On November 10, 2021, a. panel of judges held in a 4 to 1 decision that the order is invalid. *Corman, III et al. v. Acting Secretary of the Pennsylvania: Department of Health*, No. 294 MD 2021. (Pa. Commw. Ct. 2021) While the Secretary of Health has the power to issue such an order if a state of emergency has been declared, the Commonwealth Court concluded that there is no such power when no state of emergency has been declared. This decision has been appealed to the Supreme Court of Pennsylvania, which affirmed the decision of the Commonwealth Court. *Corman, III et al. v. Acting Secretary of the Pennsylvania: Department of Health*, No. 83 MAP 2021 (Pa. 2021). The Pennsylvania Supreme Court in December 2021 held that the school mask mandate in Pennsylvania is invalid. See: https://law.justia.com/cases/pennsylvania/commonwealth-court/2021/294-m-d-2021.html

The masking requirement continues to be a controversial issue in Pennsylvania school districts as well as in other school districts. On December 13, 2021, by a 5 to 4 vote, the Perkiomen Valley School Board (in Pennsylvania) decided to permit optional masking in school buildings. On January 2, 2022, the School Board, by a 7 to 2 vote, deferred the optional masking and continued the masking mandate until January 21, 2022.

On January 21, 2022, an unnamed parent on behalf of unnamed students filed a class action challenging the optional masking and requesting that masking be required unless there is a "district-approved mask exemption." The class included the school children who are at severe risk of illness and injury due to their disabilities. Out of 5,319 students in the school district, 1,080 are disabled.

U.S. District Court Judge Wendy Beetlestone granted the plaintiffs' request for a temporary restraining order until there was a further hearing so that masks would continue to be required. The claim is that the optional wearing of masks is a violation of the Americans with Disabilities Act, which is the same claim made in the Texas case discussed in this section. *John and Jane Doe, et al. v. Perkiomen Valley School District, a Pennsylvania governmental entity, et al.*, Civil Action 22-cv-287 (E.D. Pa. Feb. 7, 2022). https://www.dailylocal.com/2022/01/27/federal-judge-re-imposes-mask-mandate-on-perkiomen-valley-schoolsd

[119] *E.T. v. Morath*, No. 1:21-CV-00717 (W.D. Tex.) This is a decision in the U.S. District Court for the Western District of Texas. The lawsuit was initiated by Disability Rights Texas, an advocacy group for persons with disabilities. The challenge to the state order is based upon the federal statute prohibiting discrimination against persons with disabilities. Notwithstanding the executive order challenged in this case, the Richardson Independent School District required that masks be worn. On November 10, 2021, the district court held that the executive order violated the ADA and issued a permanent injunction.

The State of Texas appealed to the Fifth Circuit Court of Appeals, which ultimately reversed the district court and dismissed the case on July 25, 2022. The Court of Appeals found that the plaintiffs did not prove that they suffered an increased risk of injury of contracting COVID-19 due to the absence of a mask mandate. The court also found that the plaintiffs should have sued the individual school districts rather than the state government. See: https://clearinghouse.net/case/18553/. This does not affect the analysis in the text related to the period of time before the appeal was decided.

[120] This statement that the same federal law applies in Texas and in Pennsylvania presupposes that the federal law will be applied the same in both circuits in the federal system. The issue of the impact on children with disabilities was not raised in the Pennsylvania decision discussed in e.n. 123.

[121] I also discussed this statutory provision in section 6.3 in *The Judge and the Philosopher.*

[122] The ACA is at 26 U.S.C. 5000A(a) and the amendment may be found in the Tax Cuts and Jobs Act of 2017, Pub.L. 115-97, Section 11081, 131 Stat. 2092 (codified in 26 U.S.C. Section 5000A(c)). For an extended discussion of laws without penalties, see Barkun, Michael, *Law Without Sanctions: Order in the Primitive Societies and the World Community.* Michael Barkun serves as a Professor Emeritus of Political Science at the Maxwell School of Citizenship and Public Affairs, Syracuse University.

[123] *California v. Texas*, 593 U.S. _____ (2021). No. 19-840, decided on June 17, 2021. This case was a challenge to the validity of the Affordable Care Act filed by Republican state attorneys general. The Supreme Court held that the plaintiffs had no standing to challenge a law that imposed no penalties. The Supreme Court avoided deciding the constitutionality of the ACA. It is interesting to note that the Trump Administration refused to defend the ACA. The California Attorney General stepped in to defend the statute. Since the Supreme Court dismissed the case on the grounds of lack of standing, the Supreme Court was able to avoid ruling on whether the individual mandate in the Act is unconstitutional since there is no penalty for violating the mandate.

[124] The Supreme Court accepts less than one percent of the petitions for certiorari that are filed in the clerk's office. Perhaps, fewer petitions for writs of certiorari would be filed if the attorneys could make more intelligent decisions about the likelihood of acceptance. In an article written by Joan Bishupic and published on

October 17, 2021, entitled "The secret Supreme Court: Late nights, courtesy votes and the unwritten 5-vote rule," *CNN Politics*, the author discusses the customary rules that govern the actions of the Justices. For example, there is a custom in death penalty cases for a "courtesy fifth vote". It takes four affirmative votes for a case to be accepted for review. If the case is filed by someone who is scheduled to be executed, and four justices vote to hear the case, it is possible that the applicant will be executed before the case is decided. In order to ensure that this will not occur, there is a custom among the Justices that one of the Justices, even though he/she did not vote for review, will cast a fifth vote which will delay the execution (5 votes are required to do so) so that the Justices who voted to hear the case will get the opportunity to do so because the case will not become moot by the execution having occurred. https://www.cnn.com/2021/10/17/politics/supreme-court-conference-rules-breyer/index.html

[125] These are discussed in section 6.3 of *The Judge and the Philosopher.*

[126] *Conway v. Cutler Group,* 626 Pa. 660, 99 A.3d 67 (2014). This case is discussed in detail in chapter seven of *The Judge and the Umpire.*

[127] *Lightcap v. Wrightstown Township*, 25 Bucks Co. L. Rep. 145 (1974), *aff'd,* No. 1625, C.D. 1973, (Pa. Commw. Ct., 1974). See the discussion of this case in Moskowitz, David H., *Exclusionary Zoning Litigation,* Page 48.

[128] *Gohmert v. Pence,* 510 F. Supp. 3d 435 (E.D. Tex. 2021), unreported at Court of Appeals level. This case was introduced in Section 2.8 of *The Judge and the Philosopher.* It is also discussed in Section 2.5 in this book. Given modern technology, there is no longer any reason for non-publication of opinions. Non-publication became an issue because of the number of appeals in the federal courts. There are 50,000 to 100,000 appeals filed each year. Over 80% of the opinions in the federal appellate system are non-published. Consequently, non-publication has the potential of

distorting the law and clouding the divide between law and non-law, which in turn creates confusion within the rule of recognition.
[129] *People v. Elias V (a/k/a In re Elias V).*, 188 Cal. Rptr. 3d 202, 237 Cal. App. 4th 568 (Cal. Ct. App. 2015). See section 7.10 of *The Judge and the Philosopher* regarding the citing of unpublished opinions.

Chapter Six: Additional Situations That Require Reconsideration of the Rule of Recognition

[130] *Conway v. Cutler Group,* 626 Pa. 660, 99 A.3d67 (Pa. 2014). See chapter seven of *The Court and the Umpire.*
[131] *Buttes Gas and Oil Co. v. Hammer*, (1982 AC 888).
[132] *Id.* at 937.
[133] *R (on the application of Miller, Appellant) v. The Prime Minister (Respondent) v. Advocate General for Scotland (Appellant):* https://www.telegraph.co.uk/politics/2019/09/24/supreme-court-ruling-lady-hales-prorogation-statement-full/

The U.S. Constitution in Article I, Section 5 has a rule regarding this subject: "Neither House, during the session of Congress, shall, without the consent of the other, adjourn for more than three days, nor to any other place other than that in which the two Houses shall be sitting."

The limitation on lengthy proroguing of the Parliament seems to be based upon a customary rule with the force of law. In comparison to this ruling, there are other instances in which the customary rules were not followed, and it was clear that the customary rules that were involved were customary rules that lacked the force of law. For example, see Foster, Max and Said-Moorhouse, Lauren, "Queen won't return to London to appoint new British PM, for first time in her reign," *CNN*, August 31, 2022, when Queen Elizabeth decided to meet the UK's new prime minister at Balmoral rather than Buckingham Palace—a historic first in her 70-year reign. As Head of State, the Queen appoints the new prime minister. Consequently, Boris Johnson resigned, and Liz Truss accepted her appointment in Scotland. https://www.cnn.com/2022/08/31/uk/queen-elizabeth-prime-minister-balmoral-intl-gbr

[134] *Baker v. Carr*, 369 U.S. 186, 82 S. Ct. 691(1962).

[135] *Rucho v. Common Cause,* 585 U.S. _____ (2019). The North Carolina plaintiffs claim that the State's map discriminated against Democrats, while the Maryland plaintiffs claim that their State's map discriminated against Republicans. The Supreme Court held that partisan gerrymandering claims present political questions beyond the reach of the federal courts. The Court is concerned that there is no legal standard that may be applied to aid the Court in deciding what legislative district lines would be appropriate. There are no rules, just principles, and principles are not able to be applied to resolve this issue. However, as indicated in the text, the *Rucho* case may no longer be the law.

[136] *Moore v. Harper*, 600 U.S. _____ (2023). I expand upon this discussion of the impact of gerrymandering on depriving African Americans equal voting rights in section 7.5.

[137] See chapters 10 and 11 in Biskupic, Joan, *Nine Black Robes*. See also Cole, Jared P., "The Political Question Doctrine: Justiciability and the Separation of Powers," *Congressional Research Service*, December 23, 2014.

[138] *Harper v. Hall*, 380 N.C. 317, 868 S.E.2d 499 (2022) (*Harper I*).

[139] *Harper v. Hall,* 383 N.C. 89, 125, 881 S.E.2d 156, 181 (2022) (*Harper II*).

[140] *Moore v. Harper*, 600 U.S. _____ (2023). "A particularly robust reading of the theory {independent state legislature theory]—which the court turned aside—would have empowered state legislatures to make decisions on all aspects of elections, from congressional lines to how people register to vote and cast a ballot, without any opportunity for challengers to contest those decisions in state courts under state laws or constitutions. Opponents of the theory argued that it could have led to

unchecked partisan gerrymandering, and laws that would make it harder for people to vote." Montellard, Zach and Gerstein, Josh, "Supreme Court denies state legislatures the unchecked power to set election rules," *Politico*, June 27, 2023.

[141] *Moore v. Harper*, 600 U.S. _____ (2023).

[142] *Ibid.*

[143] For the risks associated with placing the pipelines close to houses, schools, libraries, etc., see the following articles: Rettew, Bill, "YEAR IN REVIEW: Mariner East pipeline work continues despite protests and lawsuits," *Daily Local,* December 29, 2021 (pipeline is very close to apartment complexes and Chester County Library) https://www.dailylocal.com/2021/12/28/year-in-review-mariner-east-pipeline-work-continues-despite-protests-and-lawsuits/; and Moss, Rebecca, "Judge: Pipeline risks not disclosed," Spotlight PA, *The Philadelphia Inquirer*, April 26, 2021. https://www.inquirer.com/news/pennsylvania/spl/pa-mariner-east-pipeline-sunoco-ruling-safety-negligence-puc-20210426.html.

   In 2018, Rebecca Britton, superintendent and safety coordinator for a Chester County school district, wrote a letter to Governor Tom Wolf complaining about the Mariner East pipelines that are roughly 500 feet from some of the schools emphasizing how difficult it would be to evacuate safely the 3,400 students should an accident occur. Spotlight PA calculated that, if there was a serious accident, up to 345,000 people and 340 schools, childcare centers, places of worship and mobile home parks statewide could be impacted by a leak.

[144] I am not contending that there are no regulations. The pipelines that I am discussing have been the subject of multiple fines and even criminal actions but there is no way to force the regulatory agencies to control the placing of the pipelines too close to houses, schools, etc. in densely populated areas. Here are some references to the civil fines and criminal penalties (which also resulted in fines) imposed upon Sunoco regarding these pipelines. See Moss,

Rebecca, "Judge: Pipeline risks not disclosed," Spotlight PA, *The Philadelphia Inquirer*, April 26, 2021 ($16 million dollar civil fine); Rubinkam, Michael, "Sunoco Must Dredge Chester Co. Lake, Pay $4M Over Pipeline Spill," The Lineup, *The Philadelphia Inquirer*, December 8, 2021 ("Energy Transfer has also been assessed more than $24 million in civil fines, including a $12.5 million fine in 2018 that was one of the largest ever imposed by the state"); and the Pennsylvania Attorney General issued 48 criminal charges against Energy Transfer for violating the environmental laws of Pennsylvania which resulted in almost $50 million dollars in fines. See: https://www.facebook.com/watch/live/?ref=watch_permalink&v= 552313295839888

[145] Much of the information in this section comes from an article written by Hagan, Willard Nelson, "Local Government Role in Ensuring Pipeline Safety," an article submitted to the School of Architecture and Planning, at the Massachusetts Institute of Technology (May 1989). See also Rellahan, Michael P., "Mariner East gas pipeline developer pleads no contest in pollution cases," *Daily Local*, August 1, 2022: https://www.dailylocal.com/2022/08/05/pipeline-developer-pleads-no-contest-in-pollution-cases/.

There is the possibility of, in some cases, private causes of action against the pipeline companies. *See* Rellahan, Michael P., "'Courts will protect them,' lawyer says of homeowners plagued by pipelines," *Daily Local*, July 6, 2022: https://www.dailylocal.com/2022/07/05/courts-will-protect-them-lawyer-says-of-homeowners-plagued-by-pipelines/

[146] As I will explain, there are federal, state, and local regulations and they will be outlined in the text and in these endnotes.

[147] For the federal regulations, see: 49 CFR, PART 195: https://www.law.cornell.edu/cfr/text/49/part-195

[148] *Flynn, et al. v. Sunoco Pipeline, L.P.*, Before Pennsylvania Public Utility Commission, No. C-2918-30061.16. p. 2018-3006 17 and

there are five additional case numbers. The evidence was heard by Elizabeth H. Barnes, Administrative Law Judge, who wrote a 207-page opinion. I read the initial decision (Non-Proprietary version). There were some redactions, but they do not affect my analysis. The opinion is dated April 9, 2021.

[149] The Pennsylvania Public Utility Code is found in 66 Pa. C.S., Section 101 et seq.: See 66 Pa. C.S.1501: https://www.legis.state.pa.us/cfdocs/legis/LI/consCheck.cfm?txtTy pe=HTM&ttl=66&div=0&chpt=15&sctn=1&subsctn=0
66 Pa.C.S. 1505: https://www.legis.state.pa.us/cfdocs/legis/LI/consCheck.cfm?txtTy pe=HTM&ttl=66&div=0&chpt=15&sctn=5&subsctn=0
See also: 52 Pa. Code
59.33: https://www.pacode.com/secure/data/052/chapter59/s59.33.html

[150] Page 81 of ALJ Barnes opinion.

[151] By a 5 to 4 vote, the U.S. Supreme Court recognized the power of eminent domain that is granted to pipeline companies in *PennEast Pipeline Co. v. New Jersey,* 141 S.Ct. 2244 (2021). The pipeline company could even condemn New Jersey state-controlled land. See also Peters, Jason N., "Sunoco's Mariner East 2 ruins quality of life in Delaware County through eminent domain," *Grid Magazine*, May 29, 2021. https://gridphilly.com/blog-home/2021/7/16/sunocos-mariner-east-2-ruins-quality-of-life-in-delaware-county-through-eminent-domain/.

[152] *Ibid.* An earlier version of this same case is *Flynn v. Sunoco Pipeline, L.P.,* No. 942, C.D. 2018, 2018 WL 1463443, (Pa. Commw. Ct. 2018). *See also, Flynn V. Sunoco Pipeline, L.P.,* 182 A.3d 1107 (2018). The Court of Common Pleas of Delaware County sustained Sunoco's preliminary objections. Plaintiffs sought an injunction to prevent the Mariner East 2 pipeline (ME2). They contended that the pipeline was contrary to Middletown Township's Subdivision and Land Development Ordinance (SALDO). The trial court agreed with Sunoco that SALDO was preempted by state and federal law.

The Commonwealth Court affirmed the decision of the trial court. Sunoco is a public utility. The PUC regulates the intrastate movement of natural gas and petroleum products through pipelines. Sunoco received Certificates of Public Convenience (CPCs) from the PUC that authorize it to install the pipeline systems. The new ME2 construction will be parallel to and entirely within the existing Mariner East 1 (ME1) pipeline easements. Sunoco has obtained PUC approval for both ME1 and ME2. The pipeline must be 75' from the dwellings. In this case, however, the old pipeline is closer than that distance to houses, libraries, etc. The new pipeline is being placed in easements that were obtained many years ago. Also, the original easements were for a substance which is much less hazardous than the substance in the new pipelines. Now, they will transport hazardous volatile liquids (HVLs) which creates additional risks. Plaintiffs contend that this statutory provision does not confer siting responsibility to the PUC and that the township's SALDO provisions should apply to the siting of the pipeline.

The Commonwealth Court affirmed the trial's court's ruling that SALDO is preempted by state and federal law. The Commonwealth Court cited as binding precedent the *Delaware Riverkeeper* case, which is the next case that I will mention.

That case involves West Goshen Township's zoning ordinance. *Delaware Riverkeeper Network v. Sunoco Pipeline L.P.*, 179 A.2d 670 (Pa. Commw. Ct. 2018), In this case, the Commonwealth Court held that the state legislature intended the Public Utility Code to occupy the field of public utility regulation in the absence of an express grant of authority to the contrary. This preemption precluded municipalities from regulating pipelines in their zoning ordinances. This case involved the same pipeline as the pipeline in the Delaware County case. Even though the PUC has not adopted specific regulations as to the siting of the pipeline, the Commonwealth Court holds that municipalities may not adopt regulations.

In contrast to the siting of the pipelines, the Commonwealth Court reached a contrary decision when PECO, a Pennsylvania public utility, wanted to construct a building that it called a "gas reliability station". The proposed facility would be a building that would have equipment to reduce gas pressure on a new pipeline before the fuel is distributed to nearby neighborhoods in Marple Township, Delaware County, Pennsylvania. Unlike the siting of the pipeline itself, from which the township is preempted from adopting regulations, the township could, and did, apply its zoning ordinance to the siting of the building.

The township denied zoning relief for the project because it was incompatible with residential and retail uses near the facility. PECO requested a special exception from the zoning hearing board to allow it to use its property for the proposed facility. The application was opposed by the residents and the township. The residents contended that PECO should find a safer and more suitable location for the facility. PECO's request was denied. As I pointed out in Appendix A to *The Judge and the Philosopher,* obtaining zoning relief is highly dependent upon whether the neighbors approve or disapprove of the zoning request.

PECO then filed a request with the PUC to approve its application notwithstanding the local opposition. The PUC ruled in PECO's favor in March 2022 holding that "PECO has the authority to place the buildings along the pipeline to manage the distribution and supply of natural gas in its pipes as long as the company operates its facilities in compliance with state and federal regulations." In other words, PECO could disregard the local municipal regulations. Zoning law, as I point out in Appendix A in *The Judge and the Philosopher*, is a smorgasbord of federal, state and predominantly local regulations.

The neighbors and the township appealed the PUC order to the Commonwealth Court, an intermediate appellate court in Pennsylvania. The Commonwealth Court reversed the decision of the PUC. The court held that the PUC has to revisit its decision to "incorporate the results of a constitutionally sound environmental impact review." The court's reasoning was that the PUC erred when it did not consider the environmental issues. The PUC is obligated to consider environmental factors because the State Constitution recognized environmental rights. See Kummer, Frank, "Pa. court overturns decision that allowed natural gas project in Delco," *The Philadelphia Inquirer*, March 13, 2023. The case is No. 319 C.D. 2022, and the decision was made on March 9, 2023. The opinion is not yet published.

In summary, PECO's claim that it is exempt from the local zoning ordinance when siting its building has not been successful. The PUC must consider the environmental issues raised by the protestants. The township has the authority to regulate the siting of the building, but the PUC may reverse the township's decision by finding that the building is reasonably necessary for the public utility to operate. The PUC erred in holding that potential explosions, noises and emissions from the building were outside of its review authority. This does not mean that the PUC will review the siting of the pipelines, even though consistency in rulings would seem to dictate that the PUC should, at a minimum, consider the environmental issues associated with the siting of pipelines. This decision also does not require that the PUC consider the safety and health issues associated with the siting of the pipelines, though it has the authority to adopt regulations or impose conditions upon the licenses it grants to consider such issues. Hence, it remains true that this is a situation in which there is authority to regulate, but there is a failure to do so.

[153] Page 90 of the opinion. The PUC regulations are in 66 PA Code 59.33. The federal regulations are in 49 CFR PART 195.

[154] These details come from the findings of facts in the opinion starting with EN 43 in the opinion.

[155] Sunoco has drafted emergency plans, but these plans are confidential. They have been shown to first responders, but the

persons who see the plans must sign confidentiality agreements. The plans are not available to the general public.

[156] See Moss, Rebecca, "Judge: Pipeline risks not disclosed," Spotlight PA, *The Philadelphia Inquirer*, April 26, 2021: "Sunoco advises people to leave uphill on foot and not operate a cell phone until they reach a safe distance but does not say in public mailers just how far is safe from the pipeline in an accident, or how to protect people with disabilities, children, and elderly individuals with limited mobility." Moreover, the public mailers did not disclose the risks of "property damage, personal injury, asphyxiation, burns, death or fatality. See: https://www.inquirer.com/news/pennsylvania/spl/pa-mariner-east-pipeline-sunoco-ruling-safety-negligence-puc-20210426.html

[157] Finding of facts 295 to 302 of the opinion.

[158] Preemption occurs when one authority may adopt the regulations and other potential regulators are prohibited from regulating the activity in question. Those who are prohibited are preempted from adopting regulations.

[159] Page 165 of the opinion.

[160] Conclusion of Law No. 36 of the opinion.

[161] Conclusion of Law No. 48 of the opinion.

[162] Conclusion of Law No. 51 of the opinion.

[163] Page 90 of the opinion.

[164] Compare siting requirements for PUC regulated high tension power lines and lack of siting requirements for pipelines: https://www.pacode.com/secure/data/052/chapter57/subchapGtoc.html

[165] Page 106 of the opinion.

[166] The applicable law is the Public Utility Code, 66 Pa.C.S. Section 101 et seq. The legislature may, of course, amend this statute to expand or contract the authority granted to the PUC. If the PUC concludes that it has no authority to control siting, there is no mechanism to force the legislature to grant the PUC such authority. The PUC clearly has authority to impose civil penalties,

and ALJ Barnes recommends that such civil penalties be imposed. But these only represent fines, and the fines are a business expense and do not provide any relief for the complainants. In my opinion, the PUC has authority to adopt siting regulations and to impose safety conditions on the permits it issues. No amendment to the statute is necessary.

[167] *Delaware Riverkeeper Network v. Sunoco Pipeline, L.P.,* 179 A.2d 670, 691 (2018).

[168] *Louisiana v. American Rivers, 596 U.S.* _____ (2022).

[169] See Grzincle, Barbara, "Supreme Court uses 'shadow docket' to revive Trump EPA clean water rule," *Reuters,* April 6, 2022. https://www.reuters.com/legal/government/supreme-court-uses-shadow-docket-revive-trump-epa-clean-water-rule-2022-04-06/. *See also* Pierce, Charles P., "The Supreme Court's 'Shadow Docket" is Looking Increasingly Shady," *Esquire Magazine, April* 12, 2021. https://www.esquire.com/news-politics/politics/a36099436/supreme-court-shadow-docket-california-churches-covid-19/

[170] https://il.usembassy.gov/statement-by-president-trump-on-jerusalem/

[171] See "Statement by President Joe Biden on Armenian Remembrance Day," issued by the White House on April 24, 2022: "Each year on this day, we remember the lives of all those who died in the Ottoman-era Armenian genocide and recommit ourselves to preventing such an atrocity from ever again occurring. Beginning on April 24, 1915, with the arrest of Armenian intellectuals and community leaders in Constantinople by Ottoman authorities, one and one-half million Armenians were deported, massacred, or marched to their deaths in a campaign of extermination. . ." The Turkish government was outraged by our official recognition of this tragedy. https://www.whitehouse.gov/briefing-room/statements-releases/2022/04/24/statement-by-president-joe-biden-on-armenian-remembrance-day-2/

[172] Presidential Records Act (PRA), 44 U.S.C. Sections 2201-2207. See Sussay, Meghan M., "The Presidential Records Act: Background and Recent Issues for Congress," *Congressional Research Service*, December 31, 2014.

[173] Langford, John, Florence, Justin, and Newland, Erica, "Trump's Presidential Records Act Violations: Short and Long-Term Solutions," *The Lawfare Institute,* June 15, 2022. https://www.lawfareblog.com/trumps-presidential-records-act-violations-short-and-long-term-solutions

[174] *Ibid. See also* Groppe, Maureen and Penzenstadler, Nick, "Trump's handling of documents proves 'toothless' records law needs a jolt, critics say. After Trump, 'toothless' records law could change," *USA Today*, September 16, 2022. The National Archives may seek the help of the Justice Department to investigate unlawful removal or destruction of governmental and presidential records. There are also other statutes that may be violated by taking, removing or destroying government records which may bar a person from viewing classified documents or from holding a federal office. https://news.yahoo.com/trumps-handling-documents-proves-toothless-100011450.html. This becomes clear with the indictment of former President Trump for his record keeping activities.

[175] Goldiner, Dave, "Trump, now facing indictment, was caught on tape admitting he can't declassify secret documents, report says," *New York Daily News*, June 9, 2023.

[176] *Gohmert v. Pence*, 510 F.Supp.3d 435 (E.D. Tex. 2021). Not only does the district court decide that the plaintiffs in this case lack standing, but there may also not be a cause of action based upon their claims. In addition, and even more important from the perspective of this case not being a precedent is that the Court of Appeals affirmed the district court decision but declared that the decision would not be published. This case is discussed in sections 2.3, 2.5 and 5.5.

[177] I am not aware of any lawsuit having been filed by a homeowner or other owner of property who challenged the use of the pipelines in an old easement for transporting HVLs. Since the HVLs were unknown when the easements were created 70 to 85 years ago, the grantors of the easements could not have anticipated or known of this potential use. Therefore, when they granted the easements, they did not agree, and could not have agreed or anticipated, the danger that would be created by the use of the easements. This could negate the use of the pipelines for HVLs.

Chapter Seven: Litigation Regarding Racial Discrimination

[178] *Alexander v. Sandoval*, 532 U.S. 275 (2001).

[179] *Chester Residents Concerned for Quality Living v. Seif*, 944 F. Supp. 413 (E.D. Pa. 1995).

[180] *Chester Residents Concerned for Quality Living v. Seif*, 132 F.3d 925 (3rd Cir. 1997).

[181] *Seif v. Chester Residents Concerned for Quality Living*, 524 U.S. 974 (1998).

[182] *Brown v. Board of Education* of *Topeka*, 341 U.S. 483 (1954). The Supreme Court recognizes that the schools are segregated because of residential housing segregation. The Supreme Court in a later case held, however, that when two school districts tried to integrate their schools that this was a violation of the equal-protection rights of the white students. The two school districts, in two different states, assigned students to schools using race as a factor to achieve racial balance and to foster integration. *See, Parents Involved in Community Schools v. Seattle School District No. 1*, 551 U.S. 701 (2007).

[183] UCLA Civil rights Project, "Brown at 60," May 15, 2014, Washington Center for Equitable Growth, "U.S. school segregation in the 20th Century," October 2019.

[184] UCLA Civil Rights Project, "Black Segregation Matters," December 2020.

[185] Fiske, Warren, "PolitiFact VA: Public schools are more segregated now than in the late 1960s," *WCVE News, The Takeaway*, June 8, 2022.

[186] *Commonwealth of Pennsylvania v. County of Bucks*, 22 *Bucks County Law Reporter* 179 (1972).

[187] *Commonwealth of Pennsylvania v. County of Bucks*, 8 Pa. Cmwlth. 295, 302 A.2d 897 (Pa. Commw. Ct. 1973). *See also* Lowry, Olan B., "Exclusionary Zoning; Mount Laurel—Seminal or Tempest-In-A-Teapot," 4 Western New England Law Review 541 (1982) and Moskowitz, David H., *Exclusionary Zoning Litigation*, Page 46.

[188] *Commonwealth of Pennsylvania v. County of Bucks,* 414 U.S. 1130, 94 S. Ct. 869, 38 L.Ed.2d 864 (1974).

[189] *Commonwealth of Pennsylvania v. County of Bucks*, 8 Pa. Cmwlth. 295, 299, 302 A.2d 897 (Pa. Commw. Ct. 1973).

[190] *Id.* at 300.

[191] *Id.* at 301. For a successful effort to accomplish a housing allocation plan among the counties in the Delaware Valley (Pennsylvania and New Jersey), see Moskowitz, David H., "Regional Housing Allocation Plans: A Case History of the Delaware Valley Regional Plan," 7 *The Urban Lawyer* 292 (1975).

[192] *Lightcap v. Wrightstown Township*, 25 Bucks County Law Reporter 145 (1974), *aff'd*, No. 1621 C.D. 1973, Pa. Commonwealth. Ct., October 18, 1974.

[193] Redlining refers to the practice of banks and other agencies of not issuing mortgages to purchasers in areas in which African Americans and Latinos want to purchase homes or to grant financing to builders of houses in areas where the purchasers are likely to be minority persons.

See Roebuck, Jeremy and Bond, Michelle, "DOJ reaches 'historic' redlining settlement with Philadelphia mortgage lender," *Philadelphia Inquirer*, July 28, 2022, about Trident Mortgage Company agreeing to reinvest more than $18 million as a result of its lending practices. Trident had denied home loans to Black and Latino borrowers in Southern New Jersey and Delaware during the years 2015 to 2019. Trident also agreed to pay a civil penalty of $4 million and to set aside $2 million to fund educational efforts.

During those years, "Trident actively avoided issuing mortgages for homes in Black and Latino neighborhoods, maintained a nearly all-white staff, and ignored warnings that its lending practices were likely in violation of the federal Fair Housing Act… Redlining practices historically have led to poverty because they have denied the opportunity to acquire net worth by appreciation in the value of homes, denied educational opportunities in better school districts and have contributed to housing discrimination. https://www.inquirer.com/news/redlining-philadelphia-trident-mortgage-company-fox-roach-justice-department-20220727.html

The appreciation in the home you own "is the way most U.S. households build wealth, especially those with lower incomes." See Bond, Michelle, "Race a factor in home wealth," *Philadelphia Inquirer*, April 20, 2023. I will return to this article below regarding the racially discriminatory increase in home values.

Redlining is not limited to discriminatory practices related to the purchasing of houses but is also a racially discriminatory practice in the leasing of apartments and housing to minority individuals. See "FTC and CFPB investigating Background Screening Issues Affecting Rental Housing Tenants," published by Saul Ewing, LLP in news@saulnews.com (March 8, 2023: "On February 28, 2023, the Federal Trade Commission ("FTC") and Consumer Finance Protection Bureau ("CFPB") issues a Request for Information ("RFI") seeking public comment on background screening issues affecting rental housing applicants and tenants in the United

States." The concern is that the initial screening practices of the rental agencies may be racially discriminatory."

In addition to these discriminatory practices, it was also common to place restrictive covenants in deeds that prevented sales to persons viewed as undesirable neighbors. While it is very time-consuming and expensive to remove those restrictive provisions from old deeds, title insurance companies now place the following language in title commitments: "This commitment does not republish any covenant, condition, regulation, or limitation contained in any document referred to in this commitment to the extent that the specific covenant, condition, regulation or limitation violates state or federal law based on race, color, religion, sex, sexual orientation, gender identity, handicap, familial status or national origin."

The effect of this statement is to not publish (not to include in the title report) the restrictive covenant. The restrictive covenant remains part of the record of the title, though enforcement of the restrictive covenant would be illegal. In other words, the restrictive covenant is in the books of recorded deeds, but it is not enforceable, just like there are laws in the statute books that are not enforceable.

Not only has there been discrimination in the form of redlining and restrictive covenants, but there has also been less increase in home values in black neighborhoods. See Bond, Michelle, "Race a factor in home wealth," *The Philadelphia Inquirer*, April 20, 2023: "Nationally, a medium-priced house is worth $190,000 more than it was a year ago.

"Black homeowners saw the smallest wealth gains over the last decade among racial groups. Asian homeowners, who as a group own more expensive homes than any other, saw the largest wealth gains, according to the report." Black homeowners averaged $115,000 in wealth gain, compared to more than $232,000 for Asian homeowners.

[194] This issue is discussed in section 1.2.

Shelby County v. Holder, 570 U.S. 529 (2013).

196 Voting Rights Act of 1965, 42 U.S.C. 1973(a).

197 I cannot discuss this issue at length in this book. Here is the situation to which I am referring. The Court of Appeals for the D.C. Circuit affirmed the decision of the District Court that Sections 4(b) and 5 of the statute were constitutional. *Shelby County v. Holder,* 811 F.Supp.2d 424 (D.D.C. 2011) and 679 F.3d 848 (D.C. Cir. 2012). The Supreme Court, in an opinion by Chief Justice Roberts, joined by Justices Scalia, Kennedy, Alito and Thomas reversed the Court of Appeals and held that Section 4(b) is unconstitutional.

Section 4(b), according to the majority opinion in *Shelby County,* exceeded Congress' power to enforce the Fourteenth and Fifteenth Amendments. The coverage formula conflicts with the constitutional principles of federalism and "equal sovereignty of the states" because the states are not being treated equally. Congress cannot subject a state to preclearance based upon its history of past discrimination.

Congress has the power to enforce the Fifteenth Amendment's right to vote that shall not be denied or abridged on account of race. The Court in the majority opinion does not reach the issue of the constitutionality of Section 5 of the Act. Section 5's preclearance requirement, however, applies only to the jurisdictions that are subject to Section 4(b) coverage. The effect of the decision is to make Section 5 inoperable.

My interest in this decision, in addition to its impact on voting rights, relates to the role that Justice Thomas played in the decision. If he had recused himself, it would have been a 4 to 4 decision and the Court of Appeals decision would have been affirmed. Therefore, his vote with the other four Justices made their decision a majority decision. His vote was essential. But he should have recused himself. I reach this conclusion based upon the following facts.

An amicus brief was filed urging the Court to make the decision which it made by the Judicial Education Project. This nonprofit corporation had received an invoice from Kellyanne Conway's firm to pay her firm many thousands of dollars for work that was never performed (Conway has been a prominent figure in Donald Trump's campaigns and in his presidency).. Her firm paid Clarence Thomas's wife, Ginni Thomas, many thousands of dollars (her firm is called Liberty Consulting). Liberty Consulting received $80,000 between June 2011 and June 2012. The request for the payment was made in January 2012. The request that the payment be made was by Leonard Leo, who was an adviser to President Trump (for whom Conway also was an advisor) regarding judicial appointments to the Supreme Court. Leo asked that Ginni Thomas not be identified by name. Justice Thomas did not disclose her connection to the firm that filed the amicus brief or the substantial payments she had received. Justice Thomas should have recused himself from participating in this decision.

[198] *Moore v. Harper*, 600 U.S. _____ (2023).

[199] *Allen v.* Milligan, 599 U.S. _____ (2023). See Sherman, Mark, "Supreme Court rules in favor of Black Alabama voters in unexpected defense of Voting Rights Act," *AP News*, June 6,2023: https://apnews.com/article/supreme-court-redistricting-race-voting-rights-alabama-af0d789ec7498625d344c0a4327367fe#.

[200] *Ibid.*

[201] *Brnovich v. Democratic National Committee*, 599 U.S. _____ (2021).

[202] The dissenting opinion notes that "native American citizens need to travel long distances to use the mail." *Id.* at Page 30. "But many rural Native American voters lack access to mail service, to a degree hard for most of us to fathom. Only 18% of Native voters in rural counties receive home mail delivery, compared to 86%of white voters living in those counties." *Id.* at Page 36. Native voters travel 45 minutes to 2 hours just to get to a mailbox. "So, in some Native communities, third-party collection of ballots—most by fellow clan members—became 'standard practice.'" *Id.* at 37.

[203] Section 2 of the VRA has two parts. Subsection (a) states the law's basic prohibition: "No voting qualification or prerequisite to voting, or standard, practice, or procedure shall be imposed or applied by any State or political subdivision in a manner which results in a denial or abridgement of the right of any citizen of the United States to vote on account of race or color." 52 U.S.C. Section 10301(a).

Subsection (b) provides the standard to apply: "A violation of subsection (a) is established if, based on the totality of circumstances, it is shown that the political processes leading to nomination or election in the State or political subdivision are not equally open to participation by members of [a given race] in that [those] members have less opportunity than other members of the electorate to participate in the political process and to elect representatives of their choice." 52 U.S.C. Section 10301(b)

[204] My focus in this book is not on jury trials and jury nullification. If the case is decided by a judge rather than a jury, it is more likely that the result will be a correct decision. This does not mean that the trial judge may not make a decision that is incorrect. In *The Judge and the Umpire,* the first case that I discussed is *O'Brien v. Desco* in chapter two. The trial judge in that case stated that he tries to make not only correct decisions but decisions that are also moral and ethical.

In a jury trial, the judge will deliver instructions to the jury about what the law is. The jury then deliberates and arrives at its decision, which may be consistent or inconsistent with the law in the judge's charge. The jury may reach a compromise verdict. Or, as in the situation of jury nullification, the jury may disregard the law. In general, in regard to jury trials, see Kalven, Harry, Jr. and Zeisel, Hans, *The American Jury.* There were 200 attempts to pass a federal statute making lynching a federal crime, but the Congress did not act. Finally, lynching was made a federal hate crime in March 2022.

For more details about lynchings, see "Lynching in the United States," *Wikipedia*: https://en.wikipedia.org/wiki/Lynching_in_the_United_States.

[205] *Johnson v. Hackett*, 284 F.Supp. 933 (E.D. Pa. 1968). This decision has been cited 120 times. Here are some of the references when it has been cited:

"It is the nature of the act performed, not the clothing of the actor or even the status of being on duty or off duty, which determines whether the officer has acted under color of law. It is a violation of civil rights only if the officer was acting under color of state law. Acts committed by a police officer even while on duty and in uniform are not under color of state law unless in some way "related to performance of police duties."

A policeman's private conduct, outside the line of duty and unaided by any indicia or ostensible state authority, is not conduct occurring under color of state law.

On-duty police officer's instigation of a physical altercation and exchange of insulting names was purely "personal pursuit".

There are references to the right of dignity in some cases decided after the decision in *Johnson v. Hackett*. See the following cases:

U.S. v. Windsor, 570 U.S. 744 ((2013): "Here the State's decision to give this class of persons the right to marry conferred upon them a dignity . . ."

People v. Ramirez, 599 P.,2d 622, 25 Cal.3d 260 (1979): "Also due process encompasses a concern for the dignity . . ."

Walker v. State, 316 Mont. 103, 68 P.3d 872 (2003) refers to Article II, Section 4 of the Montana Constitution conferring a right to human dignity.

Estelle v. Gamble, 429 U.S. 97 (1976): "The Amendment embodies broad and idealistic concepts of dignity, . . ."

Schmerber v. California, 384 U.S. 757 (1966): "The interests in human dignity .. ."

While I would not consider it to be the creation of a right of dignity, there is some reference to such a right in *Roper v. Simmons*, 542 U.S. 551 (2005). I will discuss this case at some length in chapter nine. Here are one such reference:
"By prohibiting even those convicted of heinous crimes, the Eighth Amendment reaffirms the right of the government to respect the dignity of all persons." *Id.* at 560.

Chapter Eight: Real Rules

[206] While the correct decision is always presumptively justified, the just decision and the wise decision, since they are authorized, may be justified. You may still disagree about whether the decision is just or wise. In the *Conway* case, discussed in chapter seven of *The Judge and the Umpire,* the trial court made the correct decision and found for the builder. The Superior Court reversed the trial court and decided in favor of the plaintiffs. I view this Superior Court decision as incorrect, just and unwise. The Supreme Court reversed the Superior Court and reaffirmed the decision of the trial court, which I consider to be a correct, unjust, wise decision. All three of the decisions are authorized, authoritative (until they are reversed) and binding. Justifiability is an evaluative concept.

In endnote 79, I discussed Mitchell Berman's legal philosophy of principled positivism. He wants to introduce principles into the law in order to satisfy Dworkin's criticism of Hart's legal philosophy. Hart initially declined to include principles within the law, but he, in later writings, appeared to include them. I view this as a mistake on Hart's part; he should have stayed with his original position. I agree with Berman that principles play a role in judicial decision-making, even though they are not part of the law.

Berman quotes the following from an article: "[W]e cannot establish principles by agreement because we cannot establish their weight by agreement." Berman, Mitchell, "How Practices

Make Principles, and How Principles Make Rules," Faculty Scholarship at Penn Law 2765 (2022), Page 26, fn. 76, quoting from Alexander, Larry and Kress, Kent, "Replies to Our Critics," 82 Iowa Law Review 923, 925 (1997): https://scholarship.law.upenn.edu/faculty_scholarship/2765/

This quotation presents another reason why principles should not be regarded as part of the law. Berman contends that principles are grounded in practices. Principles are sometimes similar to customary rules without the force of law. If a judge looks to practices or to customary rules without the force of law to refer to them in making a judicial decision, the principles enter into the judicial process in order to make the just decision or the wise decision. This decision would be an incorrect decision because the judge is creating a new legal rule to apply to make the decision. The judge is using the customary rule or the principle to create a new legal rule. If the legal actors are not judges, and they may not be authorized to create law, their activities (or, in Berman's terminology, the practices) may be viewed as real rules. The principles are part of the legal culture, which makes them part of the legal system. But the judges are not applying the law.

The legal theorist should distinguish the customary rules that lack the force of law from those that have the force of law. Berman discusses the prorogue case. *Id.* at 38. The U.K. has a constitution that includes legal principles, and they are used to create legal norms. When they are applied, and no other sources for the decision are mentioned, as in this instance, they are acknowledged to be the law. In this example, Berman's concept of the influence of practices is evident. The practices are similar to customary rules with the force of law.

There are also, however, cases in which new legal rules are created and there are no practices involved, though there may be principles that are referenced to create the new legal rules. The best example of this occurring is *Erie Railroad Co. v. Tompkins* (chapter six in *The Judge and the Umpire*). A new legal rule is clearly created. The new legal rule is not consistent with the practices, and, in fact, it is designed to change the practices. It is also not a customary rule with the force of law or even a customary rule that lacks the force of law. It is contrary to the customary rules.

But *Erie* is a wise decision, and it is based upon the principle that the same result should be reached in federal court as in state court in order to reduce forum-shopping. It is not the application of a legal rule of the pre-existing law. Berman would likely view it as consistent with principled positivism and I consider it to be a wise decision and consistent with creative positivism.

[207] See Moskowitz, David H., "The American Legal Realists and an Empirical Science of Law," 11 *Villanova Law Review* 480, 499 (1966) for a discussion of various versions of empirical studies of the law that could generate real rules. The body of legal rules that constitute the law has been compared to the total deposits in a bank. After the bank makes loans for 75% of its total deposits, it cannot return to all of its depositors their deposits if they are all requested in a short period of time. Similarly, the body of legal rules cannot all be administered at the same time. The legal system works as a mechanism of control of conduct only because the entire body of rules is not uniformly enforced. The rules are, therefore, selectively enforced. Those that are enforced are legal rules and the other legal rules that are not enforced are just paper rules. See Barkun, Michael, *Law without Sanctions: Order in Primitive Societies and the World Community*, Page 62.

[208] This is evident from a reading of Llewellyn's definition of "real rules": "'Real rules' are conceived in terms of behavior; they are but other names, convenient shorthand symbols, for the remedies, the actions of the courts. They are descriptive, not prescriptive, . . . 'Real rules,' then, if I had my way with words, would by legal scientists be called the practices of the courts, and not 'rules' at all. . . . 'Paper rules' are what have been treated, traditionally, as rules of law; the accepted *doctrine* of the time and place—what the

books there say, 'the law is.'" Llewellyn, Karl, "A Realistic Jurisprudence—The Next Step," 30 *Columbia Law Review* 431, 444 (1930) (Llewellyn's emphasis). *See also*, Schauer, Frederick, *Introduction to The Theory of Rules*, Page 11. This is one area of disagreement between the realists and the legal positivists, because the former, in general, agreed with Llewellyn that the rules are predictions (a form of factual statement), while the latter, in general, do not consider legal rules to be descriptive but consider them to be prescriptive (or, in H.L.A. Hart's legal philosophy, they may also be power conferring, instead of duty imposing).

[209] *Moore v. Harper*, 600 U.S. _____ (2023)

[210] Raz, Joseph, *The Concept of a Legal System*, Pages 201-02.

[211] Frank, Jerome N., "What Courts Do in Fact," 27 Illinois Law Review 645 (1932). *See also*, Moskowitz, David H., "Real Rules," *Estudios en Honor del Doctor Luis Recasens Siches* (1987).

[212] *Ibid.*

[213] Gardner, John, "The Legality of Law," 17 *Ratio Juris* 168, 174 (2004).

[214] The Challenges of Crime in a Free Society, A Report by the President's Commission on Law Enforcement and the Administration of Justice, New York, Avon Books (1968). Llewellyn raises this issue of non-obedience coupled with non-enforcement: "For without effectiveness, a rule is paper only, not backed by nor sanctioned by the State, . . ." Llewellyn, Karl, *The Theory of Rules*, Pages 61-62.

[215] Davis, Kenneth Culp, *Discretionary Justice,* Page 86.

[216] Laws against adultery in colonial America were very harsh. "Until the mid-20th century, most U.S. states . . . had laws against fornication, adultery or cohabitation." The last conviction for adultery in Massachusetts was in 1983 in *Commonwealth v. Stovell*, 389 Mass. 171 (1983). In this case, the statute was held to be constitutional. Adultery was a crime in Pennsylvania until the statute was amended in 1973. It is still a crime in 15 states. See

"Adultery Laws," *Wikipedia*:
https://en.wikipedia.org/wiki/Adultery_laws. Keep this in mind when we discuss in *The Judge and the Incorrect Decision* the theory that a precedent has been wrongly decided if it is based upon an interpretation of the Constitution that is inconsistent with the test of text, history and tradition.

[217] See Fair, Daryl R. and Moskowitz, David H., "The Lawyer's Role: Watergate as Regularity Rather Than Aberration," 2 *Journal of Contemporary Law* 75 (1975). In this article, we contend that the explanation for why so many lawyers were involved in the illegal activities that became known as Watergate was not an outlier but a common feature of our legal system. We mailed a questionnaire to 427 lawyers. There were 127 responses and 91 of those responses were from lawyers who practiced divorce law. The responses included which ground for divorce was asserted in the cases each lawyer handled. Adultery was the claim in 17% of the cases. 95% of the cases were uncontested. 95% of the uncontested cases resulted in a divorce. The lawyers responded that 60.4% of their clients lied to get their divorce. Only 21.1% of the cases were cases in which the lawyers thought their clients did not lie. In the contested cases, only 26.4% of the applicants were granted divorces. The lawyers thought that only 16.5% of the uncontested cases would have resulted in a divorce had they been contested cases. The point of the preliminary study is that lying was common in divorce cases and the lawyers knew that it was. In other words, lying was part of the system, which was facilitated by lawyers and judges, who knew that the testimony was false.

[218] Lon Fuller in *The Morality of the Law* lists congruity as the eighth principle of the inner morality of the law. There must be congruence between the paper rules and the actual administration of the law. Matthew Kramer in *Objectivity* discusses Fuller's eighth principle.

Fuller contends that, for law to exist, there must be some congruence of the real rules and the paper rules (though he does not use these terms). The paper rules must be consistent with the implementation (administration) of the legal norms. Kramer calls this "congruence between formulation and implementation." While the legal system may have some norms that are unimplemented, there must be general implementation of most norms.

Kramer contends that there will be no legal system if there are far-reaching incongruities between the paper rules and the real rules. Kramer, in *Legality,* declares that "a statement articulating the legal consequences of a pattern of conduct is true if and only if its content follows from the legal standards—
expressed in statutes, constitutional provisions, **judicial doctrines and practices,** contracts, administrative regulations, and the like— that are actually operative and applicable to such conduct within the relevant jurisdiction." (Emphasis added).

John Gardner also refers to law including that, at some relevant time and place, relevant agents "authorized it, **practiced it**, initiated it, **enforced it,** endorsed it, or otherwise engaged with it." Gardner, John, "Legal Positivism: 5 ½ Myths," 46 American Journal of Jurisprudence 199 (2002). (Emphasis added).

In order to have congruence with the law in the books and the law in practice, there must be, in general, a predominance of correct decisions.

[219] These may be found at:
https://www.google.com/url?client=internal-element-cse&cx=007572080359491747877:gul-_xwuyho&q=http://www.depgreenport.state.pa.us/elibrary/GetFolder%3FFolderID%3D4673&sa=U&ved=2ahUKEwixn_X-utH9AhXnVaQEHdZeBUwQFnoECAQQAQ&usg=AOvVaw2Dto7f3qgLz9iZqeW2YIp5

[220] *Alimota Farmers Elevator and Warehouse Co. v. United States,* 409 U.S. 470, 93 S.Ct. 701, 35 L.Ed.2d 1(1973).

[221] *Id.* at 796-97.

Chapter Nine: Alternate Sources

[222] In section 2.8, I provided the oaths taken by members of the Electoral College.

[223] The best description of Hart's internal aspect is as follows: "Though Hart never expounded the notion of presuppositions with any precision, his understanding of it was closely similar to Robert Stalmaker's broad pragmatic conception: 'A person's presuppositions are the propositions whose truth he takes for granted, often unconsciously, in a conversation, an inquiry, or a deliberation. They are the background assumptions that may be used without being spoken—sometimes without being noticed— for example as suppressed premises in an enthymematic argument, or as implied directions about how a request should be fulfilled or a piece of advice taken.'" Kramer, Matthew, *H.L.A. Hart: The Nature of Law,* Chapter 3, Footnote 3, quoting Stalmaker, Robert, "Presuppositions," *Journal of Philosophical Logic,* Page 447 (1973). Those presuppositions form the basis for Hart's internal aspect, which, in turn, forms the basis for the individual accepting the obligatory nature of the legal norms.

[224] See "Kim Davis," *Wikipedia*: https://en.wikipedia.org/wiki/Kim_Davis
Kim Davis, who had been the Chief Deputy Clerk from 1991 to 2014, was elected in 2014 to be the Rowan County Clerk. In 2016, the U.S. Supreme Court decided *Obergefell v. Hodges*, 576 U.S.694 (2016), which legalized same-sex marriage. Davis refused to issue marriage licenses to same-sex couples because of her personal religious objection to same-sex marriages. After a lawsuit was filed, she was ordered by the U.S. District Court to start issuing marriage licenses to same-sex couples.

She refused to issue the licenses. She was found to be in contempt of court, and she spent five days in jail. While she was in jail, the deputy clerks issued the licenses. A three-judge panel in the Sixth Circuit Court of Appeals denied her appeal of the stay order of the District Court and declared that "there is thus little or no likelihood that the clerk in her official capacity will prevail on appeal." The U.S. Supreme Court refused to hear her appeal from the decision of the Court of Appeals. *David Ermold v. Kim Davis*, No. 22-5260/5261, United States Court of Appeals for the Sixth Circuit, Opinion by Circuit Judge Griffin, September 28, 2022. This is an unpublished opinion.

Davis continued to defy the order of the district court, but her deputy clerks continued to issue the marriage licenses. Davis refused to sign them, but they were considered to be valid without her signature. The district court ordered that she not interfere with the licenses being issued. She lost her reelection bid in 2018.

[225] Baum, Lawrence, *Judges and Their Audiences,* Page 113 makes this observation: "Judges are socialized in their [legal] norms, and lawyers and other judges are important audiences. These judges want to see themselves as people who follow their duties under the law, and they want others to see them in the same way."

[226] These are the facts in *Roper v. Simmons*, 543 U.S. 551 (2005). The jury voted for execution and the judge imposed that sentence. In a 5-to-4 decision, SCOTUS held that the execution would violate the cruel and unusual punishments clause and that, therefore, it would be unconstitutional to execute the juvenile who was 17 years old when he committed the crime. He confessed to the crime and even reenacted it for the police to video. Justice Scalia wrote a dissenting opinion. Using the originalist approach, he interpreted the cruel and unusual punishments clause to allow for the execution because he concluded that the authors of the Eighth Amendment intended that the execution would not be considered to be a cruel and unusual punishment for committing this horrible crime even if the defendant was less than 18 years old when the crime was committed.

[227] The Supreme Court of Missouri concluded that the national consensus had developed against the execution of juvenile offenders. The sentence of execution violated the cruel and

unusual punishments clause. They sentenced Simmons to life imprisonment. The State of Missouri appealed to the U.S. Supreme Court.

[228] *Roper v. Simmons*, 543 U.S. 551, 560-61 (2005).

[229] See Gardner, John, "Concerning permissive sources and gaps," *Oxford Journal of Legal Studies*, Vol. 8, Issue 3, Pages 457-61 (1988).

[230] *Erie Railroad Co. v. Tompkins*, 304 U.S. 69 (1938). See Chapter Six of *The Judge and the Umpire*.

[231] *Knick v. Township of Scott, Pennsylvania*, 588 U.S. _____ , 139 S.Ct. 2162, 294 L.Ed.2d 558 (2019).

[232] *Cincinnati Insurance Co. v. Flanders Motor Service, Inc.*, 140 F.2d 146 (7th Cir. 1994) *(Cincinnati 1)*. See chapter four in *The Judge and the Umpire*.

[233] *Swift v. Tyson*, 41 U.S. 1 (1842). As I mention in *The Judge and the Umpire*, *Swift v. Tyson* was overruled in order to make the wise decision (in *Erie*). It was not overruled because it was an incorrect decision. Incorrect decisions may be reversed on appeal, but, if not reversed on appeal, the decision is part of the law. This distinction between correct and incorrect decisions and why decisions may be reversed on appeal because they are incorrect but cannot be overruled because they are incorrect will be explained in *The Judge and the Incorrect Decision*. The current Supreme Court seems to be confused about the difference between reversal and overruling in consideration of whether *Roe* and *Casey* should be overruled. See chapter six in *The Judge and the Umpire* for an example of how and why an established precedent should be overruled as the Supreme Court did in overruling *Swift v. Tyson* in the *Erie* decision.

[234] *Conway v. Cutler Group*, 626 Pa. 660, 99 A.3d 67 (2014). See chapter seven in *The Judge and the Umpire*.

[235] There are very few constraints imposed upon HOAs regarding the kinds of norms that they may create. In *Cape May Harbor Village v. Sbraga*, 42 N.J. Super. 56, 22 A.2d 158 (2011), the HOA community had 24 luxury single-family detached houses (worth

approximately $2,000,000 each). The defendant had lived there for many years, but she and her husband divorced. Because of a recession, she could not sell her house and she could not afford the upkeep. She wanted to rent the house. The HOA amended its rules to prohibit renting. It then sought an injunction against the defendant renting her house. The court granted the injunction. It is nearly impossible to decide if this is a correct decision because there are virtually no clear standards in the law for determining which norms are applicable to HOAs in restricting their rule-creating authority.

[236] *Roper v. Simmons*, 543 U.S. 551 (2005).

[237] *Awrod v. Ziriax*, 670 F.3d 1111 (2012). See section 4.7 in *The Judge and the Philosopher*.

Chapter Ten: Criticizing a Judicial Decision

[238] *Conway v. Cutler Group*, 626 Pa. 660, 99 A.3d 67 (Pa. 2014). See chapter seven of *The Judge and the Umpire*.

[239] *Elderkin v. Gaster*, 447 Pa. 118, 258 A.2d 771 (1972). See chapter seven in *The Judge and the Umpire*.

[240] *Roper v. Simmons*, 543 U.S. 551, 587 (2005).

[241] Lord Steyn stated in *McFarland and Another v. Tayside Health Board* [1990] 4 All ER 977 that, while courts are not expected to make moral decisions rather than legal decisions, "some of the moral answer to a question of the justice of a case, has been one of the great shaping forces of the common law." In other words, courts are authorized to, and do make, the wise decision and the just decision.

[242] John Rawls in *A Theory of Justice* considers many theories about justice. He concludes that justice is fairness. He also recognizes an innate sense of justice, like a kind of natural right. Justice, as a moral concept, may conflict with other moral norms, like the right to liberty. See also Pound, Roscoe, *Justice According to Law,* Page 2: "In different theories which have been used justice has been

regarded as an individual virtue, or as a moral idea, or as a regime of social control, or as the end or purpose of social control or so of law, or as the idea of relation among men which we work to promote or retain in civilized society and toward which we direct and control and law is the most specialized form of social control."

John Gardner points out that there may be a special connection between justice and the law. Gardner, John, "Finnis on Justice," *Reason Morality and the Law, The Jurisprudence of John Finnis,* (Keown, John and George, Robert, eds.), Page 26 in The University of Oxford Legal Research Paper Series. It is also in the SSRN Electronic Library. See also Sir Carleton Kemp, *Aspects of Justice,* Pages 54-55. Finally, justice is also an important feature of our political system. It is also a factor in the cases considered by the Supreme Court, such as *Roe v. Wade* (the legality of abortions) which is a central theme in my fourth book in this quartet, *The Judge and the Incorrect Decision.* See Appendix A for a preview of vol. 4.

It is difficult to imagine a discussion about *Roper v. Simmons,* 543 U.S. 551 (2005), the case in which the murder is committed by a juvenile defendant who was 17 when he committed this crime, without mentioning justice. The correct decision in this case would have been to apply the legal rule in the leading precedent, *Stanford v. Kennedy,* 492 U.S. 361 (1999). This was a decision that was made 16 years previously and was exactly on point. Applying the legal rule in that precedent would have led to the conclusion that execution of a juvenile did not violate the cruel and unusual punishments clause.

In the majority opinion by Justice Kennedy, he refers to the "evolving standards of decency" as the test to be employed. This sounds like a test designed to yield the just decision.

The right to not receive a cruel and unusual punishment flows from the principle that justice precludes punishment for crimes that is disproportionate to the offense. As I mentioned in chapter seven, when I discussed the right of dignity, Justice Kennedy declares the following: "By prohibiting even those convicted of heinous crimes, the Eighth Amendment reaffirms the duty of the government to respect the dignity of all persons." *Id*. at 560.

[243] Timothy Endicott would not agree with this presentation. He maintains that interpretation of legislation is an evaluative act. He insists that the court needs to make evaluative judgments about the purpose of the law and the values that can be promoted by adopting one interpretation or another to apply the law. Endicott, Timothy, *Authority, Law and Morality, Ethics in the Public Domain*, Pages 95 and 127.

He also declares that an interpretation is an explanation of how to apply a standard. He calls this an "applicative interpretation," an account of the meaning of the text that is designed as a guide to its application. *Id* at 133.

I do not want to enter into an extended discussion of this point. Endicott's approach is just not consistent with my experience interacting with judges. There is virtually no discussion of the purpose of a legal rule. There is some discussion about what the rule is, what the terms mean and how it will apply to a specific factual situation. And, as the *Conway* case illustrates, the courts will consider evaluation of the rule itself and of the effects of its application (the consequences of the legal rule). They will also consider whether making the new legal rule should be left to the legislators to decide rather than the judges (it is a policy decision for the legislature to resolve). See also Appendix A of *The Judge and the Incorrect Decision* for how the three elements become part of the oral argument before the court.

[244] A good example of a narrow ruling would be the decision in the *Webb* case: *Webb v. McGowin*, 27 Ala. App. 82, 168 So. 198 (1935), *cert. denied*, 232 Aka, 374, 168 So, 199 (1836). See Chapter Five in *The Judge and the Umpire*.

[245] Section 8.5 in *The Judge and the Umpire*.

[246] Llewellyn, Karl, *The Theory of Rules*, Page147. In *Newland v. Sebelius*, 881 F. Supp. 2d 1287 (D. Colo. 2012), *aff'd*, 542 F. App'x

706 (10th Cir. 2013), Judge John I. Kane restricts his ruling in the case to the litigants in the case. The District Court did not enjoin enforcement of the preventive care coverage mandate against any other party or individual.

[247] For unintended consequences, Texas adopted a statute in May 2021, that becomes effective on September 1, 2021. Unlike typical abortion statutes that ban abortions and provide for state enforcement of the ban, this statute calls for individuals to enforce it and they are paid an incentive to do so. The purpose of the way the statute is enforced is to insulate the statute from a legal challenge based upon a civil rights cause of action. The civil rights statute applies only to state enforcement of a statute that affects the civil rights of citizens.

The Texas law is, in effect, a total ban on abortions because many pregnant women do not know that they are pregnant in the first six weeks of the pregnancy and abortions are banned six weeks after gestation. The statute allows anyone, anywhere, to sue people involved in providing abortion care or practical support to patients in Texas. The complainant may obtain a judgment of $10,000 or more if successful.

The unintended consequence of using this technique to prevent abortions is that the same technique may be utilized to ban firearms, allowing for civil suits against gun owners. See Hurley, Laurence and Chung, Andrew, "Analysis—Texas abortion law critics warn conservatives of unintended consequences," *Yahoo News,* October 31, 2021. https://www.reuters.com/world/us/texas-abortion-law-critics-warn-conservatives-unintended-consequences-2021-10-31/

For unthought of consequences, see Wilson, Conrad, "DOJ uses Civil Rights-Era Law to Charge Protesters and Insurrectionists," *WHYY,* May 22, 2021. This article concerns the federal Civil Obedience Act, which was adopted in 1968. There were many civil rights protests and political protests during the 60's. The statute makes it a crime with a penalty of up to five years in prison for interfering with police officers or firefighters performing their official duties during a protest or civil disorder. The drafters of the statute clearly intended it to restrain protests by liberal students or African Americans.

During the last 30 years, the statute was applied in approximately 12 cases nationwide. Interestingly enough, one of them involved a protest at the Dakota Access Pipeline. See Section 4.5 for why pipelines might be protested.

After the January 6, 2021, insurrection, federal prosecutors have brought hundreds of cases against the individuals protesting at the Capitol. About one-quarter of those charged in the riot are facing charges of violation of the civil disorder statute. https://www.npr.org/2021/05/22/999180144/doj-uses-civil-rights-era-law-to-charge-protesters-and-insurrectionists

[248] *Elderkin v. Gastar*, 447 Pa. 118, 258 A.2d 771 (1972). See chapter seven of *The Judge and the Umpire*.

[249] Ladd, John, "The Place of Rational Reason in Judicial Decisions," *Rational Decision* (edited by Friedrich, Carl J.), Pages 127-28.

[250] For a case in which the trial judge was reversed for not providing the reasons for his decision, see Harrison, Judy, "Maine supreme court admonishes judge for not outlining reasons in divorce dispute over vaccinations," *BDN,* November 24, 2021. This is a case between divorced parents in which the father wanted to have his two children vaccinated and the mother refused. The Maine Supreme Court reversed the trial court and remanded the case to the trial judge to provide the reasons for his decision.

The mother claimed that the vaccinations were unnecessary and unsafe, but she offered no proof. The trial judge decided in favor of the mother. The trial judge failed to explain the reasons for his decision. The author states that "The decision does put judges who handle divorce cases on notice that they must outline their reasoning in decisions concerning parental rights and responsibilities."

See: https://www.theguardian.com/media/2022/may/17/who-owns-einstein-the-battle-for-the-worlds-most-famous-face

[251] See Warner, Daniel, "Behind Daniel Ellsberg's Whistleblowing was a Sense of Justice," *Counterpunch*, June 30, 2023. Warner concludes that it is difficult to define justice. Children often demand fairness at a very early age: and parents are often requested to justify their actions in the name of fairness and justice, although explaining these concepts is not easy to do. Ellsberg's photocopying of The Pentagon Papers (about the Vietnam War) and giving them to the newspapers to publish was based upon his belief that the Vietnam War was wrong (even though he was a hawk at the beginning) and that the public had a right to see the document. The just decision was the trial judge's dismissal of the charges against Ellsberg. The Supreme Court affirmed the decision of the trial court allowing the newspapers to publish the document. This is Warner's conclusion: "The federal judge's decision as well as the Supreme Court's ruling confirmed justice on several levels. . . Ellsberg's photocopying the Report, the press making it public and the courts' decisions all can be summarized as just. "

[252] The case is *Trump v. Mary L. Trump and Simon & Schuster, Inc..*, No. 2020 Slip Op 20175 (N.U. Sup. Ct. 2020).

Appendix A: Volume 1 and Volume Two and a Preview of Volume Four, *The Judge and the Incorrect Decision*

[253] *Erie Railroad Co. v. Tompkins*, 304 U.S. 64 (1938) is an example of an appellate court deciding a case based upon an issue that was neither raised in the trial court nor briefed in the appellate court. I discuss this case in chapter six of *The Judge and the Umpire*. The *Erie* case does not fit seamlessly into Hart's description of the legal system. Pursuant to the decision in *Erie*, federal courts attempt to

decide cases as they would be decided in the relevant state court. The federal court will apply not only state statutes and state customary rules but also state common law. After the decision in *Erie*, the federal judge will no longer apply federal common law in diversity-of-citizenship cases. This is called the Erie Doctrine.

Hart's legal philosophy offers no means by which one may explain the *Erie* decision. Not only was there no rule in the pre-existing law that would justify the decision in *Erie*, but the decision was also not based on an issue raised by the parties or briefed by the parties. It is as clear a case as one can imagine of the Supreme Court creating a new law. In doing so, the Justices are not acting like umpires.

254 To establish that lawyers arguing before courts may contend that alternate sources should be considered, I present in Appendix A of volume 4 the oral arguments in the Supreme Court in *Knick v. Township of Scott*, 588 U.S. _____, 139 S.Ct. 2162, 204 L.Ed.2d 558 (2019).

255 My example for developing a new legal rule by analogy is *Adams v. New Jersey Steamboat Co.*, 131 N.Y. 163, 45 N.E. 369 (1890). This case involves the theft of property from a traveler on a steamboat. If a traveler stays at an inn, the owner of the inn would be liable for the theft of the property. The opposite would be true for travelers on a train while sleeping on a berth in a railroad car that has multiple berths and no doors that can be locked in order to provide privacy and security for each individual berth.

Judge Richard A. Posner, a legal philosopher, and a former judge on the federal Court of Appeals, concludes that sleeping on the sleeping car in a cabin with a closed door is more analogous to sleeping in a hotel room than it is to be sleeping on a berth with multiple other passengers on berths on a train. Therefore, the owner of the steamship in the *Adams* case is liable to the passenger who suffered the loss of his property.

Analogies are used to take something that makes sense (like travelers who stay in a hotel need to feel secure and the hotel has to ensure that they are secure) and couple it with something that is being considered (do riders on trains and steamboats have other alternatives to feel safe and be safe) and by doing so determine whether riding on the steamboat is closer to staying in a hotel rather than riding on a train. This analogy works even though riding on the steamboat is more like riding on a train than like being in a hotel because the train and the steamboat are both moving, and the hotel is not. See sections 7.9 and 14.8 in *The Judge and the Philosopher.*

256 Stanley Fish, a law professor and philosopher at the Benjamin N. Cardozo School of Law at Yeshiva University, explains that the construction of the analogy in the *Adams* case is a reasoning process related to making comparisons: "Posner [Judge Richard A. Posner] asks if a precedent could be distinguished on the basis that in the earlier case the plaintiff had been left-handed and in the present case is right-handed and he answers 'it could not—but only because there is no consideration of policy or ethics that would justify so narrow an interpretation.' [Citation omitted]. The state of the culture of what it would hear as reasonable [not the force of reason itself] bars a judge, at least now, from grabbing hold of the distinction between left- and right-handedness . . ." See Fish, Stanley, "Almost Pragmatism: Richard Posner's Jurisprudence," 57 University of Chicago Law Review 1447, 1451-52 (1990).

When Fish mentions policy, ethics and the legal culture, as all having an impact upon the judicial decision, he is referring to the accepted customs inherent in the judicial decision-making process. I view the reference to ethics as consideration of the just decision, and the reference to policy as related to the wise decision. His analysis is consistent with my theory of the three elements of the judicial decision being the correct decision, the just decision, and the wise decision.

257 The most important customary rule that I will discuss is the customary legal rule that provides for the peaceful transfer of

power in the election of the president in the United States. This is discussed in chapter 3 in this book, *The Judge and the President.*
[258] While it is not absolutely clear, I conclude the Hart did accept the concept of there being a correct decision in every case. Yet, contrary to that statement, Hart sometimes seems to almost be unconcerned or disinterested in whether the decision is correct: "...[I]n the law it seems difficult to substantiate the claim that a judge confronted with a set of conflicting considerations must always assume that there is a single uniquely correct resolution of the conflict and attempt to demonstrate that he has discovered it." Hart, H.L.A., "Problems in Philosophy of Law," 6 *The Encyclopedia of Philosophy*, 254, 271 (P. Edwards, ed.) (1977). *See also* Hart, H.L.A., *Postscript* in *The Concept of Law* (hereinafter referred to as "Postscript"), Page 254: "It will not matter for any practical purpose whether in so deciding cases the judge is *making* law in accordance with morality (subject to whatever constraints are imposed by law) or alternatively is guided by his moral judgment as to whether existing law is revealed by a moral test for law." (Hart's emphasis). The *Postscript* is in the later editions of *The Concept of Law.* See endnote 119 in vol. 2. My conclusion that Hart accepted the concept of the correct decision is based upon conversations with him about this subject and other statements that he made that I refer to in volumes 2 and 3. I view the correctness of the judicial decision as an either/or concept. Every judicial decision is either a correct decision or an incorrect decision.
[259] *Mosser v. Darrow,* 341 U.S. 267 (1951). This case is discussed in chapter eight of *The Judge and the Umpire.*
[260] See Raz, Joseph, "Two Views of the Nature of the Theory of Law: A Partial Comparison," Coleman, Julius (Editor), *Hart's Postscript: Essays on the Postscript to The Concept of Law*, Page 21 and Endicott, Timothy A.O., "Herbert Hart and the Semantic Sting," in *Hart's Postscript: Essays on the Postscript to The Concept of Law*, Pages 39-40. *See also* Perry, Stephen R., "Hart on Social Rules and the Foundations of Law: Liberating the Internal Point of View," 75

Fordham Law Review 1171, 1179 (2006) for the view, with which I agree, that Hart accepts that the rules ascertained by the rule of recognition are "content independent" which means that the judge applying the rule is undertaking an analytical process and not an evaluative process in order to make the correct decision. Hart uses the internal point of view to point out that the officials who make the laws and the citizens to whom they are applied agree that the officials have the authority to make the laws. Laws are obligatory, according to Hart, because of the social fact of acceptance by the officials and the citizenry in accordance with the internal point of view. The obligatory nature of law does not require that you ignore that there are other reasons for obeying the law in addition to sanctions in the law.

[261] Dworkin finds Hart's theory of social norms to be defective because it fails to recognize a distinction between a consensus of convention presented in a group's conventional rules and a consensus of independent conviction demonstrated by the conventional practices of concurrent members of the society. Conventional social practices become comparable to constitutional conventions if they are accepted by individual members of the society. Dworkin wants to distinguish conventions from rules that demonstrate independent conviction.

Hart acknowledges that Dworkin has clarified the distinction between social practices and the normative nature of customs that have the force of law. Social customs may become legal rules, according to Hart, including part of the rule of recognition, if they are recognized by the court's law-ascertainment and law-application activities. Hart distinguishes this practice from enacted legal rules, but he does not explain whether customs become legal norms absent there being a court decision that qualifies as law-identifying and law-applying activity. Hart, if I understand him correctly, is agreeing that custom may create a rule of pre-existing law, but the custom becomes law only if the court declares that it is law. Hart may accept the possibility of self-executing customary rules being part of the law, though it is not absolutely clear that this is part of Hart's legal philosophy.

Dworkin finds the transformation from social practice to norm to occur if there is "a certain normative state of affairs." See Postscript, Pages 256-57.

[262] *Betts v. Brady*, 316 U.S. 458 (1942) and *Gideon v. Wainwright*, 372 U.S. 325 (1963).

[263] *Miranda v. Arizona*, 384 U.S. 436 (1966). This is really 4 cases combined into this decision, three of which are reversals of cases in which custodial interrogations are improperly conducted. In the fourth case, the procedure is permitted, and the lower court decision is affirmed. As I will explain, this decision is not consistent with U.S. history and tradition. It is also not consistent with the text of the Fourteenth Amendment according to the reasoning in the *Gideon v. Wainwright* case mentioned in the prior endnote.

[264] *Id*. at 467.

[265] *Id*. at 476.

[266] *Id*. at 484.

[267] *Id*. at 499.

[268] *Ibid*.

[269] *Id*. at 530.

Index

A

B

P

Paper rule	5, 154, 170. 172-4, 176-7, 182, 185, 187-8
Parliament (England)	133
Pedigree theory	102, 109, 175, 223
Pelosi, Nancy	24
Penalty	4, 43, 123, 150-3, 179, 194
Pence Card	27, 29, 68, 79, 237
Pence, Michael R.	25-33, 35-8, 50, 52, 55, 57-61, 67-8, 79, 81, 83, 87-8, 95, 127, 237, 239
Pennsylvania	16, 26, 32, 34, 37-48, 50-4, 61-3, 68, 72, 79-80, 83-4, 95, 118-22, 126, 132, 141, 150, 157, 159-61, 168-70, 177-8, 182, 204-5, 217, 237-8
Pennsylvania Public Utility Commission	141
Per curiam	19, 21, 38, 66, 161
Philadelphia	6, 38, 61, 71, 83, 86, 118, 159, 176-7, 234-5, 237-8
Pipelines	139-150, 154
Plea bargaining	179
Policing	44, 47, 85, 92, 110, 114, 143, 168-70, 174, 176-8, 183, 231-2
Pollution	148, 182
Pottstown Hospital	118
POTUS	6-7, 9, 11, 13, 18, 63, 70, 115, 238
Poverty	162
Powell, Sidney K.	82, 84, 96-8
Power-conferring	113, 150-1, 191-2, 221-2
Precedent	1, 4, 6, 11, 33, 64-5, 70, 103, 105, 107-8, 110, 113-4, 122, 124, 127-134, 154, 158, 164, 167, 169, 172, 179-81, 193, 195-9, 205-7, 218, 220, 223-4, 227-9, 233
President	1-3, 6-13, 15-18, 21, 23-39, 44, 46-8, 52-61, 67, 69-70, 73-5, 79, 81, 85, 87-91, 98-9, 103, 111, 150-3, 219-20, 239
President's Crime Commission	175

W

Wallace, George	16
Washington	*See Chiafalo v. Washington*
Washington D.C.	47, 79, 91, 98
Washington, George	61
Welsh, Carolyn "Bunny"	238
White House	26, 29, 36, 58, 94, 96, 98, 151
Willard Hotel	29
Willis, Fani	59, 89
Winner-take-all	7, 10
Wisconsin	25-6, 32, 34, 37-8, 40, 50, 52, 67-8, 68, 81, 239
Wise decision	20, 109, 111-12, 114, 157-8, 169, 171, 185, 188-90, 196-8, 203, 207, 210-17, 219, 220, 223-4, 226, 228, 232
Wolf, Thomas W.	150
Writ of certiorari	50, 77, 91, 134

Z

Zoning	99, 109, 114, 126, 147-8, 159-62, 165, 167, 201

DAVID H. MOSKOWITZ

Dave practiced law for approximately 50 years (now retired) and has been involved in entrepreneurial ventures of different types during that same period and at the present time. He spends his days working on his real estate projects or his biopharma projects, and writing books.

He is married to Marian (they have celebrated their 38th anniversary) and they have raised five children and have five grandchildren. Marian is the Chairlady of the Chester County Commissioners, and a board member of multiple non-profit institutions. They live in Malvern, Chester County, Pennsylvania.

You can contact the author via his website
www.thecreativepositivist.com

Made in the USA
Middletown, DE
22 September 2023

39020733R00201